WILL WE WAKE UP?

The Hidden Powers Behind The World Stage

Marcel Messing

Second edition, January 2022

© 2021 www.obeliskboeken.com
© 2021 Marcel Messing - www.marcelmessing.nl

Cover design and drawings: Marianne van den Dungen
Editing: Marijke Messing
Photo cover: Enith Stenhuys
Translation: Team Obelisk

By popular demand, Marcel Messing's 2006 book 'Worden Wij Wakker?' [Will We Wake UP?] has been republished in Dutch and is now also translated into English. Unfortunately, in view of a number of recent developments, it is becoming increasingly clear Marcel Messing at that time was providing a thorough preview of the very turbulent times we are now in.

Keywords: 9/11, September 11, 2001 attacks, terrorism, international politics, Gulf War, Afghanistan, Iraq, United States, CIA, RFID chip, Google, radiation, surveillance state, Big Brother, biometric passport, internet, pandemic, vaccinations, transhumanism.

First edition, December 2021; Second Edition, January 2022
ISBN: 978-94-93071-90-2
NUR: 728

Let's say that everything you know is not only wrong,
it is a carefully wrought lie.
Let's say that your mind is filled with falsehoods – about yourself, about history,
about the world around you – planted there by powerful forces,
so as to lull you into complacency.
Your freedom is thus an illusion.
You are in fact a pawn in a plot,
and your role is that of a compliant dupe,
if you're lucky.

Charles Paul Freund, 'If History is a Lie: America's Resort to Conspiracy
Thinking', in *The Washington Post*, January 19, 1992

There is nothing concealed that will not be disclosed,
or hidden that will not be made known.
What you have said in the dark will be heard in the daylight,
and what you have whispered in the ear in the inner rooms
will be proclaimed from the roof tops.

Luke 12:2-3

Yes, he who wants to reveal the truth to people
exposes himself to a lot of misunderstanding.

Omraam Mikhaël Aïvanhov, March 8, 2006

Content

The 2021 English translation

There has recently been a renewed demand for the book '*Worden Wij Wakker? Over de verborgen krachten achter het wereldtoneel*', first published in 2006 by Ankh-Hermes and until recently only available as an e-book. It was being traded at high prices on the internet without my knowledge, so I gratefully accepted the offer of the publisher Obelisk to reprint the book. It's now available again and the publisher has updated the notes and internet references.

Prior to this republication, my manifesto was published in early January 2021 *Code Red Alarm. Not primarily caused by the Corona Pandemic, but because of what is hidden behind this Cover-up*, and can be ordered at world of consciousness.com. The Dutch version of the manifesto (*Code rood: Alarm! Mensheid en planeet aarde in gevaar*) as well as the French (*Code Rouge: Alarme! Danger pour l'Humanité et la Planète*) can be found on my website. Since there are similarities to be discovered between the current pandemic and the so-called 'swine' flu, I have decided to publish the booklet *Vaccinate or not? Contribution to the discussion of making a choice* [in Dutch - Frontier Publishing, 2009, no longer available].

Inform yourself. Do not only investigate the prevailing views of specialists, scientists, and journalists, but also of those specialists, scientists and journalists who have conducted sound research, that is not or hardly allowed to be discussed in the mainstream media. Read their books and reports and if you can't or don't want to take the time, visit their websites and draw your own conclusions. Do not be put off by those who use clever words and clichés to try to silence you and who usually do not do any proper research themselves. But above all: use common sense, trust your intuition and, as far as I am concerned, never make decisions if you are in doubt. My website will keep you informed of upcoming publications.

As a result of the book "Will We Wake up?", in a podcast with Jorn Lukaszczyk (*The Truman Show*) in July 2021, I personally recounted the dramatic event of 9/11, how I experienced it in 2001, and what 'coincidences' have occurred in my life in relation to 9/11. Internationally, several authors have done in-depth research on 9/11.

It is obvious that we are living in an extremely critical time and waking up on a large scale is necessary now, more than ever before. Time is running out! Numerous events are coinciding: The pandemic, lockdowns, vaccination programs and the vaccination passport, global mass brainwashing and hypnosis, the super-fast rollout of 5G, the almost daily outbreak of revolutions and situations of civil war, the confrontation of a global refugee problem, famines, terrorist attacks, political corruption, dictatorship and terror, the collapse of established institutions and religions, the rapid degradation of the planetary ecosystem (caused in part by globalization), the decay of moral values, the many lies about the climate... Humanity, indeed all living beings, are dancing on the volcano in this 'iron age' called kali-yuga.

But right through all this, profound transformations are taking place, in which the soul, denied by countless materialistic scientists and philosophers, can awaken to its true essence. Only when we learn to understand, accept and integrate the Universal Law, among other things expressed in the archetype of the tree of life, only when we realize that all living beings in our universe and in parallel universes are connected to this and that this Law is intended to protect life and bring it to further development, can man make an enormous leap in his evolution of consciousness. Then he too will realize that it is not about vanity, arrogance, egotism, power, exploitation and demonism, but about truth, light and love.

The coming years will be decisive for planet Earth and all living beings. Everything depends on a rapid awakening in many areas through knowledge and understanding, through which a collective force of consciousness becomes feasible. I would like to wish you, the reader, all the best and much strength and inspiration at this very crucial moment. May *Will We Wake up?* give you a better understanding of the current world situation.

Marcel Messing, December 2021.

Introduction (2006)

If, therefore, it is proper for anyone to lie, then certainly for the leadership of the state towards enemies or fellow citizens, with regard to the well-being of the state: all others, however, must refrain from it.

Plato (427-347 B.C.), *The state* III, 389

Much has changed in the world since September 11, 2001 (9/11). Now five years later, we see that more and more people are questioning the official account of those catastrophic events. If a few years ago you belonged to the conspiracy theorists and were looked upon with a certain contempt or disdain by the media, lately, more and more dissenting voices have begun to emerge. Those who gave unquestioning credence to the well-known story of the U.S. government, must recognize that there is more to it. Several policy makers and media experts are beginning to get the unpleasant feeling that it could all have been a gigantic lie, as a result of which around the world far-reaching decisions have been taken with major consequences for social life. Particularly in the areas of security and privacy. The first victim in a war is always the truth. Floods of false information then reach the media. This was already the case during the First and Second World Wars. Propaganda Minister of Nazi Germany Joseph Goebbels fully understood this when he said, 'Thank god people don't think,' a quote he took from Hitler. For Goebbels, 'truth was the deadly enemy of the lie,' but also 'the greatest enemy of the state'.

The time will come, however, when people will start to think more clearly than the manipulators of the mind ever thought possible. The time will come when people wake up. For every lie, no matter how blatant, leaves its traces. First, a few individuals conducting critical research will wake up, then larger groups, and finally all of humanity. Even dictator Adolf Hitler, responsible for hideous atrocities and terrible suffering, was aware of this. In *Mein Kampf* he wrote, 'For the most brazen lie always leaves traces, even when it has been destroyed. This is a truth known to all who are masters in the art of lying, and who work relentlessly at perfecting the lie.' Many today have worked and are working on perfecting the lie. Sometimes even with Machiavelli-like traits. But whether this is always done 'in the interest of the state'? Whoever tells *one* lie, the Buddha said, will have to invent *many* thereafter to cover the first one. Until that one lie comes to light… The truth is always more powerful than the grossest lie, because the foundation of truth is light. And in the light of truth, according to the cosmic law of harmony, the darkness of the lie must yield.

In recent years, our world has rapidly descended into a level of increasing violence, growing fear, terror and devaluation of values. In many countries, the state responded by passing numerous new laws and regulations. Security quickly became more important than privacy. Since 9/11, innumerable cameras and eavesdropping devices have begun to spy on us at an ever-increasing rate. If someone behaves suspiciously for even a moment, he is subject to a strip search. Since 9/11, it is compulsory to carry an ID card at all times. (In some countries this was already the case.) The biometric passport was quickly introduced. Ingenious electronic control systems and increasingly large and sophisticated eavesdropping devices were installed. Satellite surveillance, connected to electronic equipment and mega-computers, which most people have never heard of, is increasingly permitted and considered normal. Security services are being given new programmes and tasks. In many countries, umbrella security agencies are being set up and counter-terrorism coordinators appointed. The army, police and other authorities regularly carry out exercises. After all, there may be attacks in European countries. Every day. In many countries, alarm codes orange and red have been put in place. There has never been so much talk of 'big brother' as since 9/11. Not the 'Big Brother' of cheesy soap operas or penny dreadfuls, but the terrifying, all-controlling, manipulating and dictating 'Big Brother' of Orwell's novel 1984, who in our time has become the embodiment of increasing and total control and espionage, aimed at enslaving mankind. Since 9/11, fear has been exploited on a collective scale. An atmosphere of constant threat has been created and distrust of other groups and religions is growing. Polarization is increasing and so is a climate that we ourselves unconsciously have created in which the seeds of terrorist attacks can germinate. The virus of fear and despair has nestled in every part of our society. Many people have the feeling that this virus has been deliberately deployed. As if a powerful shadow behind it all is exploiting the state of fear for its own purpose. A number of people are beginning to realize that there is much more going on than what we are told by the media. The internet is buzzing with criticism, and all sorts of conspiracy theories are shared and discussed. Although this book points out the great risks of the internet and the forces that lie behind it, this medium can also be used in a positive way to unmask those who try to manipulate us. Something we should never forget.

It is as if something snapped in human relationships since 9/11 and at the same time there is a growing consciousness which seeks to extract the truth from the murky sea of lies. In doing so, thick mud streams that cause unbridled suffering and misery, seep through the mazes of the net. Day after day, brute force opens gates of unprecedented suffering and sorrow. But day after day, the light also reveals, step by step, the dark shadow in the background, creating the possibility of bringing the great suffering afflicting our planet to a halt.

The 'war on terror', which is drawing a colossal, sickening cloud of darkness over Earth and reinforcing antagonism, hatred and suffering everywhere, seems to have reached a critical point. Paradoxically, as a result, the collective consciousness is beginning to wake up. A mighty ray of light is gradually piercing through the cloud of darkness. Certainly, he who accuses others also accuses himself. The voice that reproaches is connected to the one who utters it. The eye that looks reproachfully at another is connected to the same light.

The chaos currently created in many parts of the world shows a certain structure that refers to hidden forces behind the world stage, which seem intent on creating a totally different world order. In this new world order, modern technology, especially electronics, is deployed on many fronts with the aim of enslaving man. Every day the sacredness of life is grossly violated. Until the infringed life turns against those who caused the infringement. After all, there are laws in the universe that one cannot keep breaking. What you sow, you will reap sooner or later. As the Buddha once said, 'The ungodly shall prosper as long as the seed of his ungodliness is unripe. When the seed of the ungodly is ripe, his prosperity will come to an end.'

Suppose we have been deceived. That we have been told blatant lies for decades under the guise of truth. Suppose that there have been plans on the table for years about the destiny of this planet. Plans that we never suspected, plans that are already well advanced. This book first poses the question of whether we are living in a transitional period or end times. It then discusses hidden backgrounds of September 11 (9/11), explains President Bush's secret, reveals some of big brother's electronic control and spying techniques, and discusses the great dangers of the chip, especially the implantation of the subcutaneous microchip in humans. Finally, the role of the internet is explored, where many of the aforementioned themes converge. Not only are we in danger of being locked up in a gigantic electromagnetic cage of radiation in the coming years, which will completely dehumanize us, the forces behind the world stage are also busy getting a stranglehold on man step by step through a strangling control system. First, they make a direct attack on his privacy and then they use super-advanced electronic technologies to attack his soul quality. A power elite, consisting of a collective of top people from politics, religion, business, banks and secret services, does not hesitate to enslave mankind to its goals, its world order. This is the most brutal attack on the principle of love. An attack that makes the atrocities of 9/11 pale in comparison, because for the first time in human history the decisive spiritual evolution of humanity is being hacked into in an extraordinarily devious manner. All the more reason to wake up quickly, very quickly, and start responding appropriately, taking action where necessary. The stakes are high.

There seems to be a war going on between light and darkness, although this is an obvious black-and-white simplification. 'Gray' also participates and in each of us there is a shadow that we like to conceal, but which is waiting to be transformed. Even in the darkest consciousness of a person, a glimpse of light remains. This is what the Bhagavad Gita, one of the world's most famous wisdom stories, shows. In the final battle between the Pandavas and the Kauravas, the sons of light and of darkness meet face to face.

In our time, dark forces seem to want to dust everything over, while forces of light are actually trying to transform and transcend the dark. An intense expulsion is taking place of a process that was hitherto invisible to most people's eyes. Just as a river can flow underground for a while and then suddenly resurfaces, so it is with the 'flow' of hidden forces behind the world stage. For a certain time, the stream is visible, its course traceable. Then suddenly, it goes underground to carve out the bed of an entirely different history than that of the historians. Once above ground - and this seems to always occur at the end of a cycle - there is a short window of opportunity to see what was going on, unbeknown to us. Hidden forces built a pyramid of power and falsehood, cast a controlling all-seeing eye over the planet, waiting for the time to set their capstone of arrogance on this pyramid but oblivious to the fact, that during this underground building of the pyramid of power there is also a pyramid of light at work. In this pyramid the cornerstone is equal to the top stone, there is no hierarchy of power, which wishes to exploit the base. In this pyramid; love, compassion, wisdom and patience are central and every living being is a valuable building block in the temple of life. Within this pyramid, there is even an attempt to turn the enemy into a friend. Not through a sugar-sweet method of half-heartedness or misdirected goodness, but through the transmission of information of what is going on in the world. In the hope of thus alleviating suffering and restoring the original goodness of man, in which millions, indeed perhaps billions, of people have lost faith.

When the sacredness of life is seriously violated, where burning desire from totally sick minds threatens to destroy everything and everyone, when creation sighs in travail, the conscious human being can no longer be a silent bystander. As Martin Luther King once said, 'evil advances so rapidly because good men stay silent'. With this we certainly do not want to fall into the pitfall of dualism of good and evil, but emphasize that not every human being is trapped in a state of consciousness of demonization, which is currently raging across the world. Certainly, everything is one. But that does not mean that duality doesn't exist, although some philosophers claim so. The possibility to deny a choice is also a choice. And doubting whether truth ever comes to light exists only by virtue of not daring to doubt the doubt. The unity of being is only seen and experienced when duality is also understood and experienced. On the chessboard of black and white, one is not asked to judge or condemn, but rather to develop the gift of distinction and cleanse blends of black and white in one's own being. Only then will pros and cons disappear in the single light that shines on both good and bad.

Reality sometimes turns out to be completely different than we thought. Even when we think we have come to know it to some extent, new doors are constantly opening. The sometimes-shocking facts in this book are, of course, not intended to instill fear or promote doom and gloom, but to provide information that will hopefully enable us to deal appropriately with the problems that confront us in the years ahead. Everyone matters. It would be wrong and dishonest to conceal this and not take the reader seriously. To say that everything will resolve itself is to participate in a big lie. That is not what I am advocating. Perhaps for some people it is a free ticket to continue their complacent lives for a while. Possibly infused with a 'new-age' sauce. Certainly, to have faith that everything will be all right is ever more necessary, but equally so is our joint effort. The final act of the present world stage will not end simply by the intervention of an all-solving deus ex machina.

Finally, a word of thanks to all those friends who have been such a great help in writing this book, especially Joli Coeur. I sincerely hope that this book, which is merely an introduction to this complex theme, may touch many hearts and minds. So that we may all wake up soon! May the light of truth and love lead and guide us all in the decisive years ahead! May the Great Spirit, as our red brothers, the Indians, so often call the universal force that permeates all life, protect us on our journey.

Marcel Messing, 2006

1

The great revolution

We are at the peak of an incredible global change. A pivotal moment in which we are making decisions that will affect life on Earth far into the future of what we call time.

We can throw open the doors to the mental and emotional prisons in which the human race has been locked for thousands of years, or allow the agents of that control to complete their agenda for the mental, emotional, spiritual and physical enslavement of every man, woman and child on the planet: with a world government, world army, world bank and world money system, and a population microchipped as its foundation.

I know this sounds bizarre, but if the human race turns its eyes away from the latest soap opera or game show long enough to keep its brain busy, it will see that these events are not about to happen, but that they are already happening. The pace at which world politics is increasingly coming under centralized control, and that of business, banking, military affairs and media is increasing by the hour. The microchipping of people has already been suggested and in many cases is already taking place.

Whenever a hidden agenda is about to be implemented, there is always the period when what is being hidden must penetrate the surface for the final jab into physical reality. (...)

If you want to know what kind of life this means, unless we wake up soon, just look at Nazi Germany.

That is the world that awaits the world's population if the plan that I call the 'brotherhood agenda' will unfold from the year 2000 into the first twelve years of the new century.[1]

David Icke, author.

---

[1] Icke, D., *The Biggest Secret*, p. XIII-XIV.

1.1   Time of transition or end of time?

You will hear of wars and rumours about wars,
but see to it that you are not alarmed.
Such things must happen, but the end is still to come.
Nation will rise against nation, and kingdom against kingdom.
There will be famines and earthquakes in various places.
All these are the beginning of birth pains.

Matthew 24:6-8

The torrent of publications on the critical situation of our planet is unstoppable. Shores of illusions are being eroded by it. We can no longer close our eyes to this. And fleeing is not an option either.
Climatologists warn of catastrophic climate changes, astronomers speak of extraordinary solar eruptions, astrologers emphasize the powerful influence of the Age of Aquarius. The grim dance of Kali, goddess of strife, is said to have begun. In ancient Indian wisdom she plays an important role. She is said to have opened the creaking gate of the Iron Age several years ago and put her name tag on it. The Puranas, Sanskrit for 'ancient stories' of Indian wisdom literature, knew about it, too.[2] Thousands of years ago they already outlined our current era in startling detail. A nutcracker for the rational mind. Anger, lies, immorality, lawlessness, strife, wars, bigotry, false ideologies, degeneration of the sacred, diseases, hunger, murder and manslaughter, abortion, deranged sexuality, natural disasters, climate disturbances, degeneration of character and language, materialism, juvenile gangs, false gurus, decline of religion, disappearance of respect for life - it's all there. God-fearing ministers cannot improve it, preachers of doom cannot make it worse.

---

[2] Danielou, A., *La fantaisie des dieux et l'aventure humaine*, p. 13-37.

Not to mention, of course, the wisdom of the Indians. That is up for grabs, although obviously not every intuitive Indian is a sage and not every rational European is a fool. Mayans, Incas, Aztecs, Iroquois, Hopi and Blackfoot Indians all speak of the great upheavals of our time. Anyone who plows through the Bible again, or browses the myths and wisdom books of various cultures or consults the prophetic works of religious literature will find plentiful references to our time.

However, with prophetic proclamations, we continue to struggle. Bookshelves full of what is going to happen, should have happened, yet did not happen. Even in the granary of prophecies there is chaff among the wheat. One must wield the wand carefully and let the chaff of charlatans be blown away by the wind. Especially in the eyes of the rational Westerner. The latter accepts more easily a weather forecast based on satellites and computers or prophetic claims of scientists about computers, nanotechnology, imminent epidemics or climate changes than the warnings of biblical prophets such as Ezekiel, Daniel, Jeremiah, or the likes of Nostradamus, Edgar Cayce or Jakob Lorber. However, those who accept a certain margin in their time predictions can also learn a lot from them. The physicist, astronomer and philosopher Carl Friedrich von Weizsäcker recognized this. During World War II, he participated in the development of an atomic bomb in Germany, but had great conscientious objections to it. He once said, 'I personally believe that the growing criticism of the technocratic world is the foreshadowing of deep crises, even disasters. It is unforgivable not to listen to Cassandra and Jeremiah'.[3] Jesus noted that a prophet is not recognized in his own community. St. Paul expressed himself in similar ways. In his first letter to the Thessalonians he writes, 'Do not despise the prophetic word, but examine everything and retain what is right'. (1 Tes.5:20-21).

Regardless of how one feels about prophecies, many feel that things will come to a climax in the coming years. We are seeing all too well what is going on. More and more floods, tsunamis, earthquakes, famines, volcanic eruptions, wars, droughts, desertification, wildfires, hurricanes

---

[3] *Die Zeit* (June 15, 1979).

and insect plagues. Old values and norms are crumbling. Forecast: if we do not achieve a breakthrough at all levels on our planet before 2010, its degradation will begin at a rapid pace. This is what Professor Ervin Laszlo, international scholar, former concert pianist and founder of the Club of Budapest, said.[4] Short-term prophecy is apparently allowed these days. Especially when solutions are offered, like Ervin Laszlo does. And it remains good practice to light a candle in the hour of darkness. How about a few hundred million torches? Or even more?

For your consideration, a casual sample from the granary of prophecies. The wand did some preliminary work. It is up to each person to remain alert to whether the signs of the times are correct.

I have had visions of these times of Earth changes
and what you need to survive them.
I feel a responsibility to share my knowledge
with those who are ready,
who are open to it. If they don't want to hear it,
then there is nothing I can do about it.[5]

Sun Bear, Indian visionary from the Ojibwa-tribe

---

[4] Laszlo, E., *You* Can *Change the World*.
[5] Sun Bear and Wabun Wind, *Indian Prophecies for the Millennium*.

As it was at the time of Noah, so it will be again:
love will diminish and completely freeze.
The sense of God and the belief in a pure doctrine of life
revealed from the heavens to mankind will be changed into a dark,
dead superstition full of lies and deceit.
The rulers will again treat the people like animals
and have them slaughtered cold-bloodedly and unscrupulously,
if they do not submit to the will of the rulers without any opposition.
The powerful will put pressure on poor people and persecute
and suppress every free spirit using all possible means.
As a result, suffering will come upon the people,
such as there has never been on earth.[6]

Jakob Lorber, prophet, musician and composer (1800-1864)

We need to do everything we can to wake ourselves up and everyone around us.
We need to listen to the wisdom of the prophecies, open our hearts and minds to
the possibilities, begin to realize what is going on and then take action.[7]

John Perkins, author and economic hit man (ret.)

---

[6] Lorber, J., *De wederkomst van Christus,* in Dutch.
[7] Perkins J., *Confessions of an Economic Hit Man.*

And thus, the gods will go away from men - a grievous thing!
Only evil angels will remain, who will mingle with men and violently force
the poor wretches to commit all kinds of ruthless crimes, wars,
plundering and cheating, all things that are against the nature of the soul.
Then the Earth will no longer be balanced, the sea no longer navigable,
the circulation of the stars in the sky disturbed.
The voices of the gods will necessarily be hushed and silenced.
The fruits of the Earth will rot away, and the Earth will be barren.
Even the air will no longer be pure and in time will no longer circulate.
Thus, the era of the old world will end.
There will be no more religion, and everything will be in disorder,
all that is good will vanish.
But when all this has taken place, Asclepius, God [...] will cleanse the world of evil
by washing it away with floods of water, burning it away with fire,
or destroying it by wars and epidemics.
And He will restore to His world its original beauty
so that the cosmos will again be deemed worthy of admiration and reverence,
and God, who created and restored such a wonderful work,
will again be praised with never-ending songs of praise.
Such is the new birth of the cosmos: it is such a restoration of all things
as to make them right again, a holy and awesome restoration of all nature,
brought about in the course of time by the eternal will of God.[8]

Hermes Trismegistus to Asclepius

---

[8] Hermes Trismegistus, *Hermetica*.

1.2   September 11, 2001: attack or conspiracy?

Once, when he happened to mention the war against Eurasia,
she surprised him by nonchalantly noting that
in her opinion that whole war did not exist.
The rocket bombs that came down daily on London,
were probably fired by the government of Oceania itself,
'Just to keep the people scared'.
This was a thought that had literally never occurred to him.[9]

George Orwell, *1984*

World in turmoil

September 11, 2001. On the way from the Pyrenees to Belgium. My wife was driving. Lived in the mountains for exactly eleven years. Moved exactly on September 11, 2001. It seemed an inevitable date. Sound of the humming engine, southern warmth, soft classical music. It made one a bit drowsy. After a few hours of driving, I turned on the news. An indeterminate feeling had come over me, was palpable in every cell of my body. It was almost three o'clock. The radio broadcast was interrupted. World news. That was the first time we heard about the attacks.

At 8:45 a.m. local time in New York, 2:45 p.m. in France, a hijacked Boeing 767 (flight number 11!) crashed into the north tower of the World Trade Center (WTC 1). A full fifteen minutes later, a Boeing 767 crashed into the south tower of the WTC (2), and forty minutes later, a Boeing 757 impacted the west wing of the Pentagon in Washington DC. Not much later, with apocalyptic rumbling, driving huge clouds of dust, the south tower of the WTC collapsed. The wedge of the Pentagon that was hit also collapsed. A few minutes later, a Boeing 757 crashed into a forest

---

[9] Orwell, G., *1984*.

in Somerset County southeast of Pittsburgh, Pennsylvania, possibly destined to hit a nuclear power plant. Finally, the north tower of the WTC collapsed. Overall, nearly three thousand victims. The tragedy was deeply engraved in the collective consciousness. Radio and television stations talked about it continuously. The world was in turmoil. Statements followed. President George W. Bush announced that this terrorist attack was worse than the one on Pearl Harbor in 1941.

On the way, we watched the footage in a French café. It was repeated continuously. The collapsing WTC towers, panic, clouds of dust - images of hell itself. And of course, footage of the battered Pentagon. Everyone sat stunned in front of the television. Not a word was said. The event was not captured on my retina, but etched into it. In a non-rational way, I realized in a split second the consequences of this catastrophe. Over and over my attention was drawn to the collapsing towers. Something struck me that I could not explain at the time. Later I realized that I thought it was a most peculiar collapse. For a moment it seemed as if something was imploding from *within* as well. An absurd idea. Surely, I had not seen it clearly.

Fact of the matter was that on September 11, 2001, from 2:45 p.m. onward, a drama unfolded in America, which soon thereafter unfolded before the eyes of the whole world through television.

People started questioning it sometime later. Luckily, I was not the only one. The world's financial centre was in ruins. Was this an attack on the civilized world? Or was there something more sinister at play? The world reacted in shock. Rarely was 911 (nine eleven!), the number of the emergency services in America, dialed as often as that day.

Both prayer and war

That same evening, President George W. Bush addressed the nation. 'America and our friends and allies stand together with all who want peace and security in the world, and together we will win the war against terrorism. Tonight, I ask you to pray for all the grieving, for the children whose world has been shaken, for all those whose understanding of safety and security has been threatened. And I pray that they may be comforted by a power greater than all of us, handed down through the ages in Psalm

23: 'Even though I walk through the darkest valley, I will fear no evil, for thou art with me'.[10] He concluded his speech with God's blessing, as in virtually all other speeches related to 9/11: 'Thank you. Good night, and God bless America.'[11]

Hardly had the sounds of prayers faded away, when war was declared on international terrorism. 'A Global War on Terror'. A war according to an entirely new pattern. All over the world. The enemy was identified almost instantly: Osama bin Laden (who had formerly held relations with the CIA), the Taliban from Afghanistan (who allegedly sheltered Osama and his terrorist friends) and finally Saddam Hussein (once supported by the US government). 'The axis of evil' included some sixty 'rogue states' and from the President's lips we heard, 'Those who are not with us are against us.'

Critical authors

After the first emotions had subsided, countries had expressed their solidarity with America, statements were made, a united front was presented against this terrorist attack, 'appropriate measures' were taken everywhere, and hardly anyone dared to ask questions that differed from the official narrative, critical authors gradually began to put forward other viewpoints. Those who believed that there might be some conspiracy involved were quickly swept away by the media with the scythe of scorn, ridicule and suspicion. Anyone who wanted to be a good patriot had better not indulge in that sort of thing. However, distinguished American writers also began to interfere (Gore Vidal, Bob Woodward, James Risen), although they did not mention the possibility of a conspiracy.[12]

Meanwhile, the UN was being pressured by America, even manipulated according to some. The drum of war began to sound. Drums of doom spread to future battlefields. Soon a coalition went to war. First in Afghanistan, where thousands of bombs and grenades destroyed the

---

[10] Bush, G.W., *We Will Prevail,* 2004.

[11] Ibid.

[12] Vidal, G., *Perpetual War for Perpetual Peace,* Woodward, B., *Bush at War*; Risen J., *State of War.*

infrastructure of the Taliban-occupied territory in the shortest possible time. Mercilessly, the Taliban were hunted down and killed. Countless numbers were arrested and thrown into prisons without trial. American statements made it clear that this was absolutely not a war against Islam, but only against certain terrorists and extremists, against those who abused Islam. Sometime later, war was declared on Saddam Hussein. In front of the world community, former Secretary of State Colin Powell pulled a vial from the inside pocket of his jacket. A small bottle like that, filled with viruses or chemical poisons, was enough to wipe out an entire country, he said. Rejection everywhere. The British Prime Minister Tony Blair also made a statement to the effect that Iraq could deploy biological and chemical weapons within 45 minutes. Bush and Blair repeatedly informed their nations and the world that Iraq had weapons of mass destruction. James Risen, reporter for the New York Times, reports that the CIA 'sent the U.S.-based sister of an Iraqi scholar to her brother in Iraq to learn from him about the weapons of mass destruction. She came back with the message: Saddam does not have those weapons. The CIA leadership knew that the White House wanted to hear something different and decided to keep the information to themselves. British lawyer and professor Philipp Sands revealed early this month that he had been allowed to read a secret memorandum about a meeting between Bush and British Prime Minister Blair in late January 2003. Bush was questioning the legitimacy of the impending war. He suggested flying an American U2 plane in UN colours over Iraq in the hope that it would be shot down. It would provide the casus belli he was looking for.'[13] James Risen writes in his book *State of War. The Secret History of the CIA and the Bush Administration* that the CIA even considered sinking a ferry, resulting in hundreds of deaths, in order to blame it on Saddam Hussein.[14]

The fact that these weapons have never been found - and that the entire war is therefore in fact illegal - is now known to everyone, unless they are still stored somewhere in one of Saddam Hussein's bunkers, which is

---

[13] Dutch newspaper *Volkskrant* (February 25, 2006).
[14] Risen, J., *State of War*.

highly unlikely (in 2006 and in the meantime in 2021 as well). Possibly these will be remnants of what the West supplied to Saddam. Andreas von Bülow (German intelligence expert, former Secretary of Defense in the Helmut Schmidt cabinet and later Federal Minister for Research and Technology) and Noam Chomsky (professor of linguistics and known worldwide as one of America's leading political commentators) pointed out the extent of the West's involvement in supplying chemical weapons of mass destruction to Iraq.[15] One of the United Nations weapons inspectors, David Kelly, who visited Iraq on a total of 37 occasions between 1994 and 1997, suddenly died. On Friday, July 18, 2003, he allegedly committed suicide in the woods near Abingdon. His left wrist artery had been cut with a knife causing him to bleed to death, the official statement said. Not everyone was convinced this was the case. As recently as the Tuesday before his death, he had been questioned by a House of Commons inquiry committee on the Iraq affair.[16]

'There is no doubt that the atrocities of September 11 constituted an event of historical importance,' Noam Chomsky said.[17] But the actual backgrounds, he said, are still hidden from many. According to Chomsky September 11th was gratefully seized by Bush to further expand the already overwhelming military power of the US in the world by means of his 'war on terror' (in many ways a duplication of Reagan's 'war on terror' proclaimed twenty years earlier).[18] According to Chomsky, you can't talk about the terrorism of the weak against the powerful if you don't also face 'the unmentionable but much more extreme terrorism of the powerful against the weak.' If you look at the disregard for international treaties and the suffering inflicted upon civilian populations, he believes 'there is no fundamental difference between the attacks of Muslim extremists and America's war policies.'[19]

---

[15] Bülow, A. von, *Im Namen des Staates*; Chomsky, N., *Power and Terror*. Also see www.chomsky.info.

[16] Rétyi, A. von, *Skull & Bones. Amerikas geheime Macht-Elite*, Kopp Verlag, Rottenburg 2003, p. 238-240.

[17] Chomsky, *Power and Terror*, p. 105. Also see: http://100777.com/node/1425.

[18] Idem, p.109-110.

[19] Idem, cover text.

See also under section 9/11 the book by John le Carré 'A Fragile Truth', in which Carré, who also wrote the book The Listening Finch (section Africa on Congo), also discusses the David Kelly issue and Iraq.

Doubts about the official 9/11 narrative

Soon the number of websites with other than the usual information about 9/11 proliferated on the internet. Popular youth sites, too. Thousands of emails poured in. CD-ROMs and DVDs came into circulation, with background information, commentaries and images.[20] One of the top Dutch sites in this area is that of the Dutch journalist Daan de Wit.[21] Through a series of articles, lectures and meetings he has been working for some time to bring the truth about 9/11 to light. In the book *Die Bildbeweise. 11 September* by top manager and physicist Gerhoch Reisegger, numerous photos and images of reconstructions are included, accompanied by questions and comments. Meanwhile, many wondered how it was possible that the Boeing 757 that flew into the Pentagon left a hole much smaller than its 115 feet wingspan.

This is how Flight 77, a Boeing 757, is supposed to have slammed into the Pentagon.
Image: Gerhoch Reisegger.

The lines at the tips of the wings indicate where the plane should definitely have hit the building. Magic? A striking coincidence is that sixty years earlier, on September 11, 1941, under the leadership of Franklin D. Roosevelt, the cornerstone ceremony of the Pentagon under construction took place. October 11, 2001, in his speech at a memorial

---

[20] Hilder, A.J., '9-11, The greatest lie ever sold', 2005, 'Confronting the evidence' on YouTube. A call to Reopen the 9/11 Investigation', 2005, www.reopen911.org
[21] www.daanspeak.com

service at the Department of Defense, Bush pointed out how symbolic the attack on the Pentagon was. He related the speech Roosevelt gave on September 11, 1941 (when work began on the foundations of the Pentagon!) to the speech he himself gave on October 11 in response to September 11, 2001. Roosevelt in his speech held out to the American people the real danger of a military enemy [Japan] at a time when the American people had just become aware of the Nazi terror in Europe. Bush reminded Americans of the danger of international terrorism.[22] Roosenvelt was initiated into the 32nd degree of Scottish Freemasonry.[23] That means he knew Albert Pike's book, *Morals and Dogma of the ancient and accepted Scottish Rite of Freemasonry*, which every 32nd degree initiate has. Pike, himself a 33rd degree initiate in the Scottish rite and Grand Commander of North American Freemasonry from 1859-1869, saw a relationship between the pentagonal shape (pentagon or penta-gram) and the masonic flaming five-pointed star, which was equated with Sirius in Ancient Egypt. Behind the Pentagon rises the 'Washington Monument,' a giant obelisk. If you look at the Pentagon from the obelisk, you will see the pentagon upside down. Could this inverted pentagon or five-pointed star, also known as the inverted pentagram, have been the inspiration for the design of the *Medal of Honor*, the highest American military decoration for military personnel of the army, navy and air force? This award is always presented by the President of America, who is also Commander-in-Chief of the United States Armed Forces, 'for conspicuous gallantry and enterprise at the risk of his own life, above and beyond that required by duty, in actual combat against an enemy force.' The Medal of Honor is worn around the neck so that the inverted pentagram rests exactly on the

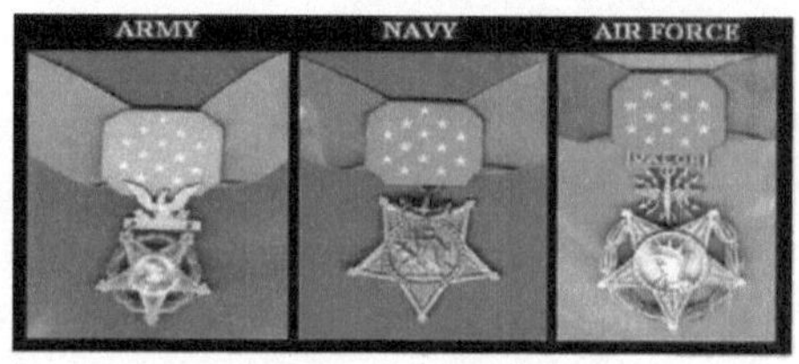

---

[22] Bush, *We Will Prevail*.

[23] When references are made to membership in Freemasonry, this book makes use of the encyclopaedic work *10.000 Famous Freemasons*, (ed.) W.R. Denslow, Missouri Lodge of Research, z.j. 4 volumes, (repr.ed. 1957-'61).

sternum.[24] No doubt it must have escaped the designers of this medal that in black magic the inverted pentagram is a symbol of demonic power and destruction.

That the cameras of the Pentagon, the electronically most heavily guarded building in the world, refused to work at the time of the crash, that a poor film is circulating on which hardly anything can be seen, that no large aircraft debris was found, that all the steel wreckage was immediately shipped to China and Japan, which processed it for the metal industry - the government gave no answer to this. Was the Pentagon perhaps under an unfavourable star sign that day? Did the computers at the headquarters of the Army, Navy and Air Force suddenly fail at the same time? Questions that many have already asked. Ronald D. Ray, former Deputy Secretary of Defense in the Reagan administration, former colonel and distinguished Vietnam veteran, recently raised his grave doubts about the official story of 9/11 in an interview. He questioned how it was possible, with a budget of some $500 billion a year, to not even be able to defend the Pentagon and was aghast that the government was ignoring 'the conspiracy theory'. Furthermore, in the interview, he gave examples of 'false-flag operations' by the US government, in particular an attack committed by Israel on the USS 'Liberty' ship - an attack, which President Lyndon B. Johnson allowed in order to blame Egypt and start a war.[25]

Just as in America, there are increasing numbers of people in the Netherlands who no longer accept the official story of 9/11. The Dutch government, however, turns a blind eye to dossiers that these groups wish to present. That September 11 and the war on terror also have major consequences for the Netherlands was described by Karel van Wolferen and Jan Sampiemon in *Een keerpunt in de vaderlandse geschiedenis*.[26]

---

[24] https://www.thebalancecareers.com/medal-of-honor-3344965.

[25] Interview by Paul Joseph Watson & Alex Jones on www.prisonplanet.com July 2006. Also important is the interview with Colonel Donn le Grand-Pre on the same website.

[26] Recommendation on the cover of this book by former Dutch prime minister Dries van Agt and André Spoor.

Blindly following the policy of the U.S. is not without risk. Susan George, author of the bestseller *Het Lugano Rapport*, expressed it very powerfully in an interview in *De Morgen*: 'The United States is doing everything it can to lead the planet to destruction. The big challenge for Europe and the rest of the world is therefore to isolate this US government. Not the American people, but the Bush administration.' [27]

A conspiracy?

Multimillionaire Jimmy Walter, who does not accept the official version of 9/11 and launched a campaign for truth, is offering one million dollars to whoever can prove that the WTC collapsed according to the official explanation of the Bush administration. Substantiated, of course, with scientific evidence.[28] Perhaps the fourteen MSc students from Delft University of Technology are going to win the prize promised as part of the Studium Generale. For an expense allowance of € 300 per week, they received an advance on this, which they must repay to the Studium Generale when they win. Last August, they spent a few weeks investigating the collapse of the WTC towers on a purely technical level. Head of Studium Generale and lecturer in Aerospace Engineering, dr. Coen Vermeeren, only wanted to work with students who do not see a conspiracy behind everything. 'That's too dangerous and I don't want that. Sobriety must prevail.' [29] The results of this investigation were published in September 2006.[30] Jan Vambersky, professor in Civil Engineering and geosciences, refused to participate in this project. 'Not serious at all,' he judged.[31] Willem Middelkoop, financial journalist, and freelance reporter and commentator on RTL Z, applauded the initiative. 'We need this.' Because conspiracy theories have long since ceased to be found only in the 'dark caves of the internet'. 'It's not just a few lunatics. It's millions of people all over the world. Bush will not be able to ignore this.' Middelkoop does believe that the attacks were carried out by

---

[27] Belgium newspaper *De Morgen* (May 30, 2005).
[28] www.reopen911.org
[29] Update: Vermeeren C., *9/11 Complex* (in Ducth).
[30] Update: published 2006, removed 2008.
[31] Bessems, K., in Dutch newspaper *Trouw* (July 31, 2006).

Muslim extremists, but that the U.S. government was aware that the attacks were coming and then planted explosives in the buildings. According to him, this major disaster gave the Bush administration the opportunity to wage long-planned wars. 'The United States attacked Iraq partly because Saddam Hussein wanted to start trading his oil in euros instead of dollars.' According to Middelkoop, the world economy is run by a small elite around the US stock exchange, the CIA and the US president. Middelkoop is actively researching the secrets of the financial system.[32] In 2017 Middelkoop wrote the book *Patronen van Bedrog* (Patterns of Deceit) about false flags and the Deep State.[33]

Last August 21, the 'Terzake Zomer' program of the Belgian television channel Canvas aired *Loose Change 2*, one of the most famous films on the internet (five million downloads in 2006). The film revolves around the question: was 9/11 a terrorist attack or a conspiracy? The filmmakers point out a whole series of contradictions and gaps in the official account of 9/11. A day later, Terzake Summer came out with a French report in which several conspiracy theories are examined. The Dutch investigative television program Zembla on September 10 attempted to answer the question whether the many conspiracy theories about 9/11 are based on any sort of truth and whether we will ever be able to find out what the truth is.

They also addressed the question of whether the media can be completely independent. Earlier (June 7, 2006) Peter Giesen wrote under the headline 'The big lie' an entire page in the Dutch newspaper *de Volkskrant* about conspiracy theories relating to September 11. 'Worldwide the trend is growing that attributes the attacks of September 11, 2001 to a conspiracy. Also, in the Netherlands people are coming together who want to tell their own truth about the collapsed WTC-towers. Now we can still say what we think.'

Much of the information in books and on websites overlaps, but new reports with convincing sources are constantly emerging. While magazines such as *Nexus* and (Dutch magazine) *Frontier* have long been

---

[32] Idem. Also see Free Magazine by Middelkoop, W.: Inveztor Nieuwsflash, August 4, 2006.
[33] Willem Middelkoop en Tim Dollee, '*Patronen van Bedrog*, in Dutch.

pioneers in providing 'alternative' information,[34] a range of authors now believe that 9/11 has all the elements of a conspiracy. Among them, bestselling authors such as David Icke (England), Andreas von Rétyi (Germany), Jimm Marss (America), Robin de Ruiter (Netherlands) and Andreas von Bülow (Germany).[35]

Tough questions

The above authors are asking critical questions and probing into backgrounds usually avoided by the established media. These 'conspiracy theorists' are now being read by an audience of millions. They make new connections, point to the interconnections between politics, business and secret societies and question the supposedly neutral '9/11 Commission'.[36] Why did the Pentagon's state-of-the-art security system (cameras, electronic devices, etc.) fail? Why were the automatic flight identification systems disabled? Why wasn't the military alerted immediately (there was plenty of time!). Why were so many 'defense exercises' held in the early morning of 9/11, 'coincidentally' to practice the impact of aircrafts into tall buildings? Why was this exercise cancelled almost immediately after the actual impact of the first plane into the north tower of the WTC, when Bush was not even aware of the attacks? Why was nothing reported about this exercise? How could hijackers with barely any decent flight training fly such complex aircrafts? Why are there no video recordings of the hijackers at the airport, while pictures of them emerged immediately after the attacks? Why were the remains of the corpses not traced? Where were the black boxes from the planes that flew into the WTC towers, which were resistant to enormous heat (1500°C)? Why are the contents of the other black boxes not disclosed? How could Mrs. Barbara Olson telephone from Flight 77 (with a borrowed credit card) to her husband,

---

[34] Dutch magazine *Frontier Magazine*, Frontier Publishing, *Nexus*, via Frontier Publishing. Update: both now no longer active.

[35] Icke, D., *Alice in Wonderland and the World Trade Centre Disaster;* Rétyi, A. von, *Skull and Bones*, m.n. p. 198-208; Marrs, J., *Inside Job*; Ruiter, R. de, *George W. Bush en de mythe van al-Qaeda*, in Dutch; Bülow, A. von, *Die CIA und der 11 September.*

[36] Idem. https://www.cfr.org/report/iraq-democracy-or-civil-war

who is attorney general of the Department of Justice, while the plane was flying extremely low and fast. Conversations are practically impossible then. In all the turmoil, how was Todd Beamer of Flight 93 able to make thirteen-minute phone calls from the Boeing 757's on-board phone?[37] How is it possible that the wallet containing, among other things, four credit cards of passenger Waleed Iskander (flight 11) was not burned in the blazing fire? What happened to the testimonies of firefighters and rescue workers who heard explosions outside and inside the buildings?[38] Questions and more questions, which the government does not answer. The authors who write about this substantiate their story with numerous sources, otherwise their books and websites had better be ignored if they had not.

Professors on conspiracies and 9/11

Books on conspiracies are not new. The internationally renowned Caroll Quigley, Bill Clinton's history professor at Georgetown University, wrote about them as early as 1966 and Anthony Sutton, professor of economics, in the 1980s. Professors in our time are also writing on the subject, although not in their capacity as a university professor. We should mention David Ray Griffin, James Fetzer and Steven E. Jones. According to them, too, the official story about the collapse of the WTC towers is flawed. There is much more to the story. From June 2-4 2006, an international conference on the subject was held at the Embassy Suites Hotel in Chicago.[39] At a Los Angeles hotel, June 25 of this year, more than 1,200 people gathered to reject the official account of 9/11. Among them were scientists, journalists, philosophers and experts on terrorism. 'A more radical movement is accusing the US government of an *inside job*'.[40] In addition, articles by 'Scholars for 9/11 Truth' appear regularly, in which reputable scientists attempt to refute the official version of 9/11. Michael Meyer, for example, a mechanical engineer, describes how the

---

[37] http://911blogger.com/node/9627

[38] https://killtown.blogspot.com/2006/02/911-rescuer-saw-explosions-inside-wtc.html

[39] http://911review.com/articles/griffin/nyc1.html

[40] Dutch newspaper *Dagblad van het Noorden* (June 26, 2006).

WTC towers did not collapse in a normal way.[41] Physicists such as David Heller and Steven E. Jones share that view. Other scientists, such as Thomas Eagar and Jan Vambersky, believe that the official reading of the collapse is quite explainable.

Testimonies on 9/11

The American professor emeritus of philosophy of religion, David Ray Griffin, in particular, is making millions think about the terrorist attacks with his shocking publications about 9/11.

The testimonies of a number of fire-fighters, police officers and Wall Street Journal reporters about the explosions they heard in the WTC towers, which, according to some of them, clearly point to a controlled demolition (controlled collapse, created by explosions) are quite revealing. These witnesses even speak of 'multiple explosions' and of 'sequenced explosions'. Mark Loizeaux, head of Controlled Demolition, Inc. explains: 'If I were commissioned to bring the towers down, I would put explosives in the foundation so that the weight of the building would cause the structure to yield.' And: '... to bring down a building the way we intend, without damaging another building', the collapse must be 'fully planned'. It requires 'the right explosive and the right scheme for applying the charge'.[42] The fact that it took so long for these testimonies to become available to us is because the city government, led by Mayor Michael Bloomberg, declined for a long time to make them available.[43]

---

[41] https://www.scholarsfor911truth.org

[42] Griffin, D. R., 'Explosive Testimony: Revelations about the Twin Towers in the 9/11 Oral Histories' (August 16, 2006). Source: https://911truth.org/explosive-testimony-revelations-twin-towers-911-oral-histories/

[43] Idem.

Bloomberg, a multimillionaire, is not only mayor of New York but also a media mogul.[44]

Specialists speak out

In his book *The 9/11 Commission Report. Omissions and distortions* Griffin exposes the lies told in the report of 'The 9/11 Commission' as well as the new lies the commission invented to cover up the previous lies. The 9/11 Commission Report, seen by Griffin as one of the most important documents ever published in the U.S., was only released in July 2004 and was quickly presented by the government as the definitive account of the 9/11 events. Griffin shows, however, that not only was the commission not 'independent' and 'impartial,' but that there was no thorough reporting. Step by step, he walks us through the 9/11 commission's conclusions and reveals how much is incorrect, omitted or distorted in them. Among other things, Griffin concludes that the Bush administration was at least complicit in allowing the catastrophic attacks on 9/11 to happen.

Another renowned investigator into 9/11 is Andreas von Bülow. He not only wrote a revealing book about the workings of secret services,[45] but also about the CIA and September 11th.[46] In an interview for GCN Radio Network, conducted by Alex Jones, he expressed his views on September 11 and stated unequivocally that the case was executed from the inside. [47] In his book on the CIA and September eleventh, he elaborates on issues that have also been raised by other authors. Extremely detailed, not hesitating to tackle precarious issues. Assuming a possible collaboration between American and Israeli security services, he raises the question of who, if anyone, warned the Israelis working in the WTC. After all, there were only a few Israeli victims. 'A discussion of these allegations immediately runs the risk of being accused of antisemitism,' he points out.[48] The range of inconsistencies surrounding 9/11 argues in favour of

---

[44] https://en.wikipedia.org/wiki/Bloomberg_L.P.

[45] Bülow, A. von, *Im Namen des Staates*.

[46] Bülow, A. von, *Die CIA und der 11 September*.

[47] www.prisonplanet.com

[48] Bülow, A. von, *Die CIA und der 11 September*, p. 214.

asking not only about the backgrounds of the conspiracy theory, but also about those of the secret services. Related to this, he recalls a quote from the former Pentagon department chief in the war on terror: one must always follow the fingers 'pointing at alleged terrorists back to the hand, the arm, the person extending those fingers and ask if the fight against terrorism is the actual motive of the person pointing the fingers.'[49] The war on terror enables a whole new geopolitics and important new key positions (military, political, economic). Von Bülow was one of the first to point out that in The New American Century, a project conceived by neoconservatives and led by Bush Senior, the blueprint for what would be implemented after 11 September had already been drawn up. Anyone who reads von Bülow's book on 9/11 is likely to see the official version of the US government in a completely different perspective. Add to this the fact that Bush senior spoke openly on 11 September 1991 in a speech to the Senate about the New World Order, as advocated by the power elite, and 11 September 2001 becomes almost a symbolic date.[50]

Anyone reading von Bülow's book on 11 September is likely to see the official version of the US government in a completely different light. Add to this the fact that Bush senior spoke openly on 11 September (!) 1991 in a speech to the Senate about the New World Order, as advocated by the power elite, and 11 September 2001 becomes almost a symbolic date.

'Dude, Where's My Country?'

Meanwhile in the US, the call for a new investigation is strong. Many are beginning to protest, ask questions, and criticize official explanations. They are no longer afraid of being called 'unpatriotic,' they are crawling out of the shelters of instilled fear, making their voices heard, fed up with the lies. A broad movement is beginning to emerge, including filmmakers, singers, actors, visual artists, authors. One of them is the internationally known filmmaker and author Michael Moore. In particular, his documentary *Fahrenheit 9/11* made quite a splash with the public. In all his books and films Michael Moore asks tough questions.

---

[49] Idem, p. 231.
[50] Idem, p. 231-237.

Not everyone appreciates that. In *Dude, Where's My Country?* he ironically asks George W. Bush: 'What was that expression on your face in that classroom in Florida on the morning of September 11 when your chief of staff said to you, 'America is under attack'?'[51] Moore examines the president's schedule on September 10 and 11 and shows that a lot of things don't add up. Especially not regarding the event at the school he visited. Apparently, no one bothered to inform the president immediately after the horrendous attacks. 'You arrived at that school after the first plane in New York hit the North Tower. Three months later, at a rally at Orlando City Hall, you told a kid from school, 'I was standing in the hallway waiting to go into that classroom, and then I saw a plane flying into that tower - the TV was apparently on, and I used to be a pilot myself, and I said, well well, that's one lousy pilot. I said, that must have been a terrible accident. But I had to go in quickly then, I couldn't think about it for long.' You repeated that same story a month later at another one of those town hall meetings in California. The only problem with that story is that you didn't see at all how that first plane crashed into the tower - no one saw that live on TV, because that footage wasn't broadcast until the next day. But that doesn't matter; we were all confused that morning. You went into that classroom around nine o'clock and the second plane hit the south tower at 9:03 am. Just a few minutes later, your chief of staff Andrew Card came in, as you sat in front of that classroom full of children and listened as they read out; he whispered something in your ear. Card was evidently telling you about the second plane and that story that we were 'attacked'. And at that very moment you began to stare into the distance, not really a blank stare, but more like paralyzed. You showed no emotion at all. And then ... you just kept sitting there. You sat there for about seven minutes and did nothing. That was, to say the least, strange. Creepy. You just sat there on the little chair, and you listened to the children reading, very peacefully, for five or six minutes. You didn't look worried, you didn't say you had to leave, you weren't hurriedly led away by your Secret Service advisors. George, what were you thinking? WHAT was going on in your head? What did that expression on your

---

[51] Moore, M., *Will they ever trust us again?*

face mean? 'Of all the questions I've posed to you, this is the one that puzzles me the most,'[52] Michael Moore said.

It's oily business.

Many an oil specialist believes that 9/11 was engineered in part to gain possession of the oil fields. This would allow pipelines to be routed through the region immediately. Karl W.B. Schwarz, director of Patmos Nanotechnologies, LLC and I-Nets Security Systems, reports a number of interesting facts on his website.[53] Taliban-ruled Afghanistan, bordering Pakistan, former Russian states like Georgia, Turkmenistan and Uzbekistan, and Iran (which in turn borders Iraq), is an extremely oil and natural gas-rich area. In order to extend pipelines to the West, one must first gain control over these areas. All kinds of interests are at stake here. For instance, in Uzbekistan the companies Enron, Mayer Brown and Rowe & Maw (Washington law firm) shared a joint office. They anticipated large profits through oil and gas. But that required pipelines to export the natural gas. From Rowe & Maw, a certain Richard Ben Veniste is senior partner. But Ben Veniste is also a member of the '9/11 Commission'. Enron, a major sponsor of George W. Bush, also in oil, recently went bankrupt due to a variety of scandals. The Taliban and General Rashid Dostum (who controlled Northern Afghanistan) had signed agreements with Argentina's Bridas Corporation. This was to enable the construction of a crucial pipeline through Afghanistan.
After 9/11, revolutionary developments take place all of a sudden in this entire area. The Turkmenistan government is succeeded by a new one, the president of Georgia suddenly dies at age 41, and the Pakistani government of Bhutto, which had also signed agreements with the Bridas Corporation, toppled. Because the Taliban were allegedly sheltering al-Qaeda, America soon declared war on Afghanistan. Since then, little is heard of the Bridas Corporation. According to Schwarz, these are facts that were never brought forward by the '9/11 Commission'. In this government-appointed commission, which is supposed to investigate all

---

[52] Idem, p. 48-50.
[53] Update: https://keywiki.org/Karl_W._B._Schwarz

matters relating to 9/11, a lot of conflicting interests can be found. And in the background, big companies like Bechtel and Main play an influential role. Just as they did before in Kosovo, these companies hope to be able to win billions for projects in Iraq and Afghanistan. And, of course, there is also the influence of large oil companies in America, such as Rockefeller's Standard Oil and money lenders such as Rothschild, Schwarz says on his website.

The Freedom Tower: 1776 feet high

A new tower will rise from the ashes of the World Trade Center. It is destined to become the pride of America, a symbol of freedom and determination. A very tall, glassy tower, looking a bit like a launch pad. On top of the tower is an illuminated, spiky pole, which is supposed to resemble the torch of the Statue of Liberty. Of course, heavily secured and equipped with special structures. For Jewish architect (and gifted musician) Daniel Libeskind, who survived the Holocaust, it is his most prestigious of projects.[54] A new tower will rise from the ashes of the World Trade Center. At 1776 feet (including the pole), it is taller than its predecessor. Lovely figure, by the way: 1776. It commemorates the year of America's independence. The new tower will no longer contain asbestos, as was the case in the Twin Towers. Rétyi, as well as other authors, points out that just before the attacks, the CIA had been warning of the impending attacks, but these never reached the people who worked in the WTC. It is also rumoured that the WTC, (the construction of which closely involved both David and Nelson Rockefeller) closed a new rental contract for the next 99 years with a new tenant, Larry Silverstein, some six months before the catastrophe. Silverstein planned to remove the dangerous asbestos, previously used in construction. An expensive undertaking. Fortunately, he had each building covered by insurance - over 3 billion per tower - just before the collapses. The insurance companies paid him $4.1 billion after the dust had settled. Silverstein's initial investment involved not more than 14 million of his own money.[55]

---

[54] https://en.wikipedia.org/wiki/Daniel_Libeskind
[55] https://www.reuters.com/article/us-usa-sept11-insurance-idUSKBN1KN2OL.

The special number 1776. We will encounter this number several more times in the remainder of this book, including in connection with the founding date of the highly secretive Order of the Illuminati. Various authors are linking this Order to that of Skull and Bones, of which a number of powerful Americans are members, including several members of the Bush family. But first, let's examine the bigger picture and see what 'Bush's secret' might be. Perhaps then we will better understand the 'Global War on Terror'. After all, the truth is at stake.

'… and the truth shall set you free'

Over the CIA's main entrance in Langley, Virginia, we can read a remarkable proverb: 'Thou shalt know the truth, and the truth shall set you free'. The proverb is taken from John 8:32.

Von Bülow draws our attention to this and adds his own comment: 'But the CIA's motto in itself is deceptive and is inconsistent with its mission and it is too good to ever become the truth. Only the informed citizen can overcome the consequences of colossal disinformation. The true patriots of the USA have a job to do![56]

Orwell formulated it in *1984* thus: 'The Ministry of Truth differed strikingly from everything else to be seen. It was a magnificent structure, a pyramid of gleaming white concrete rising in terraces three hundred feet high. From where Winston stood, he could just read how in ornate letters the three slogans of the Party were carved into the white façade:

WAR IS PEACE

FREEDOM IS SLAVERY

IGNORANCE IS STRENGTH.'[57]

---

[56] Bülow, *Die CIA und der 11. September*, p.252.
[57] Orwell, *1984*, p. 9-10. (Newspeak is the official language of Oceania.)

1.3   Bush's secret

I recognize that the government does not have the right to propagate a religious belief, or directly fund religious exercises or religious education. That is not a matter for the government. [58]

George W. Bush to members of a conference held by the White House on projects of organizations relating to communities and faith. Philadelphia, December 12, 2002.

The president of Good and Evil

Australian philosopher Peter Singer, professor of bioethics at Princeton University, known for his high-profile book *Animal Liberation. Between Death and Life*, is considered one of the most influential contemporary philosophers in the world. He also wrote a book about George W. Bush, *The President of Good and Evil.* Singer points out that it has not happened since time immemorial that a president has spoken so often about good and evil. He examined a considerable number of Bush's moral statements and analysed his thinking. As a prominent moralist, the President of America, who calls himself a Christian, does not act on his moral statements.

'George W. Bush is a Christian. His heart, he has told us, he has entrusted to Jesus. When war with Iraq was imminent, he read the Bible every day. He also prays daily. He believes in a 'divine plan that supersedes all human plans.' He takes his faith into his public life. He thinks a president should testify of 'the power of faith'.'[59]

---

[58] Singer, P., *The President of Good and Evil.*
[59] Ibid.

The *reborn Christian*

Who is this president of the United States, who just before the invasion of Iraq asked his father for advice? No, not Bush senior, but his 'father in heaven'. Many accuse him of numerous contradictory statements; that he often uses lies and that his moral statements do not correspond with his actions. So how is it that this president is still in power? Is he really the most powerful man on earth? Where does his habit come frome, of having numerous speeches delivered by his speechwriters, end with a dry and monotonous, 'God bless you' and 'God bless America'?

Who is this *reborn Christian*,[60] who feels a connection to the Christian Coalition, a coalition of mostly right-wing, sometimes ultra-right-wing 'reborn Christians'? This coalition is committed to a total transformation of society and is against the theory of evolution, abortion, homosexuality, euthanasia, cloning, and in favour of the sanctity of marriage and family. Many a member of this coalition envisions 'the end of times,' with Bush as the leader of Armageddon, after which theocracy can reign. Who is this *reborn Christian*, influential oil baron and member of Skull and Bones, who begins every cabinet meeting with a prayer, who asked God to bless General Tommy Franks (who was to attack Iraq) and U.S. troops, who regularly praises his Creator, quoted the prophets from the Bible when the space shuttle Columbia crashed, effortlessly connects sword and Bible, and rules with imperial elegance? Who is this man, who before becoming president was an alcoholic, like his grandfather Prescott and his brother James, and was arrested several times for being drunk and misbehaving? [61] Who is this man, who after his conversion to a reborn Christian swore never to touch a drop of alcohol again? Who is this man, who at the death of Pope John Paul II, together with the President of Russia, Vladimir Putin - former head of the KGB, the Russian Secret Service - stood close to the coffin and praised the deceased prince of the Church as 'a gift from God'?

Who is this man, who on September 11, 2001, stunned the entire world by his sluggish response, and a few days later emerges as the leader of the

---

[60] *Reborn Christian*: a mixture of methodist and christianity.
[61] Kelley, K., *The Family, The Real Story of the Bush Dynasty*.

free world, declares a global war on terrorism, violates treaties and conventions, turns a blind eye to inhumane prisons, torture, CIA renditions of Guantanamo Bay detainees, and meanwhile tirelessly talks about freedom and democracy, human rights and privacy? Who is this man who acts in such a lethargic way with disasters? Think of the catastrophic tsunami on Boxing Day 2004, which wiped out entire areas of Indonesia and India, and of the monster Hurricane Katrina, which flooded New Orleans on August 29, 2005. Who is this man, who often stays at his ranch in Texas during critical situations? For example, when Cindy Sheehan, whose son Casey was killed in Iraq at the age of 24, went camping in front of Bush's ranch to explain to him that the majority of Americans are against the war?[62] Who is this man, who without flinching sends a few hundred thousand soldiers into war to fight terrorism and seems emotionless when fallen soldiers return at night by plane in a body bag? According to experts, he did not properly perform his own military duties (Vietnam) and his military file was allegedly 'accidentally' destroyed during an attempt to salvage decaying microfilms.[63] Who is this man, who leaves his ranch to prevent, by signing a controversial law, euthanasia from being applied to Terri Schiavo, who had been living a vegetative life for 15 years on a feeding tube, but when he was governor in Texas had 152 executions carried out effortlessly? Who is this man, who hates political reporters, is, by his own admission, 'disgusted with the Washington establishment,' while at the same time caving in to it and not allowing his executive power to be eroded?[64]

Spin-doctors, Rasputins and lobbyists

Who is this man, who is pushing for the appointment of Jewish multi-billionaire and philanthropist Ronald Arnall from Los Angeles as ambassador to the Netherlands, while Arnall was involved in many mortgage scandals (hastily reaching a settlement with the victims), has interests in oil and gas, insurance, real estate, and as one of Bush's major

---

[62] Dutch newspaper *Volkskrant* (August 16, 2005).
[63] Dutch magazine *De Tijd* (July 10, 2004).
[64] Dutch newspaper *Volkskrant* (February 25, 2006).

sponsors once said, 'America finally has a leader of great integrity and courage, who will deliver the world from the scourge of terrorism.'[65]

Who is this man, replacing liberal and moderate judges with neoconservatives? Who is this man, who appoints someone like Elliot Abrams as coordinator of the new international democratization program of the United States and not much later uses his influence to appoint the controversial neoconservative politician John Bolton as ambassador to the United Nations? Abrams (hawk, was a supporter of Sharon's politics) is friends with hawks like Perle, Feith and Wolfowitz and served as a divisive figure in the Iran-Contra scandal as recently as the 1980s.[66]

Who is this man, surviving the collapse of energy giant Enron, home to major sponsors of his, and the resignation of his adviser Tom Delay? Delay, a former bug killer, was the influential chairman of the Republican Party in the House of Representatives and a ruthless businessman, who had to resign on charges of illegal party funding. Delay's fall also got Delay's friend, Jewish businessman Jack Abramoff, a lobbyist in Washington, in trouble. He was arrested on suspicion of political pay for play. Close associates of Delay were also suspected of corruption.[67] Who is this man, surrounded by 'spin doctors', Rasputins and lobbyists, who seem to have him dancing to their tunes rhythmically?

Full of contradictions?

Who is this man, who has divided the world into the *good guys* and the *bad guys* on the basis of the concept of 'the axis of evil' (a term used by the former author of Bush speeches, David Frum, who mainly referred to Iraq, Iran and North Korea[68])? Who is this man, who time and again presents the threat of international terrorism to the entire world and at the same time swiftly enforces all kinds of laws that substantially restrict freedom and privacy and expects Europe to do the same because there are at least eighty thousand potential terrorists in the world? Who is this

---

[65] Dutch newspaper *Trouw;* Dutch newspaper *Brabants Dagblad;* Belgium newspaper *de Stentor,* all on February 10, 2006.

[66] The illegal sales of American arms to Iran, that were used against Iraq.

[67] Dutch newspaper *Volkskrant* (April 5, 2006).

[68] Laurent, E., *Bush's Secret World.*

man, who befriends the multi-billionaire Bill Gates, founder and owner of Microsoft, who is committed to the rapid implementation of smart cards, biometric passports and chips and who controls the market in America and Europe with his mega-corporation? Who is this man, whom Dutch Prime Minister Balkenende and NATO Secretary-General De Hoop Scheffer support so strongly, while so many renowned authors and politicians warn about the dubious aspects of American power policy? Who is this man, who ignores the Geneva Conventions, refuses to endorse the Kyoto Treaty, antagonizes countless intellectuals? Who is this man so full of contradictions?

Influential evangelists, top industrialists and media tycoons

Who is this man, who maintains close contacts with a circle of wealthy and influential television ministers such as the multimillionaire Pat Robertson, who once aspired to become president and has built his Kingdom of God all over the United States and, like writers such as Mark Hitchcock and Tim LaHaye, has already convinced some one hundred million Americans of the End Times in which we live, the imminent Last Judgment, the coming of the Antichrist and the Second Coming of Christ? Who is this man, who, just like his father before him, is friends with the South Korean minister Sun Myung Moon (of the Moon sect), founder of the conservative Washington Times, who supports the Bush family (and Reagan at the time) and invests in South and North Korea?[69] Who is this man, who maintains good relations with the world's most famous evangelist Billy Graham, who had a tremendous influence on many presidents? Who, at the same time was their 'errand boy,' though and who is a regular pastor at inaugural speeches, is known to many heads of state and kings, knows how to take the thousands of people in stadiums almost to God's throne by his exhilarating sermons and is completely familiar with all aspects of politics, is seen as God's own representative of values and norms and is, at the same time, befriended by many top industrialists of sometimes dubious standing? Who maintains excellent relations with multi-billionaires like the Rockefellers

---

[69] Idem.

and Rothschilds and media tycoons like Rupert Murdoch?[70] Billy, already elderly, has since handed over his empire to his son Franklin, who was allowed to lead the service in honour of Bush's inauguration into the White House in January 2001.

Royal bloodline

Who is this man, who like many U.S. presidents descends from a royal bloodline? David Icke pointed out that of the 43 presidents of the United States, from George Washington to George W. Bush, 34 of them can be genetically traced back to the lineage of Emperor Charlemagne (742-814), leader of the Franks (present-day France) and emperor of the Holy Roman Empire. All of these presidents form dynasties, just as much as the royal families of Europe, to which their bloodlines can be traced. For centuries, Europe, and more recently the United States, have been defined by these royal bloodlines, as several researchers have shown. Icke bases his work, among other things, on Burke's Peerage (a kind of 'bible' about the hereditary lines of the blue-blooded nobility), which shows, among other things, bloodlines between American presidents and various royal families. Burke's book thus puts a damper on the idea that anyone can become president in the United States. Presidential candidates with the most powerful genetic kingdoms appear to win elections time and time again. Is this just because they are of 'royal' or 'noble blood,' or do the descendants of these 'hereditary lines' also have the greatest influence? For example, George W. Bush is related to the British royal family. He is the thirteenth cousin of the Queen Mother, who died in 2002, and is therefore also related to Queen Elizabeth and Prince Charles. Bush's bloodline goes back to Henry II (1154-1189) of the Plantagenet royal family. Also, Bush is related to Mary Tudor, sister of Henry VIII, and to Charles II of England. Presidential candidate Al Gore was not only a cousin of President Nixon, but also of Bush.[71] Both Gore and Bush are members of Skull&Bones. Anyone who studies royal

---

[70] Burns, C., *Billy Graham and his Friends*, p. 387-388, 422.
[71] Icke, D, *Tales from the Time Loop*, Also see Springmeier, F., *Bloodlines of the Illuminati*, p. ii-iii.

bloodlines[72] will come to the disconcerting conclusion that kings, queens and other noblemen are not only related to each other, but have ruled the world for centuries and still exert great influence on modern democracies, even if in some countries it is only a 'symbolic' function.

'European Royals one big family,' headlined the July 12, 2004, *Vlaamse Nieuwsblad.* The article shows the family tree of the Royals and a number of royal faces. One big family, going back to a certain Johan Willem Friso Nassau-Dietz, who inherited the title 'Prince of Orange' in 1702 from a distant cousin. That most royal families are very wealthy and have been involved in many wars over power, land and serfdom is common knowledge. Less well known is that they are well versed in occultism and often consult esotericists who exert great influence inside and outside the royal family. A few examples. The Russian monk and occultist Rasputin (1863-1916) was an advisor to Tsarina Alexandra Fyodorovna and had great influence on Russian politics. In sixteenth-century England, the occultist and hermetic philosopher John Dee (professor of Greek and mathematician, sponsored by King Edward VI) was protector and advisor to Queen Elizabeth I. He also, along with his companion Edward Kelley, offered his services to the eccentric and occult German Emperor Rudolf II in Prague, who employed the alchemist and occultist Michael Maier as advisor and body physician.[73] Queen Juliana had Greet Hofmans as an advisor, who was a friend of the esotericist Johan Willem Kaiser.[74] The late US President Ronald Reagan would never make any important decision without consulting his 'court astrologer' Joan Quigley, who had a great influence on the entire Reagan administration.[75] In the sixteenth century, the French physician, seer and astrologer Nostradamus gave advice to many princes in Europe and his predictions were diligently read

---

[72] See Paradin, C., *Alliances genealogiques des rois et princes de Gaule.* (Gaule is the old name for France.)

[73] Van Lennep, J, *Alchemie*, in Dutch.

[74] Bredenhoff, A., & Offringa, J.T., *Greet Hofmans*, in Dutch.

[75] Quigley, J., *'What Does Joan Say?'*

at the French Court by Catherine de Medici and many other noble people.[76]
That not only many American presidents stem from ancient bloodlines, but also various other powerful people in the world, may be less known to many. Many kings and world leaders are not only related, but also members of some occult lodge, order or occult society. Very few historians study this extremely important topic, possibly due to lack of knowledge of esotericism.

So, who is this man 'of royal blood,' George W. Bush, who is presenting the world with a big mirror and thereby paradoxically initiating a process of consciousness that will allow us to wake up from our long, long sleep of ignorance? Is he 'a leader of the old world,' as Irene van Lippe-Biesterfeld of the Dutch royal family said in the *Volkskrant* of October 8, 2005? Or is he the leader of a New World Order in the making? To project him outside ourselves is like not daring to look at our own inner wars, our own contradictions. Only those who have the courage to look within themselves first can enter the battlefield of the world unarmed, without associating themselves with it.

Even if one were to defeat a thousand times a thousand men
in a single battle,
he who overcomes only one man, himself,
is the greatest hero.[77]

Dhammapada, verse 103

---

[76] Hogue, J., *Nostradamus the New Revelations;* Messing, M., 'Nostradamus: profeet van de toekomst', in *Prana* 69 (Feb/Mar 1992), p. 5-9, in Dutch.
[77] *Dhammapada. Des Buddhas Weg zur Weisheit,*

So, what is Bush's secret?

Eric Laurent, an investigative journalist with *Le Figaro*, exposes the entire religious, political and economic webwork behind Bush in *Bush's Secret World*. This book has created quite a stir, as has his other book *La Guerre des Bush* - why the United States invade Iraq. Laurent reveals that Bush is primarily a product of the Bible Belt, that religion is central to his life and that he sees himself as the chosen one. Even before he became president, he once said of Islam, 'The God of Islam is not the same God as the Christian God. I consider Islam an evil, wicked religion.'[78] Bush not only likes to surround himself with many reverends. He also seeks the advice of hawks like Richard Perle (former top advisor to the Pentagon, good relations with arms industry, nicknamed 'Prince of Darkness') and Karl Rove (major shareholder of Boeing who has many activities in the military). But Paul Wolfowitz (former second-in-command of the Pentagon, succeeded James Wolfensohn as president of the World Bank, partner of the Rothschilds and formerly working for the Rockefellers) is also among his advisors. Other advisors who regularly pop up around Bush include John Bolton, Dov Zakheim (Orthodox rabbi, secretary of state for defense, chief financial officer at the Pentagon) and Richard Armitage (secretary of state for foreign affairs, former adviser to Boeing and to arms manufacturer Raytheon, which produces, among other things, Tomahawk cruise missiles and GBU-28 Bunker Busters that have been used in Iraq to penetrate bunkers).
Furthermore, the Bush administration maintains close ties with another giant in the armaments field, Lockheed Martin. The ultraconservative Lynn Cheney, wife of the vice president, was on the board of Lockheed Martin until February 2001. Dick Cheney himself, according to Laurent, perfectly embodies the entanglement between political and military-industrial power. Under Bush senior, Dick Cheney was in charge of the Pentagon and then became the top man at oil giant Halliburton. Halliburton not only builds oil pipelines, but also builds military prisons, handles the logistics of U.S. military personnel (including in Afghanistan and Iraq) under the slogan 'Pride to serve our troops!' and negotiates with

---

[78] Laurent, E., *Bush's Secret World*.

countries described by the Bush administration as 'terror states' and with countries that are among the worst dictatorships in the world. Thanks to Cheney, Halliburton came into contact with the top echelons of politics, as far away as the Arab world. When he left the company, he took approximately $45 million in stock options with him. After the bombing of Iraq, Halliburton received most of the contracts in that country. Even though Bush had said that 'Iraq's oil belongs to the Iraqi people', on May 12, 2003 the U.S. military signed a contract with Kellog Brown & Root (KBR), an affiliate of Halliburton, which had maintained close ties with the U.S. military since the Vietnam War. KBR was awarded the license to extract the Iraqi oil in a region of northern Iraq. KBR has built numerous bases and military camps around the world, including the military prison at Guantánamo in Cuba.[79]

The New York Times reported in February 2006 that KBR had received a $385 million contract from the Department of Homeland Security thanks to Bush to build detention centres on U.S. soil, in addition to the hundreds of detention camps already in place.[80] Laurent writes that KBR is a good sponsor of politicians and political parties and was involved in fraud and malpractice.[81] Cheney and Rumsfeld (Secretary of Defense), he says, are old timers in the business and know all the pitfalls in the Pentagon, White House and Congress.[82]

Halliburton has been under attack lately for numerous malpractices and falsely charging millions of meals to American soldiers and charging far too high prices for supplied food packages.[83]

Bush and Jesus

However, Bush finds the greatest inspiration not from the ministers and advisors surrounding him, but from Jesus. That is his secret. Jesus is his

---

[79] Idem, p. 122-139. For Wolfensohn see: Icke, D., *... and the truth shall set you free*, p. 247. For Guantánomo also see: Pastouna, J., *Guantanamo Bay*.

[80] *Power of Prophecy* (July 2006). Source: www.powerofprophecy.com.

[81] Laurent, E., *Bush's Secret World*.

[82] Idem.

[83] Witte, G., 'Iraq: Army to End Expansive, Exclusive Halliburton Deal', in *Washington Post* (July 12, 2006).

favourite philosopher, 'because he saved my heart'.[84] In the words of Jesus 'He who is not with me is against me' (Matthew 12:30) we recognize the source of inspiration of Bush's adage: He who is not for us is against us. How, however, we are to reconcile the 'war on terror' with the life and teachings of Jesus will escape many who are familiar with another saying of Jesus: 'If someone strikes you on the cheek, offer him the other also' (Luke 6:29). The book *Bush at War* by the internationally renowned investigative journalist Bob Woodward, reporter and editor of *The Washington Post* for more than thirty years, makes it abundantly clear that Bush never even considered this…

---

[84] Laurent, E., *Bush's Secret World*.

1.4   The War on Terror

I will not forget the wound to our country and those who inflicted it.
I will not yield, I will not rest, I will not relent in waging this struggle
for freedom and security for the American people
The course of this conflict is not known, yet its outcome is certain.
Freedom and fear, justice and cruelty, have always been at war,
and we know that God is not neutral between them.
Fellow citizens, we will meet violence with patient justice,
assured of the rightness of our cause and confident of the victories to come.
In all that lies before us, may God grant us wisdom
and may he watch over the United States of America.[85]

Following the text of President's Bush's address to the joint session of Congress and the nation on the 20th of September 2001

For every terrorist you kill
two or three will rise up.
The leaders think only in terms of punishment,
destruction and fear.
America uses fear to destroy fear
and thereby makes people even more fearful.
On the other hand, you have people who abuse faith for their mission.
It is beginning to look like a holy war. Very dangerous.[86]

Thich Nhat Hanh

---

[85] Bush, G.W., *We Will Prevail*.
[86] Belgium newspaper *De Stentor*, May 13, 2006.

Military means against terror

On September 18, 2001, George W. Bush signed Joint Senate Resolution 23, the 'Authorization for the Use of Military Means. This gave him constitutional authority as president to use force against imminent terrorist acts, with the possible use of the military.[87]
According to Noam Chomsky, the military part of the current war on terror is headed by Donald Rumsfeld and it's diplomacy handled by John Negroponte.[88] Secretary of Defense Donald Rumsfeld, along with Vice President Cheney, a key promoter of the war on terror, maintained numerous relationships with the military-industrial complex and business in general. John Negroponte, former ambassador to the UN and employee at the Vietnam Embassy (1964), friend of Henry Kissinger and ambassador to Honduras under Reagan, charged with suppressing the Sandinista revolution and preparing the war against Nicaragua, currently coordinates all fifteen U.S. spy agencies. As Director of National Intelligence, he rules over two hundred thousand personnel with a budget of forty billion dollars. This position was recommended by 'The 9/11 Commission', which concluded, among other things, that there was a lack of communication and coordination within the intelligence agencies.

'They hate our freedoms'

Since September 11, 2001, not a day goes by that the media does not talk about terror, terrorists or the war on terror. In both words and pictures, we are spoon-fed on a daily basis, reinforcing the perception of an enemy. Why do the people we call terrorists actually hate us? Bush answered that in his speech on September 20 2001, 'Americans ask: why do they hate us? They hate what we see here in this room - a democratically elected government. Their leaders have appointed themselves. They hate our freedoms - our freedom of religion, our freedom of speech, our freedom to vote and to assemble and to disagree. (...) We know their kind. They

---

[87] Bush, G.W., *We Will Prevail.*
[88] Chomsky, N., *Power and Terror.*

are the heirs of all the murderous ideologies of the twentieth century. By sacrificing human life in the service of their radical fantasies - by giving up every value except the will to power - they are following the path of fascism, Nazism and totalitarianism. And they will follow that path to the end: into the nameless grave of discarded lies of history.'[89]

George W. Bush predicted a prolonged war, as did John Bolton, who even spoke of a new kind of world war. In a speech to FBI employees on September 25, 2001, Bush said, 'Our nation is a nation that doesn't want revenge, but we do want justice. And I don't care how long it takes to root out terrorists, we're going to do it. We will put in the time and effort and resources necessary, not just to find those culprits who did what they did to America on September 11 - it's a larger campaign against anyone who hates freedom, anyone who can't stand what America and our allies and friends stand for.'[90]

In many of his speeches following 9/11, Bush puts the civilized world up against the cruel, ruthless, terrifying terrorists, whom he likes to call 'barbarians'. To fight this war properly, money is needed, a lot of money. In a speech to civilians and military personnel in North Carolina on March 15, 2002, Bush says, 'I have asked Congress for a one-year increase in defense spending of over forty-eight billion dollars. That is the largest increase for defense in a generation - because we are at war, and Congress must pass this budget.'[91]

Operation Enduring Freedom

Operation Infinite Justice was conceived. A number of countries united at America's request or under emotional pressure to fight against countries suspected of terrorism or harbouring terrorists. Afghanistan and Iraq were at the top of the list. But because of fierce criticism from Islamic groups, that only Allah can provide infinite justice, a new name was chosen for the operation: Enduring Freedom.[92]

---

[89] Bush, G.W., *We Will Prevail*.
[90] Idem.
[91] Idem.
[92] Kavonis, Y., *'Operation Clarity: The Politics of Naming'*.

Hardly anyone protested when freedom was soon mocked at home and in numerous other countries that followed America's example. It is finally dawning on the world opinion that through the actions of a state which itself sows hatred and fear are highly questionable and that the seed of hatred spreads with each and every bombardment and one dead terrorist will create another 10 and that freedom and justice is violated on a big scale.

Other points of view

However, there are other answers to consider as to why terrorists hate 'us'. This is not a question of pro or con, but an attempt to understand an extremely complicated matter. When Vietnamese Zen master Thich Nath Hanh, who lived through the war in his country, was once asked what he would do if he had a conversation with Osama bin Laden, his answer was that he would first listen carefully to his grievances.

Let's look at a few viewpoints that attempt to explain why terrorists might hate 'us'. The American economist David C. Korten, in The Business in Power (a book lauded by The Financial Times and by Archbishop Desmond M. Tutu, winner of the Nobel Peace Prize), points to the disastrous impact of the growing power of the multinationals, which governments have long lost control of. They determine the course of the world economy and maintain the appalling contrast of rich and poor. Corruption, degradation, the widening of antagonisms, the exploitation of other countries and the destruction of the environment are the results of globalization. He is extremely critical of the risky rise in power of American corporations.

The internationally renowned critic of capitalism Jean Ziegler talks about 'the downsides of predatory capitalism' in The New Rulers of the World. He vehemently opposes globalization. The word globalization was introduced in the 1960s by media expert Marshall McLuhan and by the American politician and advisor to various presidents, Zbigniew Brzeziński, who maintains good contacts with Israel. In his book, Ziegler makes a passionate plea for justice.[93] For him, globalization refers to the predatory nature of the powerful in business and politics. The millions of victims who have fallen and still fall daily because of this system will one day start a revolt, he concludes. The misery of the world stretches to the doorsteps of the White House. By some curious curse, world power fails to conceal the countless casualties it inflicts every day. Like the waves of a raging sea, they beat against the Capitol. But the ayatollahs of the Bretton Woods Institutions 'are blind as bats, deaf as doornails and unable to smell anything. They don't even notice the casualties they create every day. Not a single doubt clouds their conscience.'[94]

Joseph Stiglitz, professor and 2001 Nobel laureate in economics, former economic advisor to the U.S. government under President Bill Clinton and former top economist at the World Bank, provides a unique glimpse of the IMF, the World Bank, the World Trade Organization and the U.S. Treasury Department in his book *Perverted Globalization*. He shows that behind the so-called globalization hides a power-politics that increases the poverty of countless, is disastrous for the environment and destabilizes the world economy. 'Globalization, as was hitherto advocated, often seems to replace the old dictatorship of national elites with a new dictatorship of international finance.' [95] Stiglitz makes a plea for 'globalization with a human heart'.[96] In *Another World Is Possible*, leading 'other-globalists' (writers, scientists and activists representing sixty organizations in twenty-five countries) give Alternatives to Economic Globalization, as the subtitle reads.[97]

---

[93] Ziegler, J., *Die neuen Herrscher der Welt und ihre globalen Widersacher*, Goldmann Verlag, München 2005, p. 29.

[94] Idem. The Bretton Wood Institutes are the IMF and World Bank, established in 1944 after the Bretton Woods, New Hampshire, conference.

[95] Stiglitz, J., *Globalization and Its Discontents*.

[96] Idem

[97] Title of the International Forum on Globalization. Also see Ellwood, W., *The No-Nonsense Guide to Globalization*.

An economic hitman's story

John Perkins wrote a shocking book in 2004, *Confessions of an Economic Hit Man.*[98] It became a bestseller worldwide. Perkins knows the world of multinationals inside out: building and construction companies like Main and Bechtel, oil giants like Halliburton and Standard Oil (Rockefeller), and investment companies like the Carlyle Group. He is also well informed about the international financial world (IMF, World Bank and the Rockefellers' Chase Manhattan Bank). For example, Perkins believes that under the presidency of Robert McNamara, former president of the Ford plant and former secretary of defense under Kennedy, the World Bank was made an instrument of the world empire by trickery and deceit 'and on a scale hitherto unheard of.'[99] He sees the Rockefellers as the central power in the world. He mentions that the WTC towers were once nicknamed David and Nelson.[100] Perkins knows better than anyone the intertwining of business, banking and politics.

'For example, George Schultz served under Nixon as Treasury Secretary and Chairman of the Economic Policy Council, was President of Bechtel, and then became Secretary of State under Reagan. Caspar Weinberger was vice president and head of Bechtel's legal department and later became Secretary of Defense under Reagan. Richard Helms was director of the CIA during Johnson's time and became ambassador to Iran under Nixon. Dick Cheney served as Secretary of Defense under George H.W. Bush, was president of Halliburton and Vice President in the George W. Bush administration. And President George H.W. Bush began as founder of Zapata Petroleum Corp, was U.S. ambassador to the UN under Nixon and Ford, and director of the CIA under Ford.'[101] Perkins also describes the conflicts of interest between the United States and the Saudi Arabians.[102]

---

[98] Perkins, J., *Confessions of an Economic Hit Man.*
[99] Idem.
[100] Idem.
[101] Idem.
[102] Idem.

For forty years Perkins worked as an economic hit man (EHM). Among others, for Bechtel. A well-paid job. Task: to extort billions of dollars from poor countries all over the world on behalf of a powerful and wealthy elite, dressed up as a well-educated and highly paid economic 'pirate'. Countries are advised to take out loans for the development of infrastructure: power plants, highways, ports, airports, industrial parks. The condition here is that their execution is assigned exclusively to American companies. Once these countries are bankrupt and can no longer pay their debts, their natural resources (oil, for example) are confiscated, military bases are seized or they are forced to cast a pro-American vote in the UN.

An EHM thus lends himself to the American empire, which seeks a world empire based on economic power. To this end, people, nature and governments are mercilessly and unscrupulously being sacrificed. This empire, this elite consists of top executives from large corporations, international banks and governments. Perkins calls this elite the *corporatocracy*. What an EHM fails to accomplish is pursued by the 'jackals' of the CIA, and when they fail, as in Afghanistan and Iraq, the military is deployed, Perkins writes; Exposing a world of corruption, intimidation, lies, World Bank and IMF malfeasance, rigged elections, bribes, sex, extortion and murder.

As painful as the number of victims of the New York attacks (3,000) is, Perkins says they pale in comparison to the 24,000 people [now many more!] who die of starvation each day and the 30,000 children who die daily from treatable diseases because they are denied the necessary medicines.[103] [these numbers date back to 2004]
'Some attribute our current problems to an organized conspiracy. I wish it were that simple. Members of a conspiracy can be tracked down and brought to justice. However, this system is fuelled by something far more dangerous than a conspiracy. The driving force behind it is not a small group of people, but a concept that has now been accepted as gospel: the idea that all economic growth is good, and that the greater the growth,

---

[103] Perkins, J., 'Het nieuwe economische wereldrijk gebruikt slaven om de eigen leiders te verrijken', in Dutch newspaper *NRC Handelsblad* (March 25-26 2006).

the more people will benefit. In addition, this belief has the consequence of believing that those who excel at stoking the fires of economic growth should be glorified and rewarded, while those born in distant lands should be allowed to be exploited.'[104] In his view, while the corporatocracy is not a conspiracy, 'its members share common values and goals': to maintain, expand and strengthen the system by encouraging us to consume more and more.[105] His conscience was increasingly troubled. He saw how the beautiful Earth was being destroyed, how his daughter Jessica and all the other children of this generation would have no future. Despite threats and bribes not to write this book, he wrote it to clear his conscience.

'We must do everything we can to wake up ourselves and everyone around us. We need to listen to the wisdom of the prophecies, open our hearts and minds to the possibilities, start realizing what is going on, and then take action,' he concludes.[106] Perkins offers concrete solutions, focusing on helping the peoples who have been exploited and enslaved to enrich the small group at the top of the pyramid using the existing networks. 'It will be the great task of the 21st century to inform the American people of the truth behind the Empire, and to urge them to undo this process.'[107]

A new Pearl Harbor and the PNAC

PNAC means Project for the New American Century. It is a think tank that had been working out plans for the realization of the American world empire for years before 9/11. Belgian philosopher Lieven Decauter discovered this project by chance on the internet in January 2003. He discovered that there is indeed a plan for world domination through a high-tech army. From April 14 to 17, 2004, he dedicated *The Brussels Tribunal* to it (inspired by *The Russells Tribunal*: the hearings of philosopher Bertrand Russell, following the Vietnam War). The author drafted a petition signed by five hundred Belgian intellectuals and

---

[104] Perkins, J., *Confessions of an Economic Hit Man.*
[105] Idem.
[106] Idem.
[107] Idem, and Perkins, J. [103]

artists.[108] With the cooperation of former President George H.W. Bush, the PNAC think tank was founded in 1997 by Donald Rumsfeld, Paul Wolfowitz, Dick Cheney and Richard Perle. It includes only neoconservatives such as John Bolton, Elliot Abrams, John Negroponte, Douglas J. Feith (Secretary of Defense and Pentagon policy advisor), David Frum and William Kristol (publisher of The Daily Standard, son of Irving Kristol, one of the founders of the neoconservative movement).[109] All of them have excellent international relations with the business community (especially the oil industry), the military-industrial complex, and religious (business) circles. Several members of the PNAC also have close relationships with conservative to ultraconservative politicians from Israel. A number of names are mentioned in Perkins' book. Possibly the close ties to Israel can be explained by the fact that the above-mentioned politicians, with the exception of Negroponte, are of Jewish descent.

Authors such as von Bülow, Rétyi and Icke also wrote about the PNAC.[110] The goals of the Project for the New American Century are outlined in *Rebuilding American Defenses: Strategies, Forces and Resources for a New Century*. Among other things, this PNAC document states that wars should be fought simultaneously and that bases in Iraq are required.[111] Their 'blueprint of conquest' or 'process of transformation' would likely be long and slow unless a catastrophic and catalysing event - such as a new Pearl Harbor - were to occur. With the attacks of September 11, 2001, America got 'our Pearl

---

[108] Dutch magazine *De Tijd* (April 10, 2004).

[109] For the positions of the persons listed here, which are not mentioned, see the previous paragraph.

[110] Bülow, A. von, *Die CIA und der 11. September*, p 231-238; Rétyi, A. von, *Macht und Geheimnis der Illuminaten*, p. 229; Icke, D., *Tales from the Time Loop*, p. 80-88 (for background on members of PNAC and others who were referred to in the previous note).

[111] http://www.visibility911.org/wp-content/uploads/2008/02/rebuildingamericasdefenses.pdf

Harbor,' as Bush called it.[112] Not to mention that this PNAC document had been drafted exactly one year before the 9/11 attacks and two and a half years before troops were actually deployed in Iraq.[113] Moreover, Von Bülow and other authors argue that Americans knew about the Japanese attack on Pearl Harbor in advance, but that the attack was an appropriate *casus belli* for participation in World War II.

'What happened at Pearl Harbor was the beginning of a long and terrible war for America. But out of that surprise attack grew a firm determination that made America the defender of freedom. And that mission - our great calling - exists to this day, as the brave men and women of our military fight against the forces of terror in Afghanistan and around the world,' George W. Bush said in a remembrance address for Pearl Harbor Day on December 7, 2001 aboard the USS Enterprise, Norfolk, Virginia.[114]

Who reads *The New Pearl Harbour. Disturbing Questions about the Bush Administration and 9/11*, the impressive and extremely well-documented book by David Ray Griffin, will agree with the author that at the most critical moment in American history, the world press failed to conduct a thorough investigation of this 'New Pearl Harbour', associated with numerous unanswered questions.[115] Griffin also knew about the PNAC early on and agrees with von Bülow that the 'New Pearl Harbour' and the subsequently created 'war on terror' was used to propagate aggressive American imperialism around the world.

Numerous attacks around the world

As a result of 9/11, the massive defense budget requested by Bush for his global war on terror was quickly approved. The armoury was to be renewed (including outdated nuclear weapons). A sinister script is kicking in. At the same time, a nearly bottomless Pandora's box opens, from which suffering, sorrow, grief and fear escape. Since the war in

---

[112] Icke, *Tales from the Time Loop*, p. 80.
[113] Idem., p. 71.
[114] Bush, *We Will Prevail*.
[115] Griffin, D.R., The New Pearl Harbor, p. XII en XIII.

Afghanistan and later in Iraq, numerous terrorist attacks around the world follow one after the other. A black shadow spreads its wings.

April 11, 2002: Tunisia (resort in Djerba); October 12, 2002: Bali (tourists on Kuta Beach); October 24, 2002: Russia (musical theatre in Moscow); November 28, 2002: Kenya (hotel in Mombasa). May 16, 2003: Morocco (Western and Jewish targets in Casablanca); November 15 and 20, 2003: Turkey (synagogues, British consulate and a British investment bank in Istanbul); February 6, 2004: Russia (metro in Moscow); March 11, 2004: Spain (trains in Madrid); September 3, 2004: Russia (hostage drama school in Beslan); July 7, 2005: England (subway and bus in London); July 11, 2006: India (trains in Mumbai) … and many more would follow.

And in between all these attacks, a series of attacks in Afghanistan, Iraq, Pakistan, India, Israel and on the territory of the Palestinians... And many stories about what could have happened but didn't. The terror remains, hostile images between populations, cultures and religions are reinforced. The idea of a third world war is beginning to take hold, especially now that tensions are running high in the Middle East. A war against terrorism erupts, often forcing the U.S. military, equipped with modern weapons and supported by a number of allies, into guerrilla warfare. The drum of psychological warfare is beating vigorously, disinformation spreads on the winds of lies, and above all, electronics begin a silent, stealthy attack that is not immediately noticeable.

Patriot Act and Guantánamo Bay

After the 9/11 attacks, the Patriot Act is passed with the speed of lightning. By 98 votes to 1 (1 abstention). Civil rights and privacy are thoroughly reversed in America. Fear of not being a good patriot emerges. Suspicions and snitching rise.

After the bombing of Afghanistan, we hear of beatings and torture at the Abu Ghraib prison near Baghdad and at Guantanamo Bay in Cuba. Some American soldiers no longer know how to restrain themselves. The Geneva Conventions are being violated. The UN and Amnesty International publish reports. *The Torture Papers* are published. This '1250-page book gets compared to the 1971 *Pentagon Papers*, the well-documented revelations about war crimes in Vietnam. (...)

'Read these pages and weep for our country,' Michael Ratner, director of the Center for Fundamental Rights' wrote about the *Torture Papers*.[116] There is indeed torture, humiliation, intimidation (with dogs; sexual).[117] Suicides are taking place at Guantanamo Bay ('as an act of war, directed against us,' Admiral Harry B. Harris, commander of the camp, says).[118] 'You are in a place where there are no laws - we are the law.' That's how a U.S. intelligence officer characterized Guantanamo Bay.[119] Secret CIA flights to covert penal institutions leaked out.[120] After a Supreme Court ruling, the Bush administration pledges to abide by the conventions.

On 7 September 2006, the Dutch newspaper *NRC* headlined: 'Bush: 'CIA prisons exist' and two days later we read in Dutch newspaper *Trouw*: 'George Bush tries to legalise torture as a method of interrogation'. Trouw refers to an investigation by *The New York Times*, supported by lawyers from, among others, the American Army. The newspaper studied the Bush administration's proposal for the establishment of military courts that will, among other things, try the prisoners at Guantanamo.

Many people fail to see that the Bush administration wants to apply martial law to civilians step by step. By doing so, it removes the trial of so-called (terrorist) suspects from the control that applies to the normal criminal law procedures. With this, the basis for the rule of law, which was created precisely to protect citizens against arbitrariness and abuse of power by the government, falls away and the way is paved for a dictatorship in which countless people will be outlawed.

Alarms, antiterrorism laws, 'build-up mission'

Alarming situations everywhere. Green, orange, red follow each other faster and faster. Control increases, Big Brother is born in a cradle of fear, with electronics as godfather and meek officials as godmother. Internet providers are forced to pass on customer data. In many European

---

[116] Greenberg, K.J., and J.L. Dratel, *The Torture Papers*.

[117] Dutch newspaper *Volkskrant* (February 11, 2005) and (April 25, 2006).

[118] Dutch newspaper *Volkskrant* (June 12, 2006).

[119] Van Scharen, H., and I. Van Daele, 'Wij zijn de wet', in Belgium magazine *Knack* (August 2, 2006), (Europa speeltuin van de VS, dl. 1: Guantanamo).

[120] Idem.

countries anti-terror laws are spreading like wildfire or are being reinforced (in Russia, for example). In the Netherlands, in 2005, leaflets with warnings are dropped in every resident's mailbox: *What is being done about terrorism? And what can you do?* Further loss of privacy and civil rights takes place. 'We don't have anything to hide, do we? International counterterrorism exercises at sea, on land and in the air. NSA (National Security Agency) electronics are called in by Bush to eavesdrop on suspicious citizens in their own country, completely anti-constitutional. Secret services are centralized. Additional security at air and sea ports (electronic detection portals, cameras, scans), electronic monitoring of planes, buildings, passenger lists. And meanwhile, the war on terror propaganda machine is running at full speed, the *Voice of America* is screaming through the airwaves in Iran, voices are heard talking about even more wars: Iran, Syria, Korea...

In early January 2006, the Netherlands are pressured into sending soldiers to the Afghan province of Uruzgan. Senior officials of the UN (Kofi Annan), NATO (De Hoop Scheffer and the American General Jones) and the EU (Vendrell, EU envoy in Afghanistan) warn of the negative consequences if the Netherlands do not participate. In the International Herald Tribune, NATO Secretary-General De Hoop Scheffer says, 'You can't say: sorry, it's too dangerous, we're not going. I won't accept that. Then why do you have armed forces?'[121] Representatives of the Afghan government address the Dutch parliament. 'Terrorism is international. If Afghanistan becomes a safe haven for terrorists again, it will backfire on all of us,' Afghan Defense Minister Wardak warned.[122] Soon after, the decision was made that the Netherlands would join a reconstruction mission. By that time, 35 countries are already militarily involved in Afghanistan. Wat was called a reconstruction mission slowly becomes a combat mission. Fatalities were inevitable.

Many people feel that there is something fundamentally wrong with freedom and justice.

---

[121] Dutch newspaper *Volkskrant* (January 31, 2006).
[122] Dutch newspaper *NRC Handelsblad* (May 26, 2006).

Respect for human dignity and individual liberty affirms a core principle of
civilized nations everywhere.
With this important commemoration honouring our Bill of Rights and for
human rights around the world, all Americans can celebrate the universal
principles of freedom and justice that define our dreams and inspire our hope
as we face the challenges of a new era.[123]

From the presidential proclamation of Human Rights Day
and the Week of the Bill of Rights on December 9, 2001.

There is no such thing as non-violence if we only love those who love us.
There is only non-violence when we love those who hate us.
I know how hard it is to obey this great law of love.
But aren't all great and good things hard to accomplish?
Loving the one you hate is the hardest of all.
But by the grace of God, even this most difficult of things
becomes easy to fulfil if only we will.[124]

Mahatma Gandhi

Good and evil are not equal. Repel (evil) with what is best,
and you will see that the one you had mutual enmity with him
will turn as if he were a close friend.

The Qur'an, sura 41, verse 34

---

[123] Bush, *We Will Prevail*.
124 Gandhi, *All Men Are Brothers*. Gandhi was inspired by the Sermon on the
Mount of Jesus.

TO THINK ABOUT

- Every day, some 80,000 people die due to the lack of clean water, food, clothing, medicine and other basic necessities. That is 288 million a year.
- In 2006, 11 million children under the age of five alone will die of diseases. With a few million dollars, more than half of them can be saved.
- Every year, 300,000 people in the US die of obesity.
- Worldwide, 2 million children are infected with HIV.
- Every minute, someone goes blind.
- About 3 billion of the 6.5 billion on Earth live in poverty.
- They earn the same amount of money as about 190 countries spend on war.
- Two billion people live on less than $2 a day, more than half of them in the most deplorable conditions.
- 20% of the world's population (including the US, United Emirates, Singapore) consume 86% of the total world consumption.
- Of which, the US with only 300 million inhabitants (or 5% of the world population) consumes about 54%.
- America's national debt is about $8,500 billion, over $28,000 per capita. (In 2021 this number has gone up to $58,600 per capita)
- In 2005, the military budget for the entire world was $1100 billion. That's about $160 per person. Half is accounted for by the US.
- The war in Iraq cost between $40 billion and $60 billion annually.
- In 2006 the US spent 44 billion dollars on espionage.
- Per year the whole world spends about 79 billion dollars on development money.
- Every day, around 500,000 researchers and engineers around the world are developing new weapons. engineers are developing new weapons technologies.
- Their total salary costs are approximately 50 billion dollars.
- Worldwide, no more than about 2,000 people are doing research related to peace.
- The annual cost of the UN is about $20 billion.
- Billions of dollars are wasted annually in exchanging useless information by phone and cell phone.
- With that money you can solve the poverty of a country of 25 million people.
- The estimated wealth of the 300 richest families is a staggering Trillion dollars - $1,000,000,000,000 (one thousand billion dollars).

- The wealth of two families is not officially known: the dynasty of the Rockefellers and of the Rothschilds.
- Their combined wealth is estimated at between two and eight Trillion dollars.
- This money alone could solve the world's poverty problem.

QUESTION:

WHAT 'WAR ON TERROR' ARE WE REALLY TALKING ABOUT?

COULD THERE BE SOMETHING ELSE GOING ON?

2
Electronic warfare

Soon it will be possible to have almost constant [electronic] surveillance
of the most personal information of citizens.
This data can be immediately accessed by the authorities.[125]

Zbigniew Brzeziński, national security adviser under the Carter
administration and confidant of Rockefeller

Of course, it was impossible to know
if you were being watched at any given time.
How often or according to what system the Thought Police tapped someone's
line was a matter of conjecture.
It was even conceivable that they were constantly monitoring everyone.
In any case, they could switch on whenever they wanted.
You had to live - and you did live, from what became a habit
that became an instinct - on the assumption that every sound you made
was heard and that every movement, except in the dark, was monitored.[126]

George Orwell, 1984

---

[125] Marrs, T., *Project L.U.C.I.D. The Beast 666 Universal Human Control System*,
p. 176. Brzezinski predicted this 'technotronic era' in his book *Between two Ages:
America's Role in the Technotronic Era* (1976).
[126] Orwell, G., *1984*.

2.1   How big is Big Brother really?

At the top of the pyramid is Big Brother.
Big Brother is infallible and omnipotent.
Every success, every achievement, every victory, every scientific
discovery, all knowledge, all wisdom, all happiness, all virtue is
represented as stemming directly from his leadership and inspiration.
No one has ever seen Big Brother.
He is a face on the billboards, a voice from the telescreen.
We can be reasonably certain that he will never die, and there is
already a great deal of uncertainty about when he was born.
Big Brother is the mask behind which the Party wishes to show itself to
the world. [127]

George Orwell, 1984

Electronic giant

In Orwell's visionary book *1984*, the portrait of Big Brother regularly
appears on the telescreens. He is everywhere. Everywhere there is his
lurking cold gaze. The 'Ministry of Truth' manipulates everyone through
lies.
In the meantime, we are now several decades down the road. What 1984
describes has not only been accomplished, but vastly surpassed. Big
Brother has even lost his face. His portrait is missing, but his means of
spying on us have become extremely sophisticated as a result of
electronics. They seem to constitute the modern mask behind which in
our time Big Brother hides to carry out the Party's program. More than
ever, his influence is everywhere. In a few decades he became a giant. An
electronic giant without flesh and blood, without a beating heart, without

---

[127] Orwell, G., *1984*.

breath flowing through lungs. Many people don't realize it (yet). Big Brother's propaganda machine says we must be monitored and controlled. For our safety. Its decisions hardly involve us, if at all. Big Brother takes care of everything himself.

Power of the state

How did Big Brother become so big? Why is his name so often written in capital letters? Because we do it ourselves. Because in the past we failed to rip his portrait from the walls, not daring to look behind his mask. And today we tolerate the biometric fingerprints he invented, the ubiquitous cameras, satellites, eavesdropping devices and other monitoring systems. Are we ignorant? Brainwashed? Gullible? Surely security trumps privacy? Surely someone has to protect us? The state?

As early as 1835, the French historian, political scientist and former foreign minister of France, Count Alexis de Tocqueville, in his four-volume work *The Democracy in America*, warned of the centralization of state power and the threat to individual freedom in America, which he called the New World.[128] In addition to appreciative words for various institutions and traditions, he mainly criticizes the highly patronizing power, which provides bread and circuses and guards the destiny of each individual. The power of the state imprisons man, gradually eliminates free will, and finally deprives every citizen of the right to self-determination. Step by step, the individual is transformed by the cunning of the state into a docile instrument and thus loses his free will, becomes entangled in a system of rules and regulations. The state does not tyrannize, but slows down, depresses, silences. That was Tocqueville's conclusion. Almost two centuries ago.

No 'face on a billboard'

In its fight against global terrorism, is the New World (especially the US) trying to ensnare the Old World (especially Europe) in its nets? Some researchers think so. Since 9/11, the New World has been positioning

---

[128] Tocqueville, A. de, *Oeuvres complets*.

itself as big brother, preferably written in capital letters. But from now on, we'll decapitate the BB capitals. Those who are 'for' him, adapts and can count on his protection.

Those who oppose him are at great risk. Far-reaching measures for our safety are needed, thinks big brother. For our good. Step by step, however, free will is being clamped down on. In our time, electronics make possible what many a dictator dreamed of in the past. In his time Hitler had to make do with the punched-card machine (the forerunner of the computer), developed by American Herman Hollerith and taken into production through IBM's German subsidiary, Dehomag. This enabled the

Overview of punch cards of Hollerith, poster of Dehomag (German subsidiary of IBM), nazi-Germany

Nazi authorities to use standard cards with punched holes to store all kinds of data on Jewish people, gypsies, homosexuals and many others destined for the Holocaust. 'The third hole meant homosexual, the eighth indicated a Jew,' Edwin Black (son of parents who survived the Holocaust) writes in his book *IBM and the Holocaust*. According to Black, thanks to IBM technology Hitler was able to carry out his extermination program of the Jews. He further states that IBM's founder, Thomas Watson, received the 'Cross of Merit' from Hitler (his second largest client in the world), the second highest German award given to foreigners who were significant to the Third Reich. According to Black, IBM almost single-handedly brought modern warfare into the information age and with it the 'blitz' of war. Registration, identification and food allocation were done through punch cards. More than 2,000 IBM punch card machines had been installed in Germany alone and thousands in countries occupied by Germany. The main purpose was the rapid and efficient extermination of the Jewish people.[129] The punch card systems have since been replaced by ultramodern electronic databases, binoculars by satellites, and old-fashioned cameras by digital ones. And the chip seems to be the pinnacle of the total control process. Paranoia? Delusion? Conspiracy?

In our time, big brother is no longer a familiar 'face on a billboard,' but an amorphous body with a number of electronics companies engaged in surveillance, security, prevention and control as its limbs. American electronics companies hold a key position. All these companies together are the embodiment of the digital age. The U.S. government gratefully uses the limbs of big brother, encourages their growth, maintains some excellent relations with them, frequently alerts the Old World to their existence. 9/11 created the appropriate climate in which big brother could run at high speed around the world with his electronic giant feet. After all, who doesn't want security? Explosive developments began. Beyond the layman's comprehension. Convenient for the decision makers. For example, the attacks of 9/11 seem to have created not only a new Pearl Harbor, but also a climate in which many electronics company could engage in electronic bombing for the safety of the state and its citizens. There is already mention of electronic warfare. What is going on? Is there something lurking behind the mask of big brother that we never suspected? Were we indeed not awake? Too gullible? Did we put too much faith in the state? And... who, by the way, controls the controller of the controller?

A series of surveillance programs

In December 2003, investigative journalist Martin Crag wrote the article 'Big Brother. The terrorist threat gives him wings'.[130] Crag shows that since September 11, 2001, a number of programs were rapidly constructed with major implications for our privacy. The CAPPS II program (Second-generation Computer Assisted Passenger Pre-

---

[129] For more information: www.ibmandtheholocaust.com/

130 Crag, M., 'Big Brother. La menace terroriste lui donne des ailes', in *Science et vie* 1035 (2003), p. 126-129.

Screening Program), part of a much larger program, is already being implemented. Since 2004, all airline passengers bound for the United States have been traceable. All passenger data must be sent to the U.S. in advance, in violation of European privacy laws: name, address, date of birth, phone number, credit card number, seat number, meal choice, hotel if applicable, car rental. A total of 39 details must be provided. Penalty: € 5000 per passenger and the possibility of losing landing rights if the list is not filled out properly or incompletely.

Just before his farewell, European Commissioner Frits Bolkestein received the Big Brother Award in October 2004 for transferring passenger data to the US without the permission of the EU. This award had been established by Bits of Freedom (BOF), an independent Dutch organization dedicated to digital civil rights that regularly presented Big Brother Awards to agencies and individuals who had seriously violated privacy.[131] As of September 1, BOF stopped its activities.

August 2, 2002, John Poindexter (former Vice Admiral, National Security Advisor to President Reagan), appointed by Bush to head the Information Awareness Office, unveiled a project that within a few years must monitor the entire planet with its tentacles: Total Information Awareness (TIA). However, the word 'Total' reminded some of Hitler's *der Totale Krieg*. So, TIA became the acronym for Terrorism Information Awareness,[132] since it was meant to track terrorists, right? With advanced technologies, TIA can recognize us from a distance and see what we are doing. The Defense Advanced Research Projects Agency (DARPA), the Pentagon's research agency, brought in Poindexter's TIA project and launched a multi-million-dollar global project to search for suspicious patterns in publicly available databases through facial and language recognition, among other things.[133]

Soon TIA will have access to *all* the databases of the entire planet. Then all databases can be linked. A state of each individual is maintained electronically: information on personal life, bank records, medications, marital status, telecommunications, health insurance, nightlife, and so

---

[131] Felius, J., 'Big Brother Award 2004', in Dutch *Frontier Magazine* 10 (2005).
[132] Crag, 'Big Brother...', ibid.
[133] Demets, F., 'Hoezo, privacy?', in Belgium magazine *Knack* (13 april 2005).

on. TIA costs twenty million dollars a year. It contains software that can analyse a multitude of petabytes of data in a second. For example, the eighteen million books of the Library of Congress can be put into one petabyte fifty times. One petabyte can store forty pages of information about each of the 6.5 billion people on earth. Total control in the near future.

The U.S. Department of Homeland Security also has numerous measures in place since 9/11 to improve the security of U.S. citizens and visitors from abroad. For example, the United States Visitor and Immigrant Status Indicator Technology project was launched in 2004. Soon, over four hundred digital border crossings will be ready for digital visa verification. From now on, travelers who need a visa to the U.S. must first go to the U.S. Embassy in their respective countries. There, biometric data is collected, two digital fingerprints are taken plus a digital photograph. This data is then printed on a smart card and linked to the travel documents. With these travel documents and the digital identity document the visitor reports to a border official in the US. The border official scans the fingerprints, checks the biometric data and doesn't bother to ask why someone is coming to the U.S., how long they are planning to stay, and so on. This has already been sorted out in the country of origin.[134]

Spy machine in action

Meanwhile, a little brother to TIA saw the day of life: the Lifelog program. This program dumps all private data into a giant database. Emails, websites, phone calls, what TV programs were watched, what magazines were read, what was eaten, which movie was attended, in which bank money was withdrawn, the name of the supermarket visited plus purchases made. Lifelog stores everything centrally, supported by the much-vaunted GPS system, which also records where, on what day and at what time you went where. Audio-visual sensors further monitor what you say and see, while biomedical monitors track your health. Science fiction? Not; Alas. Experiments are already underway. The masses just

---

[134] Dutch magazine *Het Financieele Dagblad* (June 8, 2004).

don't know it (yet). And why is it happening? To trace the threads of an individual life, to discover patterns and habits that will protect us even better against terrorism.[135]

'No place to hide'

The benchmark on all the accelerated measures that took place since 9/11 - how electronics companies and government officials began to develop monitoring systems to make the nation 'safer,' about electronic information and surveillance technology in relation to the right to privacy - was published in 2005: *No Place to Hide* of Robert O'Harrow jr, reporter at *The Washington Post*, member of the Center for Investigative Reporting and winner of, among other things, the Pulitzer Prize for articles on privacy and technology.[136] *No Place to Hide* shows how our privacy is being systematically destroyed. Everything is already being monitored, especially in urban areas. Where you live and work, the value of your home, the names of your friends and family, what you read, eat, buy, what car you drive, what loyalty or credit cards you use, how many bank accounts you have, what websites you visit, what digital newspaper you read or what TV program you watch on the internet, every e-mail or fax you send, plane trip you take, how much money you withdraw from the bank, who you call, where you drive, what train you take, what time and where you go, who your doctor is, what coffee shop you visit - everything is centrally stored. Privacy is something of the past. Countless electronic devices, O'Harrow says, are watching us without us even knowing it. Not only through computer software, but also through sensors, micro-cameras, household appliances, chips, satellites, and especially through countless private companies with matrix-like technology.[137] O'Harrow tells the *inside story* of the key players in this 'New World,' from software inventors to secret service officials. He reveals how, since 9/11, the U.S. government has been creating a 'national security infrastructure' with the help of the Department of Defense,

---

[135] Schachtman, N., 'A Spy Machine of Darpa's Dreams'. Source:
   https://www.wired.com/2003/05/a-spy-machine-of-darpas-dreams/
[136] O'Harrow, R., jr., *No Place to Hide*.
[137] Idem.

secret services and private electronics companies, and shows the disastrous conse-quences for our privacy, civil liberties and autonomy.

He, too, goes into detail about the CAPPS II program (developed by Acxiom, a multi-billion-dollar data industry, with details on almost every adult in the United States), DARPA and TIA, but especially about the Multi-state Anti-Terrorism Information Exchange (MATRIX!) project. MATRIX was developed by computer specialist Asher with his company Seisint (short for Seismic Intelligence). This system links commercially available information on citizens to millions of records on criminals and to government documents. In July 2004, the acquisition of MATRIX by information giant LexisNexus was announced. Whatever name the new technology from MATRIX (or TIA et al.) operates under, or whether it is opposed by privacy and civil rights advocates, that it will continue is certain, says O'Harrow. Under a different name and a different structure, the main actors will simply proceed with their technologies.

Under the banner of 'for your safety', our privacy is being destroyed. Step by step we are growing into a surveillance society. '... The details of our lives do no longer belong to us, but to the societies that gather them and to the government agencies that buy or retrieve them for our security's sake.' 'Since 9/11, our lives have been stored, we have no control over these electronic diaries and don't even know what they say about us. And there is no place to hide.' O'Harrow concludes.[138]

When Kafka meets Orwell

ICAMS is the abbreviation for 'International Campaign Against Mass Surveillance'. On the (Dutch) website of the same name we read: 'Global 'security' and a 'war on terror' now dominate the world political agenda. Mainly driven by the United States, a growing web of security and anti-terrorist measures is being taken around the world. This new idea of 'security' is being used as an excuse for repressive anti-terrorist measures, the reversal of rights and freedoms and an increase in the powers of law enforcement with the aim of gaining more and more control over indivi-

---

[138] Idem.

duals and populations.' What we are now witnessing amounts to the construction of a global infrastructure for registration and surveillance.

An extremely well-documented report by ICAMS, *The Rise of a Global Infrastructure for Mass Registration and Surveillance*,[139] lays out the entire history of how, since 9/11, all kinds of laws began to change, both in the United States and around the world, how step by step, under the guise of security, extremely far-reaching measures were taken that will ultimately completely take away our privacy and civil rights and lead directly to a totalitarian state, where Kafka (the officials of the state) and Orwell (big brother) meet. The report debunks the myth that with all the measures taken, including sacrificing our privacy, things will get safer. Anyone could soon be a potential suspect. Those who genuinely criticize the loss of civil rights run the risk of being arrested as supporting terrorists. An all-encompassing *gulag* (based on Solzhenitsyn's *Gulag Archipelago*) threatens to envelop the entire world with uncontrollable prison camps in which torture is used against all conventions under the pretext of 'they are terrorists'. The report shows how, since 9/11, registration and monitoring systems have become active worldwide at an accelerated pace via an almost unbelievable electronic technology, how the biometric passport has been introduced, lists of passengers' names are checked (and debunks the myth that this facilitates travel), electronic surveillance is deployed everywhere (with gigantic profits for the companies concerned), the RFID (Radio Frequency Identification; see p xxx) and other chips are rapidly emerging, databases such as TIA, MATRIX, CAPPS II are being set up everywhere (debunking the myths 'those who have nothing to hide have nothing to fear' and 'the technology used is objective and reliable')

Police and security services are being integrated. Through a dozen pointers, it shows how our democratic world is disintegrating and increasingly losing its moral dignity, while believing that it must stand up for democracy or the establishment of democratic institutions in other countries. The report concludes that the Universal Declaration of Human

---

[139] 'Emergence of a Global Infrastructure for Mass Registration and Surveillance', April, 2005.

Rights has lost its validity. After World War II, human dignity was made central and recognized as an inalienable birthright of every human being. The right to privacy (art. 12), the prohibition of discrimination (art. 2), the right to life, liberty and security of his person (art. 3), the prohibition of torture, inhuman or degrading treatment (art.5), the right to recognition and equality before the law (arts. 6 and 7), the right to effective legal assistance (art. 8), the prohibition of arbitrary arrest, detention or exile (art. 9), the right to a fair and public hearing of his case by an independent and impartial court (art. 10), the legal presumption of innocence unless proven otherwise (art. 11), the right to freedom of movement (art. 13), the right to freedom of thought, conscience and religion (art. 18), freedom of opinion and expression (art. 19), freedom of peaceful assembly and association (art. 20) and the right to the existence of a social and international order in which the rights and freedoms set forth in this Declaration may be fully realized (art. 28) - all these articles stand in stark contrast to everyday reality in our time.[140] One can even question whether an organization like the UN still has any meaning when its foundation, the Declaration of Human Rights, has disappeared.

'Human Rights' and UN scandals

As early as 1964, the American best-selling author and film producer G. Edward Griffin described the abuses at the United Nations. Even then, the rights of man, through all kinds of punitive measures in the Universal Declaration itself, were being curtailed. The bottom line is that a person may be legally denied any individual right if, according to the politicians, it is 'necessary to protect state security, public order, public safety, public health, public morality, or the rights, freedom, or reputation of others.'[141] With the many scandals plaguing the UN lately ('food for oil,' food for sex) and the increasing criticism of the system (in which a number of peoples such as Tibetans, Inuit, Moluccans, Kurds, Aborigines and Hopis

---

[140] Idem. More information: summary of the Universal Declaration of Human Rights: https://www.un.org/en/about-us/universal-declaration-of-human-rights
[141] Griffin, G.E., *The Fearful Master*, p. 124-126.

are not represented), the dominant role of the United States and the big countries that can veto everything, many wonder what the value of 'human rights' is worth today.

Questions

Perhaps something already went wrong at the creation of the UN. On March 25, 1947, John D. Rockefeller presented a check worth $8,500,000 to Trygve Lie, the first secretary-general of the UN. This amount was intended to purchase the land on Manhattan Island to establish the UN building. This land was owned by the Rockefeller family itself.[142] Questions arise. How is it that at least fourteen of the eighteen secretaries-general of the UN were or are members of the Council on Foreign Relations (CFR), which was already established in 1921. Why is it that the last eight directors of the CIA, including Bush senior, were CFR members? And why is it that in the last four decades several candidates for the presidency and vice-presidency of both the Democratic and Republican parties were (or became) members of the CFR. We mention: Eisenhower, Kennedy, Nixon, Carter, Ford, Nelson Rockefeller, Bush senior, Clinton, Bush junior).[143]
Official sources describe the CFR as an independent organization, think tank and publisher. It is headquartered in New York, and some offices are located in Washington D.C. The CFR is said to have no affiliation with the U.S. government, but in fact the CFR consists of a number of top international personalities from business, banking and law firms, who visibly and invisibly - as a kind of shadow government - are behind the policies of world politics. One of the most influential people in the CFR is David Rockefeller, former chairman. Brzeziński's name also pops up here. Rockefeller is also chairman of the influential and secret Trilateral Commission, which was established in 1973, 'seemingly in an attempt to divert public attention from the activities of the CFR'.[144] The official goal of the Trilateral Commission is to achieve closer cooperation between

---

[142] Griffin, G.E., *The Creature from Jekyll Island*, p.401. Alo see: Icke, D., *and the truth shall set you free*, p.154-158.

[143] Icke, D., *...and the truth shall set you free*, p. 157.

[144] Marrs, J., *Rule by Secrecy*.

Western European countries, Japan and North America. Antony Sutton and Carroll Quigley refer to the CFR and the Trilateral Commission as secret societies that have an extraordinary influence on world affairs.[145]

'Nazi methods'

That the proliferation of control systems and loss of privacy sometimes provokes fierce reactions is demonstrated by that of world-famous singer Harry Belafonte (78). At a conference of entertainers in January 2006, Belafonte accused the government of America of using 'Nazi methods' and argued that the 'new Gestapo of the Heimat Ministry' had already rendered many civil rights inoperative. 'You can be arrested without charge and detained without the right to legal counsel,' he fulminated. At the conclusion of his speech, he called Bush 'the biggest terrorist' in the world. This to the fury of the White House.[146] In a speech on Sunday, January 15, 2006, Belafonte remarked: 'What is the essential difference in the quality of humanity between those who committed the cruel and tragic act of flying a plane into a building and killing 3,000 innocent Americans, and those who lied and threw the nation into a war that killed hundreds of thousands? Forgive me, fellow citizens, if the connecting line becomes a little unclear to me.'[147] The media paid little or no attention to his sometimes-fiery speech the following day, in which he said, among other things, 'Our laws and our foreign policy always brought about the death of the poor. They were brought about over the backs of those who are needy, by those who already have too much.'[148]

'Privacy – a dirty word'

Karin Spaink, publicist and former chairwoman of the digital civil rights organization Bits of Freedom (BOF) wrote an article in the Dutch daily newspaper *de Volkskrant* of 28 January 2006 entitled: 'Who will take on Big Brother?' Her analysis is spot on and razor-sharp.

---

[145] Sutton, A., *Wall Street and the Bolshevik Revolution*; Quigley, C., *Tragedy and Hope. A History of the World in our Time*.
[146] *Het Laatste Nieuws* (January 25, 2006).
[147] He did that on newsbusters.org
[148] Idem.

'We live under the paradigm of prevention these days: the thought that something or someone *might commit* an act of terror in the future is enough to warrant drastic countermeasures. (...) We are therefore taking measures that at any other time would be described as draconian, and they follow one another in rapid succession. We have made stop-and-search possible (2003). We have camera surveillance in more and more places. The obligation to provide identification has been introduced (January 2005). We have considerably lowered the threshold for requesting personal data from banks, supermarkets, insurance companies, libraries, associations, telephone companies and internet providers - now any policeman can do that, without a court order (Dutch Data Requisition Act, July 2005). At European level, we have accepted the retention obligation, which means that the so-called traffic data of all telecommunications of all citizens must be recorded and stored: when and with whom we send mails, send text messages or chats (December 2005). Yet, it is not enough. The public transport chip card that will be introduced this year will make it possible to meticulously record the movements of all passengers on public transport. The idea of storing everyone's DNA profile is being considered. The forthcoming citizens' service number will allow for quick and easy access to all the files that exist on a person within the state administration. We will have biometric identity cards. Security cameras will soon be able to recognize faces. We are becoming as transparent as the breath of an immaculate little soul. The question of whether such measures are still proportionate, whether they are feasible or effective, how much power the government gains with them and whether there is any control over the diligence with which they are carried out no longer seems to bear any relevance. The fact that such measures more often than not contravene our fundamental rights certainly does not enter into the discussion. After all, security comes first. In the fight against international terrorism, we gladly sacrifice our privacy. (...) Privacy itself has become a problem. Chief of police Welten from Amsterdam expressed this thought concisely: 'Privacy is the hiding place of evil.' In fact, he says that everyone who cares about their civil rights and who does not want to be transparent without question, becomes an accomplice of terrorists and criminals. Shout 'terrorism' three times and 'security' twice and you will get any measure passed, as the practice of recent years has shown. (...) The leap from guarding citizens' rights to guarding them is surprisingly small. (...) Privacy has become a dirty word. Those who love their privacy are in league with the enemy'.

Controlling Big Brother

In a parliamentary democracy, parliament monitors the government. Not out of distrust, but to ensure that everything is done democratically. Open, honest, not in secret. A democracy in which more and more decisions are taken behind closed doors, where, under the guise of 'security', the citizen and his or her rights are ignored, is on a slippery slope. Totalitarian states are created by setting aside the democratic ground rules or allowing them to be set aside. Democracy thrives best when there is trust, openness, patience and peace. In a democracy, citizens have the right to know what the government is keeping in its databases, and why it is taking certain measures for our safety. Why, for example, Swift, the Society for Worldwide Interbank Financial Telecommunication (which regulates the money transfers of some eight thousand banks around the world from Brussels) has, with the knowledge of the National Bank of Belgium, been giving access to its immense database to the CIA since 2002 for the purpose of fighting terrorism,[149] why there are more and more hidden cameras, of which citizens are often not even aware and that they are being recorded. How can citizens in the Netherlands still trust and respect each other when the leaflet 'What is being done about terrorism and what can you do?' says that 'over two hundred thousand professionals have joined forces to fight terrorism', but that at the same time everyone should keep an eye on each other without distrusting one another?[150] That this is counterproductive has already been demonstrated. The government's measures to combat terrorism encourage radicalization. Scientists as well as relatives and friends of terrorist suspects say that the tough policy is counter-

---

[149] Van Cauwelaert, R., 'Beroepsgeheim', in Belgium magazine *Knack* 27 (2006).
[150] For more information: www.nederlandtegenterrorisme.nl.

productive. Also, in intelligence circles there is growing concern about the negative effects of the current counter-terrorism policy. This was shown in a study by the Dutch Newspaper De Volkskrant.'[151]
Maybe Big Brother has become so big because we have kept ourselves so small for so long. It is high time that we start controlling him. Let's point the cameras at him and find out if he has a valid passport to this planet!

---

[151] Groen, J. en A. Kranenberg, 'Bestrijding terrorisme kan verkeerd uitpakken', in Dutch newspaper De *Volkskrant* (Juli 22, 2006).

2.2   The all-seeing eye

Ignoring traditional liberal values, this elite will not hesitate to achieve its political goals by using the most modern techniques to influence people's behaviour and keep society under strict surveillance and control.[152]

Zbigniew Brzeziński

Big brother's all-seeing eye

The lurking gaze of Orwell's Big Brother has now turned into the all-seeing electronic ubiquitous eye. As early as the beginning of the 19th century, Jakob Lorber predicted that in 'the end times' man would invent 'artificial eyes' that could see into the deepest depths of the starry sky. And the Hopi predicted: 'And at the end of time there will be roads visible, very high in the sky.'[153] Not only airplanes and space probes are now circling high in the sky, but also satellites, 'artificial eyes'. After years of research, Big Brother has designed a system to spy on everyone. Most people do not even know it. Under the symbol of the all-seeing eye, the whole planet is being watched. But which all-seeing eye? The all-seeing eye, attributed to God, which can be seen in Masonic and alchemical depictions and in engravings in the work of Jakob Boehme? Or an all-seeing eye that appeared on posters of IBM's Hollerith punch card system in Hitler Germany?

Initially, the TIA project mentioned earlier, also had a logo. A pyramid with an all-seeing eye hovering over the top with the motto

---

[152] Begich, N. en Manning, J., *Angels Don't Play This Haarp*, p. 177.
[153] Soeten, D. de, *Hopi*, in Dutch.

Scientia est Potentia, knowledge is power. Around it is a circle with the words: Information Awareness Office. Due to the storm of protest against this logo (the idea of a pyramid with a capstone and an all-seeing eye had already been used for the one-dollar note), it was quickly withdrawn.[154] Many felt that 'the eye of God' as a symbol of God's loving presence had turned into an all-controlling eye. It appealed to Big Brother.

Satellites: Spying Eyes in the Sky

GPS: everyone can be traced

Satellites have opened up an almost inexhaustible range of possibilities for communication, television broadcasting, military use and espionage. Few people are aware of the fact that satellites are frequently used for espionage and that special systems have even been designed for this purpose. The much-praised GPS (Global Positioning System) not only serves our convenience in knowing which route to take to reach our destination or knowing exactly where we are. GPS was invented by the US Army and has been used for military purposes since 1987. Gradually, it was introduced for civilian use. The system consists of 24 navigation satellites orbiting Earth at an altitude of 20,200 km. There are six orbits with four satellites each. They carry an accurate clock and simultaneously transmit their position to the GPS receiver. The receiver combines the position data and the time differences and calculates its own position. Deviations can be adjusted. Many GPS systems in the car immediately store the data in a central database. Where you were, at what time, and so on. Everyone can be traced. Via GPS, you can be warned about speed cameras, which alternative roads you can take in the event of traffic congestion, or where the nearest petrol station is. A great deal of military and civilian information is stored in central databases via the electronic eyes of GPS.

---

154 Ström, P., *Die Überwachungsmafia*, p. 33-34.

Galileo is able to see a ping-pong ball

'All security policy starts with gathering information and that is what is being done today by satellite', says the European Space Agency (European Space Agency).[155] In order to avoid dependence on the American GPS system the ESA and the EU took the initiative in December 2001 to develop their own satellite navigation system, Galileo. This is because of fiddling with the exact positioning. e.g., during the war in Bosnia disabling the Yugoslav army to use the GPS system; because of satellites being unavailable due to 'maintenance', like after 9/11; because of monitoring of Europe by the American secret services. It uses around 30 satellites at an altitude of 15,000 miles. Since 2005 a large part of Galileo is already in use. In 2008 the system should be ready and more accurate than the American system. Galileo is not only intended as a satellite navigation system, but, like its American counterpart GPS, it will also be used to control traffic, for telecommunications, cartography, transport surveillance, and so on. The satellite can image everything accurately up to a few centimetres in length, even a ping-pong ball! The Pentagon was not happy with the Galileo project and even predicted possible conflicts. Since 9/11, American opposition to this project has grown. Russia has the Glonass system, with 24 satellites (the same number as the GPS system) orbiting Earth at an altitude of 19,130 km to keep an eye on everything.[156]

Sat Nav: a basic necessity of life?

The electronics company Navman has now developed a portable navigation system, which accurately guides you to your destination on the basis of a number of photos.[157] These days, you can also use a navigation system on your mobile phone. Looking for a nice restaurant? Enter the data, which is then immediately dumped into a central database, and presto, there is the restaurant! The Dutch company TomTom in Amsterdam is currently the world leader in portable

---

[155] Dutch newspaper *Algemeen Dagblad* (January 17, 2006).
[156] See Reischl, G., *Unter Kontrolle*, p. 161-164.
[157] Dutch newspaper *De Telegraaf* (May 12, 2006).

navigation systems.[158] Also in Amsterdam is Route 66, number one in the field of navigation software for mobile phones. Navigation is 'a basic necessity of life', Peter-Frans Pauwels, *chief technical officer* at TomTom said. In 1997, there were no more than a hundred thousand cars with navigation systems in Europe, but by 2005 there were nine million. A huge world market has opened up. In a few years' time, most Europeans will be connected to GPS via their smartphone, car and pocket computer. The romantic aspect of map-reading, getting out of the car to ask for directions, together with a little chat, following the flow of the landscape and the unplanned break under a beautiful tree will soon be exchanged for the GPS-guided straight route of the digital highway. 'A TomTom pretends to open up the whole world for you, but it is the thing that knows the way. You don't know where you are. If the device fails, you are immediately confronted with a total sense of loss', philosopher Martin Drenthen comments.[159] Digital maps and voice technology soon determine our travels.[160] Will we be dumbfounded?

Satellites keep an eye on farmers, cows and soil

Satellites are capable of many things. They are increasingly used for surveillance. As of 2005, 10% of the agricultural land of the European Union is already monitored by satellites. Within a few years, all farmers in the 25 member states will be monitored by satellite. To prevent fraud with subsidies. After all, we are talking about an annual budget of forty billion euros. 'We will not zoom in on the farmers' living rooms. The only thing we want to achieve in the end is that the tax money of the European citizens is well spent', says the spokesman of the European Commission. [161] In the dairy sector, the aim is to use a satellite navigation system within a few years to control the livestock. The cows are given a receiver with

---

[158] Dutch newspaper *NRC Handelsblad* (May 6, 2005) and *De Telegraaf* (April 27, 2006).

[159] Van Raaij, B., 'Je weet niet waar je bent', in Dutch newspaper De *Volkskrant* (Aug 5, 2006).

[160] Vandormael, U., 'Rijden à la carte', in Belgium magazine *Knack* (26 juli 2006), p. 52-54.

[161] Dutch newspaper *Eindhovens Dagblad* (December 22, 2004).

which their behaviour can be influenced using sounds and electric shocks. The modern dairy farmer will soon be using a computer, satellite navigation and chips.

Eavesdroppers

An item in the Dutch newspaper *Algemeen Dagblad* of March 1, 2005: 'The Ministry of Defense wants to install eavesdropping dishes on the KPN satellite ground station in Burum in Friesland. This will enable the Ministry of Defense to intercept communications that are received and transmitted a few yards away via the dish of KPN [Dutch Telecom]. It concerns thirteen satellite dishes of the eavesdropping organization NSO (National Sigint Organization)'.[162] The NSO was established in 2003 as a project organization of the intelligence services AIVD and MIVD[163] for interception of satellite traffic. The Cabinet wants to privatize the NSO so that a third secret service will emerge in the Netherlands. Through the new satellite dishes, the NSO can intercept telephone calls, fax messages, data traffic and, increasingly, internet traffic on a large scale. To make the installation of the dishes possible, the Ministry of Defense wants to buy up part of KPN's terrain.'

In 2007, the world's largest radio telescope, LOFAR (Low Frequency Array), will be completed in Exloo (Drenthe). Tens of thousands of inconspicuous antennas, spread across Drenthe, Gelderland, Friesland and Germany, will soon capture the low-frequency radio waves from the cosmos. This way, the 'early years' of the universe can be studied, among other things. Cost: fifty-two million euros. LOFAR is called 'an unprecedented technological challenge'. And it's not just astronomers who will benefit: LOFAR's sensor network, which is linked via fast fibre-optic connections to one of the most powerful supercomputers in the world, will also be used by geologists, agricultural engineers and meteo-

---

[162] Sigint is short for 'Signals Intelligence'. One of the departments of the NSA is also called Sigint.

[163] Dutch newspaper *Eindhovens Dagblad* (December 22, 2004).

rologists.'[164] There is no doubt that TIA and Lifelog will be delighted with this project. To check the early years of every human being perhaps?

Spying cameras everywhere

Since 9/11, the number of cameras used to protect people, goods, buildings, traffic circuits, motorways, railways, shops, homes, banks, post offices, airports and shipyards has increased alarmingly. *Big brother is watching you!* Security firms are making millions in profits. The exploitation of fear has begun. Previously an unexplored territory, now there is money to be made. Insurance companies are increasingly making cameras mandatory and in cars, the black box will soon be storing all the data. A few years ago, theft, burglaries and robberies were commonplace in the Newham district of London.

The Newham area was at risk of becoming depopulated. The American company Visionics in particular was allowed to install the software for cameras there. Now, some three hundred cameras monitor everything via a closed-circuit television from a private security centre. Thieves moved elsewhere. Newham is safe under the prying eyes of cameras and became a model for camera surveillance.[165] In response to the IRA attacks in London during the last two decades of the previous century, 30,000 cameras were installed. Terrorists were 'unfortunately not caught', although people who parked their cars incorrectly and burglars were, the officials of the surveillance system said. An additional benefit would be that people behave better in public because of the presence of the cameras.[166] London is now the most surveilled city in the world. Around half a million cameras spy on everything and everyone. For safety's sake! Yet the attacks of 7 July 2005 could not be prevented. Since 1 January 2006, every citizen of London is monitored whenever he is outside until he returns home. Everyone is filmed at least dozens of times a day. 'Safe

---

[164] Schilling, G., 'Laagland: Luisteren naar het heelal. Van Dwingeloo tot LOFAR: reportage over vijftig jaar radiosterrenkunde in Nederland', in *National Geographic Nederland·België* (April 2006), p. 24-33, in Dutch.
[165] Reischl, *Unter Kontrolle*, p. 73-75.
[166] Idem., p. 10-11.

under the watchful eye', says a roadside advertisement. Orwell's 1984 has been richly outdone.
Could the current Prime Minister of England,
Tony Blair, be related to the deceased British
writer George Orwell, pseudonym of Eric Blair,
who worked with the British police in Burma for
a while and whose books serve as a model for Big
Brother? (BB, Blair & Blair?). Germany, in any
case, seems to be imitating England's example
with half a million cameras, while Austria, with
a hundred thousand cameras, is doing its best to
keep up.[167]

Facial recognition and the end of free communication.

Visionics also designs the facial recognition software (Facelt).[168] A closed
TV circuit ensures that citizens get into their cars safely, shop safely and
sit safely on their terraces. Big brother is the digital guardian angel,
recognizing everyone's face. Spying eyes keep an eye on everything and
society does not need to ask the question why we are so unsafe. Within
the EU, all kinds of far-reaching decisions have recently been taken at a
rapid pace that have completely escaped most people's attention.
Whether Visionics is also itching to install its Facelt software at the
external borders of the Schengen countries, we do not know. But: 'In the
meantime, the next generation of the Schengen Information System (SIS
II)[169] is being worked on diligently, which should already include

---

[167] Idem., p.148-149.

[168] Idem., p. 74.

[169] Schengen is a village in Luxembourg, where the Schengen Agreement was
concluded in 1985. It comprises several agreements between 13 EU Member
States and Norway and Iceland on the abolition of border controls and asylum
applications, competences of border police, extradition, etc. In fact, the agreement
is used for cooperation between the various police forces in investigating criminal
matters, whereby their own borders may be crossed. The Schengen Information
System (SIS I), a database system used by the countries concerned for the security
and surveillance of their borders, was used for this purpose. SIS II is considering
the use of biometrics. Source: http://en.wikipedia.org/wiki/Schengen-information-

biometric data (fingerprints, facial scans). 'It is about time that parliament and public opinion got ready for a public debate on civil liberties and security. Even if Europe dictates a number of measures, there is still the possibility for the member states to implement them with the greatest possible respect for freedoms', writes a collective of authors in Belgium newspaper *De Morgen*.[170] This collective is also deeply concerned about 'the disappearance of free and confidential communication', since the European Ministers of Justice and Home Affairs adopted the European directive on the retention of telecommunications data in Brussels on 21 February 2006. Thus, not only our telephone conversations become more transparent, but also our faces. Losing face is almost impossible with modern technology. Rajeev Sharma, professor at Penn University (Pennsylvania), has already designed software that can distinguish between the faces of men and women with almost one hundred per cent certainty. Ideal for monitoring 'dormitories, changing rooms or toilets', he says.[171] Perhaps his invention is also suitable for telephone booths. There are two more waiting before you...

Mini cameras and electronic eyes

Big brother has a *little brother*. Little brother is mainly concerned with mini cameras the size of a pinhead. An incredible market.[172] Mini spies in the shape of an insect make it possible to eavesdrop and spy on everyone. Handy on the window, in a plant or in the bedroom. Or rather in your pen?[173] Handy too for eavesdropping on your partner, recording a secret meeting, tracking your competitor. Everyone can now be a James Bond. A niche market, but also a loophole in the law and without legislation everybody with a little knowledge of electronics can venture into this unethical field of espionage and experiment. Net Eye 2000 is a Swedish

---

system. See also: www.statewatch.org/news on the relative value of the Schengen countries' 'free borders'.

[170] Vander Velpen, J., P. De Hert en J. Maebe, 'Terreurbestrijding brengt privacy in gevaar', in Belgium newspaper *De Morgen* (7 maart 2006).

[171] Reischl, *Unter Kontrolle*, p. 75.

[172] Hanus, B., *Drahtlos überwachen mit Mini-Videokameras*.

[173] Wahl, G., *22 neue Minispione*.

product. This facet eye does not need a PC. It immediately provides suitable images for the internet. 'Obviously this eye is only used for remote monitoring of production processes, maintenance of machines and meetings via the net.' (sarc...) The plans are ready to integrate the pinhead camera into televisions and computers. We will soon be well safeguarded, without being able to see or control it. An 'electronic artificial eye', which reacts and registers just like the human eye, is also in the making. It is 'intelligent' and can be programmed to recognize people or events.[174] Whether the boundary of the ethically permissible has not long since been crossed is apparently not discussed by the designers of all these spy devices. There is no doubt that soon, electronic eyes will be communicating with each other about things that cannot stand the light of day [this is now called *The Internet of Things*].

Is this allowed?

In the door-to-door brochure 'What is being done against terrorism? And what can *you* do?' contains a number of frequently asked questions and answers. A few examples. 'All those security cameras in the street and stations, is that allowed?' – 'Yes, that's allowed. Increasingly more surveillance cameras are in streets and at stations. And there are also more and more surveillance cameras on top of buildings. For our security, we have to sacrifice a little bit of our privacy.'
'Are we becoming a police state?' - 'No. Our security requires vigilance. In situations of increased risk, there will be more control. But even then, the rights of citizens are protected.' But, compromising a little privacy every time, paves the way for a police state. It is characteristic of a state that is step by step on its way but will never admit this. The most precious thing in interpersonal relations is mutual trust, the basis of society. If this is rapidly dismantled by imbedding itself in far-reaching measures that do not require us to look at the underlying causes of terror, a state is in great danger of gradually moving into a police state.

---

[174] Sunn, F., *666. Die Zahl des Tiers im Internet*, p. 63.

'Privacy – an illusion'

'They know everything about you', was the headline of the article by Olof van Joolen and Kees Wessels in the *Algemeen Dagblad* of 28 January 2006. The police and the judiciary are gradually being given more power to keep an eye on everyone. Hans Franken, professor of Information law and a member of the Senate of the CDA, says in the article: 'Citizens lose rights which were hard fought. In this way we create a society that is based on mistrust, whereas people should be able to rely on the government.' The vision of the Belgian VLD MP Karel Pinxten is also remarkable: 'The right to privacy is an increasing illusion.' He estimates that the average Belgian is in about six hundred databases, but what data exactly is known and what it is used for and by whom no one can say for sure. More and more personal data is stored in databases by the state. Soon also the DNA pattern of everyone and the fingerprints. The European Network of Forensic Science Institute (ENFSI) stores as much data as possible in order to be able to exchange it as quickly as possible in the event of crime and terrorism. And the Data Claims Act in the Netherlands, which took effect on 1 January 2006, obliges social institutions, companies, banks and insurance companies to transfer personal data of their clients to the judicial authorities if it requests it for an investigation. Investigators are on the alert everywhere. Needless to mention, everything happens for... precisely yes, our safety![175]

Electronic sniffer dogs of the intelligence services

Sniffer dog Echelon

Fortunately, there are also well-trained electronic sniffer dogs that guard us. The sniffer dog *Echelon* is strictly speaking an eavesdropping-program that through seven advanced satellites intercepts almost all civilian and military information and communications around the world outside the United States. The most expensive satellite costs more than 1

---

[175] Dutch newspaper *Metro* 1005 (May 3, 2005).

billion euros. In a broader sense, however, Echelon is a global network that electronically intercepts and analyses signals. Echelon is used by the intelligence services of the so-called UKUSA countries: Besides the United States (USA) and the United Kingdom (UK), these are Canada, Australia and New Zealand.[176]

Echelon also proved to be a good international corporate spy. Boeing, which works with Lockheed and Dupont and is held in a power stranglehold by the Rockefeller family, contributed to the creation of Echelon. [177] Echelon effortlessly plucks around ten billion text messages, four billion e-mails, four billion telephone calls (three billion via fixed devices and one billion via mobile phones) from the airwaves every day. Per second, 155 million bits can be sent into space, which is equivalent to 15,000 pages per second. [178] If you use the ATM? It will be stored. Your code to lock your mobile phone? Stored. Internet password? Stored. We don't have to worry about anything getting lost, going missing. In addition, the telephone companies keep track of who calls who, when and for how long making mobile phone calls, also from where. We may not take that into account, but we do pay this bill every time.

Sniffer Dog ETSI

Europe was furious about the espionage activities that Echelon unleashed. Although she herself also had an electronic sniffer dog in training, known by the police files as *Enfopol 98,* this animal was not yet known to the outside world. [179] You never have to let him out, he wags his tail in all directions, always finds his own way and equals the UKUSA sniffer dog. Under the name *ETSI,* the European sniffer dog became better known. ETSI, which stands for European Telecom Standards Institute, developed a standard, which serves as the basis for telecom-munications-surveillance in the EU. The standard is called ETSI ES

---

[176] Keefe, P.R., *Chatter. How everyone worldwide is bugged*, p. 24-25, 311, 313.

[177] Springmeier, F., *Bloodlines of the Illuminati*, p. 117 and 212.

[178] Keefe, P.R., *Chatter*, p. 67. 'The speed at which digital information is transmitted is measured in bits per second, with each bit representing a one or zero', writes Keefe.

[179] Reischl, G., *Unter Kontrolle*, p. 138-139.

201.671, which every provider and internet user must adhere to. Behind this letter-number combination is an eavesdropping system that must be built into the digital system, enabling police and secret services to watch and eavesdrop. Spicy fact: It is not they who finance this spying system, but the providers and internet users![180] Another bill.

Is the NSA eavesdropping on everyone?

Within the UKUSA partnership, the US has the largest and most secretive intelligence service: the NSA (National Security Agency), whose mission it is to ensure America's security. The NSA employs 75,000 people, 40,000 in the U.S. and 25,000 at eavesdropping stations[181] around the world. The NSA controls more than two thousand of those and has an annual budget of ten billion dollars. More than three billion dollars goes to decoding machines, computers, *scramblers* and other electronic equipment. Because of its mysterious nature, the abbreviation NSA is sometimes interpreted as *No Such Agency* (to deny its existence) or *Never Say Anything* (because it rarely shares information). Before 9/11, almost no American knew of the existence of this, largest, secret service in the world, located in a giant black mirror glass building in Fort Meade, Maryland, called Crypto City by some. In 1952, it was the Truman administration that secretly, outside of Congress, founded the NSA[182] and in early 2002 President Bush – also in secret – instructed the NSA to monitor and eavesdrop on telephone conversations, e-mails and other internet communications *within the US* on a large scale, albeit prohibited by the Constitution. And he did so without a search warrant or new law, with as motive to ensure the safety of citizens against possible terrorist attacks. This was partly at the instruction of the director of the NSA, Lieutenant General of the Air Force, Michael Hayden, who initiated the 'terror surveillance program' within the NSA. He was director of the NSA from 1999-2005 and has since been appointed director of another U.S. intelligence agency, the CIA (Central Intelligence Agency). On May 11,

---

[180] Idem, p. 138-141.
[181] Keefe, P.R., *Chatter*, p. 312.
[182] Idem, p. 21-22.

2006, the world was shaken up by this major eavesdropping scandal, involving the three largest telecom companies AT&T, Verizon and Bellsouth. It was the first time since Watergate that the NSA had eaves-dropped on its own citizens.[183] In mid-August 2006, the Detroit federal judge banned President Bush from further eavesdropping without the consent of a specially designated Court. Bush is of the opinion though, he can continue 'because of the threat of terrorism'. The final word on this has not yet been said. Why Nixon had to resign and Clinton had an impeachment hanging over his head because of the Monika Lewinsky affair but Bush can remain where he is, the sniffer dog Echelon has still not tracked down yet.

Supercomputers and Dan Brown

Under the codename 'Platform', the NSA developed a global computer network from 1983 to connect the government computer systems from some 52 countries. Via the electronic superhighway, all the information that the NSA wants comes to Fort Meade. Every signal that is transmitted can be tapped into. The NSA's Cray supercomputers can handle 64 billion instructions per second, giving them 'the largest concentration of computing power in the world.'[184] But even more powerful computers are being worked on, computers that can deliver unimaginable super-perfor-mances, that is beyond any layman's comprehension. In The *Juvenalis Dilemma* by bestselling author Dan Brown, the NSA's supercomputer TRANSLTR – called 'the beast' – plays a central role. Susan Fletcher, head of the NSA's cryptology department, points out during a conversation with Greg Hale that the NSA is not an advanced 'Peeping Tom'. 'This organization was only created with one goal: to guarantee the security of this country. If it so happens that we occasionally have to shake a few trees to find the bad apples, so be it. I think most citizens would love to give up some privacy if they realized that perpetrators could no longer go about their business unnoticed.'[185] Dan Brown as an advocate for a little

---

[183] Dutch newspapers: *De Telegraaf* (May 12, 2006); de *Volkskrant* (May 19, 2006); *NRC Handelsblad* (February 18, 2006); also see Risen, J., *State of War*.

[184] Keefe, P., *Chatter*, p. 22.

[185] Brown, D., *The Juvenalis Dilemma*, p. 126.

less privacy and more control? Would he have been aware of the fact that the most crucial computer and communication networks used by the US government and the Military are secured by encrypted software prepared by an Israeli 'codebreaker' affiliated with the Scientific Weizmann Institute in Israel?[186] Fascinating theme perhaps for an exciting science fiction film with the theme how the Israeli Secret Service re 9/11 breaks the code of the Cray supercomputers of the NSA with the title: *The Seniors Dilemma.*

'The Beast 666'

If in Dan Brown's book, the NSA's supercomputer TRANSLTR is 'the beast', for author Texe Marrs on the other hand, 'the beast' is the L.U.C.I.D. system that underpin the powerful NSA control and espionage network. Marrs is an insider. As a former Airforce officer, he is at home with global electronics communication systems. He taught 'American Defense Policy and Strategic Weapons Systems' and 'history of space technology' for five years at the University of Texas, Austin. At two other universities he taught political science and international relations. In the astounding book, *Project L.U.C.I.D.* he clarifies how the NSA, with all its supercomputers, information systems, networks and connections with other secret services, is working on using the L.U.C.I.D. system to *totally* control every citizen of the world via the most advanced electronic systems, biometrics, satellites and chips. As a result, man is in danger of becoming a slave of a power elite or shadow government, of which most people are completely unaware. L.U.C.I.D. is not only the trademark of the Advanced Technologies Group from New York, which has many financial interests in big-brother systems, but also stands for the Universal Identification System, an extremely advanced computer system, which collects, assembles - merges -analyses and manipulates information from *all* sources. All sources means: 'every government agency, every service, every bank and financial institution, every

---

[186] Bollyn, C., *Critical U.S. Government and military computer networks using Israeli 'Security' software*, American Free Press. Source: https://www.bollyn.com/the-israeli-code-on-us-government-computers/

company, every university, every salesman and representative, every police service, every army department, every researcher, and so on.' According to Marrs, L.U.C.I.D. is currently at the heart of the giant NSA spider web and is destined to become the universal human control system under the name 'the Beast 666'.[187] He brings this in relation to certain biblical prophecies from the Book of Revelation.

Antony Sutton (1925- 2002), a former scientific researcher at the Hoover Institute (Stanford University) and professor of economics at the State University of Los Angeles, California, pointed out years ago in one of his newsletters, *Phoenix Letter*, the undermining of privacy should the L.U.C.I.D. project go ahead. Once L.U.C.I.D. is in the hands of the government, the government can no longer be trusted according to Sutton. Sutton also points out how close the word *LUCID* is to LUCIS or Lucifer and hopes that the name is not a Freudian mistake. [188]

The evil eye and the eye of love

Now that we have seen how the all-seeing eye of big brother is everywhere to 'guard' and 'protect' us. Since 9/11 things are speeding up as well as in the loss of trust in each other, loss of the direct eye contact with each other. We are progressively manipulated by those who exploit fear as a means to control and dominate. Is it possible that the millions of electronic eyes that spy on us every day in the form of cameras, satellites and 'artificial eyes' uncover our broken manifest contra the unity of existence? All these electronic eyes are compressed into a pseudo-all-seeing eye, which seems to provide pseudo-security and pseudo-protection, but increasingly resembles the 'evil eye', in which the light has died and which makes the artificially created duality of 'terrorist' and 'non-terrorist' more blatantly visible than ever before. This evil eye makes it clear to us that we are in danger of losing our original face, ignoring our common true identity, an identity independent of papers, passports and electronics. In a thorough intercultural study on the magic of the eye, the German eye specialist Seligmann pointed out how widespread the

---

[187] Marrs, T., *Project L.U.C.I.D.*
[188] Idem.

belief in all cultures is with regard to the 'evil eye', which is seen as non-human. For example, he points to the rigid and enchanting gaze of the serpent. The Latin *draco* (Greek: *drakon*) and the Greek ophis mean not only 'snake', but also 'he who looks chilling'. In Sanskrit, the snake is called Drishti *visha,* 'whose face has been poisoned'. Just as small animals can become paralyzed by the hypnotic gaze of a snake, so man cannot escape the influence of this gaze.[189] It is interesting how many stories circulate in world literature about 'fallen watchers' (angels), also called 'fallen sons of the serpents', who have the evil eye, as opposed to the loving eye of the 'not fallen' watchers.

An experiment. Keep a magnifying glass above the eye in the top stone, which floats above the pyramid on the fragment of a one-dollar bill, depicted here. What do you see? What do you feel? Until today, these notes change hands billions of times every day, but soon all money transactions seem to have to go via the internet.

The eye in which I see God,
is the same eye in which God sees me?
My eye and God's eye, that's one eye
and seeing one and loving one.[190]

Master Eckhart (1260-1327)

---

[189] Seligman, S., *Die Zauberkraft des Auges und das Berufen*, p.163-172.
[190] Eckhart, *Love God like no one.*

2.3   The enforced biometric passport

In recent years, an attempt has been made to convince us to accept practices of control that have always rightly been regarded as inhumane and abnormal, as humane and normal dimensions of our existence. For example, everyone knows very well that the control exercised by the state by using electronic objects, such as credit cards or mobile phones, has reached levels that were previously unthinkable.

However, it would not be possible to cross certain limits in the control and manipulation of the body without entering a new biopolitical era, without going one step further in what Michel Foucault called the gradual compaction of man, and which is established by the most advanced techniques. The electronic storage of fingerprints and of the retina, the subcutaneous tattoo and similar practices contribute to determining this boundary. The security reasons put forward to justify this should not impress us. They don't matter. (...) By applying these techniques, which are designed for the 'dangerous classes', to the citizen, or rather to man as such, the states, which should actually be the forum of political life, have made him, the citizen, the suspect par excellence, and so much so that humanity itself has become the dangerous class for them. (...) The biopolitical tattoo that the United States is now enforcing on those who want to enter their territory may well be the harbinger of what will later be asked of us to accept as the normal identity registration of the ordinary citizen in the mechanisms and the machinery of the state. That is why we must oppose it.[191]

Giorgio Agamben, (professor of philosophy in Venice and until recently in New York)

---

[191] Agamben, G., 'No to Biopolitical Tattooing', in *Le Monde* (January 10, 2004)

Violation of the intimacy of the body

The 'humiliating circumstances' (fingerprints, retinal scan) to which a person is exposed when he wants to enter the United States were a reason for the Italian philosopher Giorgio Agam in 2004 to stop giving lectures in New York. He called on colleagues and students to do the same. He sharply rejects the violation of the intimacy of the body on ethical grounds, even referring to the registration of deported Jews in concentration camps such as Auschwitz. Agamben believes that what is happening now in the US could herald a biometric identity system that will soon be accepted everywhere.

America demands biometric passport

The time when a nobleman only had to wave his business card when crossing a border is already several centuries behind us. Since 9/11, the territorial drive seems to be coming up strongly in several countries. Animals marking their territories or sniffing at each other; police, inspectors and border officials do *their* sniffing around with extra attention into papers of those whose breed, religion, age, country of origin or other special marks give reason for that. Since 9/11, the production of a new type of passport has also been accelerated. Of course, you guessed it, because of our safety. The many forgeries, the almost endless influx of immigrants, the infiltration of terrorists and 'criminal elements' – this became intolerable. If this was not an urgent problem before 9/11, after 9/11 the climate for these measures was overripe. Hard data (figures, facts, documents) weigh the heaviest. Humanitarian considerations count less.

With the United Nations anti-terror resolution (number 1373) in hand, after 9/11, it was quickly established that a biometric passport should be introduced, internationally. Forgery of a biometric passport by terrorists could practically be ruled out, or so it was maintained. It was an important motive used to justify this passport. Few people were aware of resolution 1373. The United States demanded that from now on everyone who wanted to enter the country must have a biometric passport. If you didn't already have one, fingerprints and an iris scan would be taken on the spot. Reischl calls the demands of the US paradoxical, because 'in the US one does not even have ID cards'.[192] But that has changed. Despite heavy criticism on the security of RFID passports, the American government decided on 14 August to start issuing digital travel documents. They found something to prevent 'skimming' (unauthorized reading) and 'eavesdropping' of the RFID chip by equipping the passport with a foil that should protect against this type of practice. (The question arises: how will the competent authorities themselves read out the data?) According to the U.S. government, a change of the data on the chip from the outside can be prevented by an electronic signature. Furthermore, it claims that a random, unique identifier diminishes the risk of tracking down the owner of an e-passport.[193]

Biometric passport as a weapon

The information in the new passport is stored on an RFID chip. That means personal data can simply be picked up – captured by people with no more than an antenna and an RFID reader.[194] It has been known for some time that biometric passports are not 100% secure. In February 2006 it became known that a Dutch company had succeeded in cracking the RFID chip in the new passport by 'smartly' guessing at the code.[195] And in April 2006, at the Black Hat Conference in Las Vegas, security analysts from the flexilis company showed a four-minute video of an experiment with an RFID passport that could detonate an explosive with remote control. Flexilis has notified the U.S. Department of Homeland Security of this experiment and the Ministry of the Interior and Kingdom Relations (BZK) deny the danger.[196] 'There is no way one can simply pick up all sorts of signals from the chip', says a spokesperson, 'That is only

---

[192] Reischl, *Unter Kontrolle*, p. 88.

[193] https://2001-2009.state.gov/r/pa/prs/ps/2006/70433.htm

[194] Ström, P., *Those Überwachungsmafia*, p. 134.

[195] Persson, M., 'RFID-chip blijkt niet onfeilbaar', in Dutch newspaper De *Volkskrant* (March 15, 2006).

[196] https://usatoday30.usatoday.com/tech/news/computersecurity/2006-08-03-flexilis-rfid-passports_x.htm

possible if you have the passport in your hands,'[197] because the communication between the chip and the reading device is encrypted and one needs to read a strip first in the passport. According to computer hackers, it doesn't matter that the chip is encrypted. Most codes end up being cracked anyway. [198]

EU countries give in to America

Biometrics has become a slogan. The word comes from the Greek: *bios* (life) and *metreo* (measure). Every person has unique patterns in his body, recognizable in, for example, fingers, palm, eye, voice, facial features, DNA. These patterns can be measured, digitally recorded and stored in a chip.

On 13 December 2004, the European Union decided to introduce the biometric passport with portrait photo and fingerprints as a rapid introduction.[199] The law was introduced in 2005 and it should be commonplace in 2008. Following the EU measure that no one will be able to travel abroad without a biometric passport, the 25 EU countries eventually gave in to America. Big brother has spoken. The United Kingdom did not sign the agreement, but had adopted the Identity Cards Act a month earlier, which introduced the new biometric identity card (in fact a passport) in phases.

'New generation' of travel documents

Conscientious objection to the biometric passport does not count. This was communicated in February 2005 in the Netherlands by the then Minister of the Interior, De Graaf.[200] The then Minister Pechtold for Administrative Renewal and Kingdom Relations (BVK) introduced the new model passport and the National Identity Card on 24 April 2006. 26

---

[197] Belgium newspaper De *Stentor*, August 5, 2006.

[198] Idem.

[199] Nield, M., 'The Police State Raod Map', September 2004. Bron: http://www.hiddenmysteries.org/freebooks/studies/policestateplanning.pdf

[200] *Nederlands Dagblad* (February 17, 2005). The Dutch minister replies by letter to questions from Mr. J. Spaans from Hoogeveen, who suggests that the United States are forcing things.

August 2006 the introduction of this 'new generation of electronic Dutch travel documents' took place. Elsewhere on the website of the Ministry of the Interior and Kingdom Affairs, there is talk of 'electronic travel documents with biometric characteristics'.[201]

The biometric passport has a chip, that in addition to the personal data, includes the passport photo. The colour photograph must be recent, taken head-on and in the technical format prescribed by the EU. No more smiling anymore. We 'have to look neutral and keep our mouths closed'.[202] The Netherlands has followed the example of England. Smiling would complicate the electronic facial scan. Already a forerunner of the big-brother state? Furthermore, on the chip are: name, first names, date of birth, gender, document number, social security number (in the future citizen service number) and end date of the validity of the document.

The fingerprint will be introduced later, once the EU has adopted all the 'technical specifications'. The chip allows the data to be electronically controlled by comparing it with the characteristics of the carrier of that passport and with the printed data in it. For example, by introducing the biometric passport, the Netherlands also complies with the agreements that the EU has made to 'increase security'. The Ministry of the Interior and Kingdom Affairs designed 'the travel curriculum' to realize this.

What the Minister of the Interior does not tell (or does not know) is that the data stored in databases of the biometric passport are immediately transferred to a central database, where big brother complements and/or checks the picture of every world citizen! The Dutch government no longer has to dream of such a database.[203] It's already there. In addition, biometric databases can be cracked. Everyone will fit into the system. And no one is allowed to say, 'I pass.' That's the time to be careful!

---

[201] Published on the website of the Dutch 'Ministerie van Binnenlandse Zaken en Koninkrijksrelaties': passport with chip; en
https://www.theregister.com/2005/12/01/jahc_biometric_id_standards/
[202] https://www.nu.nl/algemeen/779379/lachen-mag-niet-meer-in-nieuwe-paspoort.html
[203] Persson, M., 'De wereld van Orwell lijkt bijna onvermijdelijk', in Dutch newspaper De *Volkskrant* (February 25, 2006).

A contemptible feeling

Many a citizen suddenly begins to realize that he has been presented with something that he has not only not asked for, but which also makes him feel unworthy. After the adoption of the law on body searching and the law on the identification duty, the biometric passport was introduced fairly quickly in the Netherlands. Despite the protests here and there, there was no mass resistance. In the eighties, almost the entire public opinion in the Netherlands was mobilized when introducing the postal code, now the majority seems willing to be carried to the biometric 'data slaughter bank'. Because of safety.

A message from *De* of 8 December 2005: 'Officers will soon be able to take fingerprints of suspicious persons on the street. The mobile computers of police forces will be provided with this possibility as a trial next year, so that officers can establish the identity of suspects on the street.'

Biometrics are not new

Fingerprinting is not new. The Babylonians and Chinese already used it when concluding a treaty. A little ink on the finger and hup, the fingerprint was ready. The Englishman William Herschel was the first to use the fingerprint for police purposes. Commissioned by the English crown, he was in charge of the distribution of salaries and pensions in Calcutta (late 19th century). Because there was fraud, he entered the fingerprint as identification. 20 years later, the general inspector of police in Calcutta, the Englishman Edward Henry, introduced the dactyloscopy. (The Greek *daktylos* = finger; *skopein* = see.) Dactyloscopy is the science that studies the lines and patterns of the fingers, especially the fingertips, hands and feet. When Henry became police commissioner in London four years later, he also introduced dactyloscopy in England and Wales. Germany followed in 1903 and not much later the whole world. 'Brittania rules the 'finger-waves'?'

A billion-dollar company

Biometrics creeps in everywhere. There's a huge market for it.[204] The leading biometric companies are mainly based in America. They are often connected to companies that produce weapons or supply the technology for weapons (Lockheed Martin, Raytheon, General Dynamics).[205] When America mandated the biometric passport and Europe had to follow, America simultaneously gained a monopoly over the biometric industry. Biometric Technology Today had a turnover of 230 million euros in 2000. In 2001, turnover had already doubled. Biometrics has become a multibillion-dollar company and is advancing everywhere. The 'biometric eye' is already following us and in Germany identification via an iris scan has already been introduced, for example at Hanover airport. (Fig. 8) Airports, restaurants, swimming pools, recreational resorts, banks and companies are increasingly adopting biometric identification. Every time a finger, iris, palm or voice pattern is scanned, the number that the scan gives is quickly compared with the stored data in the chip. We have been reduced to a digital number. Of course, for our safety. 'Experts are convinced that within five years in shops and sports centres and most offices the issuing of a scan is mandatory.'[206] Motto: 'He who has nothing to hide, needs not fear anything.' And vice versa / vice versa? 'He who has nothing to fear does not have to hide anything.' By the way, what does the state keep hidden from us? Should the citizens not monitor the lost memory sticks and computers of the state better?

From *Ausweis* to *Auschwitz*

Nazis, fascists and communists have always been obsessed with identity cards and national registrations. Before the horrific holocaust began on Jewish people and every Jew had to wear a Star of David, the Nazis had created complete card systems through IBM's Hollerith punch card system to quickly track down Jewish people, gypsies and homosexuals

---

[204] Ström, P., *Die Überwachungsmafia*, p. 130-144.
[205] Reischl, G., *Unter Kontrolle*, p. 87-88.
[206] *PZC* (November 11, 2005).

(see section 1 of this chapter). No valid *Ausweis* (proof of identity) made the road to the horrific Auschwitz concentration camp shorter. The commander of this camp once declared: 'Our system is so terrible that no one in the world will think it possible (...). If someone were to manage to escape from Auschwitz and inform the world about it, the world would label him as a fantasist and liar'.[207]

The massacres in Rwanda in 1995, in which one million people were killed in a horrendous way, were carried out so 'efficiently' because the Hutus could see on the mandatory identity cards whether they were dealing with a Tutsi or a Hutu at the checkpoints and raids.[208] In Iraq, Sunnis are asked for passports during raids. If there is Shia on it, a neck shot follows.

'However, if the social-political climate changes, biometrics can change from a useful instrument to an instrument of oppression. (...) Suddenly, instead of countering deception, this technology can serve to track down political dissenters and exercise state control,' said Beth Givens of the Organization Privacy Rights Clearinghouse in San Diego.[209]

Where is this going?

The biometric passport appears to be an intermediate stage. After all, no matter how resourceful this passport is, it can be lost or stolen. This also applies to all kinds of other passes. Our wallets are full of them. And if it gets stolen, you lose all the passes at once... If the passport has disappeared, then also the chip with all the information. It is therefore 'better' to give the chip a safe place where it is not lost. In our body, under the skin. Big brother is already busy with it, has big plans. Most people do not notice it. It is all perfectly timed, we'll see. Reduced to a digitally stored face and recognized by face scanners, we are in danger of losing the awareness of our original face. Even a smile is too much to ask...

---

[207] Breitman, R., *Heinrich Himmler*, 2005, p. 12.
[208] Marrs, T., *Project L.U.C.I.D.*
[209] Ström, *Die Überwachungsmafia*, p. 140.

If you seek the truth, don't run after things any longer.
Stop thinking about what is right or wrong but just like now see what your
original face looked like before your father and mother were born.[210]

Zen master Hui-Neng (637-714)

WHAT CAN WE DO?

- Find other sources of information than the usual: consult other books, journals and websites, create an archive and set up a small library of effective information.
- Open a website for your information. Follow verdicts in the field of privacy and civil rights. Create working groups and/or discussion groups.
- Contact newspaper, radio, television, local government, national politicians. Express your concern. Ask questions. Follow political decision-making concerning privacy, civil rights, security. Create a leaflet to inform your neighbourhood. Distribute pamphlets. Anything creative. Realize that a well-organized action is effective. Trust your own strength and influence. Be genuine, sincere and peaceful in your possible action.
- Contact ICAMS for more information. Address NGO's and human rights organizations. Scrutinize the UN charters., If necessary, start a trial collectively against violation of civil rights.
- Check and find out how much surreptitious control takes place in your own environment. Via cameras, for example. Other means of control may also be the subject of your investigation. Publish it. Ask why. Start a dialogue.
- Make a study of the various aspects of the biometric passport. Show your dissatisfaction with fingerprints and iris scans. Even though the new passport is a fact, make sure that you are aware of this kind of thing in the near future. Make your voice heard from now on. Talk to government agencies. Ask questions about databases.
- Tip: a simple piece of aluminum foil wrapped around your passport, breaks the contact with a possible GPS control system.

---

[210] Bancroft, A., *Zen*, p.14.

3

The dangers of the chip

It is technically possible to inject any newborn with a microchip that can serve to identify the person for the rest of its life.

Such plans are secretly discussed in the United States without any public debate on the aspects involving privacy (...)

Implanted people can be followed anywhere. Their brain functions can be remotely controlled by supercomputers and even altered by frequency modulation.

The 'elite' experimenters used prisoners, soldiers, nerve patients, disabled children, deaf and blind people, homosexuals, single women, the elderly, schoolchildren as guinea pigs for secret experiments, or any group of people who were considered marginal for that matter.

The published experiences of prisoners in the state prison of Utah (USA), for example, are shocking for the conscience. Today's microchips respond to low-frequency radio waves.

Via satellites, the implanted person can also be traced anywhere in the world. (...) Today's super technology that connects our brain functions to computers via microchips (or even without them, according to the latest technology) via satellites in the US or Israel, is the greatest threat to humanity.

The latest supercomputers have sufficient capacity
to control the entire world population.

What will happen when people are inclined to agree to have microchips placed into their bodies under false pretences? …presenting the microchip as an ID, as the decoy.

Even a mandatory legislation that treats the removal of an identity implant as a crime was covertly proposed in the US.

Are we willing to robotize humanity and totally eliminate our privacy, including the freedom of thought? How many of us would want to hand over their entire lives to big brother, including our most secret thoughts?

But the technology to create a totalitarian new world order exists! Veiled neurological communication systems are installed to nullify independent thinking and to control social and political activities for the benefit of selfish private and military interests.

When our brain functions are already connected to supercomputers through radio implants and microchips, it will be too late to protest. This threat can only be averted by informing the public about bio-telemetry using the available literature and by exchanging information at international conferences.

Time is running out for changing the direction of military medicine and ensuring the future of human freedom.[211]

Rauni-Leena Luukanen-Kilde, doctor of medicine, former chief officer of the Finnish Health Service.

---

[211] This quote comes from the article 'Microchip Implants, Mind Control and Cybernetics', in *Spekula* (year. 36, 3rd quarter, 1999). *Spekula* is read by all Finnish medical students and all doctors in northern Finland.
Source: www.conspiracyarchive.com/NWO/microchip-implants-mind-control.

3.1   Chip for modern slaves

And it was given to him[212] to give life's breath to the image of the beast, so that the image of the beast could also speak, and cause that all who did not worship the image of the beast were slain.
And it causes all to be given, the small and the great, the rich and the poor, the free and the slaves, a mark on their right hand or on their foreheads, and that no one can buy or sell anything if he does not bear that sign, the name of the beast or the number of his name.
Wisdom is needed here.
He who has reason can calculate the number of the beast, for it is the number of a man, and his number is six hundred and sixty-six.

Book of Revelation 13:15-18

'Ace of spades' trumps

Big brother comes up with all sorts of tricks to make our purses and wallets, which are full of all kinds of cards, coins and papers, a little lighter. Bank cards, loyalty cards, health insurance card, entrance card for work, driving license, Public Transport card, pensioners card, telephone card, biometric passport, in Belgium the electronic identity card, with a special space in the chip to mention a possible noble status,[213] and so on. And each card has its own number and/or code.
In order to speed up the payment system, the banks introduced the *smart card* or chip card. Smart as in being intelligent, but also cunning. It is a

---

[212] By 'him' is meant the other beast, the beast 'rising from the earth' (Book of Revelation 13:11).

[213] The chip in the Belgian electronic identity card has a file of 160 bytes, in which is stored: a serial number of the card, the first two first names, family name, national register number, nationality, place of birth and date, and the gender of the owner. Source: the website of mailplan.ohv.

plastic card housing a chip, covered by a golden contact layer of 1 cm^2. The chip itself is not bigger than a few millimetres. The chip is a kind of minicomputer which can store the necessary functions and data. The old euro cards with built-in chip and all other cards with magnetic strips are the forerunner of the smart card. With the smart card, computer operations can be carried out without external intervention. The stored data on such a card is read by a special reading device *(Smart Card Reader)*. There are also chip cards that can be read remotely.[214]

Thanks to smart cards, biometric passports and electronic identity cards, we are gradually getting used to the chip. Smart! Unquestionably everyone knows that there is the calculation machine and the telephone chips in almost every new car and car key, in all kinds of household and other appliances, e.g., computer, television, and the radio remote not to mention the modern boiler. All safe *outside* our bodies. Big brother is smart, really knows what makes us tick. It takes some getting used to the idea that such a chip is getting nearer. Through bracelets on our wrist or ankle, or a chain around the neck, that is already getting closer to the skin, and what next? Underneath the skin? Once you begin to understand the card game you will soon realize that the smart card has become the 'ace of spades' in this game. 'Ace of spades' is trump, carefully eliminating all other cards. It is not difficult to see certain patterns in this card game. With the naked eye, without a camera and an alert mind, you can scan and screen the game (a simple SS method). Step by step a plan is carried out. It's hardly noticeable. Clever and shrewd! The smart card as an ace of spades in the card game! Gone with the cheques! Gone with the old coins! Replaced by the euro. Telebanking is the slogan. This is much faster and cheaper than the 'old-fashioned' money transactions. Did anyone ever ask you at the bank, whether you came from the Stone Age? (Not such a bad time at all by the way; the pyramids were built then.) Bank and post office services are gradually reduced. Small offices are closed and more ATMs introduced. Pinning larger amounts 'out of the wall' is no longer possible. And whilst the customer must once again show his passport or a copy at the request of the bank according to Law

---

[214] Reischl, G., *Unter Kontrolle*, p. 180-181; Sunn, F., *666*, p. 96.

Identification when giving service (to prevent 'money laundering' and is aimed at combating terrorism), the customer is yet again reminded of the great convenience of telebanking. Are our interests and security not beautifully taken care of, or are they?

Front stages on the digital highway

Electronic payment traffic is going into the next gear. Only a few years left they say and everything will be done via the internet. Tax, buying and selling, reservations, accounting, travel, holiday plans. Soon there will be no way back anymore. We are racing down the digital highway without having to hold the steering wheel ourselves. We are being steered by Big Brother with only one card left in our hand. The smart card. The smart card as 'ace of spades', the trump card in the game of cards. But that trump card can be stolen, we can lose it, it can be abused. So, one day the chip from that card will fly right *into* our hand, since also the trump card must disappear from the card game, however not the chip from that card we were holding. Well done smartcard. We don't need your card anymore, but we *do* need your chip. Without it, we can't buy or sell anything you see. Cash is no longer needed. So, the cards have been shuffled and now even the trump card is removed from our hands. Sceptics like to say, 'Oh, it won't happen that easily', the 'chiptics' think otherwise. Suppose there is a player who cheats. Who is cheating on us, outplaying us? Imagine....

'Goodbye to cash?'

In several countries, the idea is gradually beginning to sink in that it is best for everyone to organize everything via the internet. All those cards and passwords, all those cards and numbers, all that cash, what a hassle! As early as 1991, the American *OMNI Magazine* reported that cash and credit cards will soon be superfluous.[215] 'Farewell to cash' was already on the front page of the Swiss magazine

---

[215] Sunn, ibid.

FACTS in 1996.[216] Different times present themselves. Switzerland, the country of central banks par excellence, of gold bars and silver coins, of neutrality and activity, is leading the way.

Clever thinking. Should an economic world crisis ever arise or an attack be committed which pales 9/11... Then things will be organized in no time at all. A society without cash. Unique for our safety!

Chips on the rise

In 1996, *GEO* published the article 'The glass man', preparing the reader for an era without all those cards. During a coffee break at a conference concerning the plastic cards and the cards with chips, one of the advisors toyed with the idea of shooting a chip in the buttocks of every baby after birth, as in the easiest way... This man's business card showed that he was a marketing leader of a world company. [217] Around 2000, the Sint Lucas Clinic in Solingen and the university hospital in Lübeck decided in Germany that all newborns should wear a wristband or ankle bracelet with a chip. It contained the details of the babies and those of their mother. This is to prevent unauthorized persons from abducting a baby. This, again, for safety reasons.

In the meantime, there is serious thought given to a subcutaneous chip in the *right hand* or in the *forehead.* In 2000, a large Swiss bank designed a placard that shows a woman's head, placed in a cage the shape of a globe. Her eyes look towards the sky. In the middle of her forehead: a *mark.* Below it the text: 'Take part in the e-revolution.'[218]

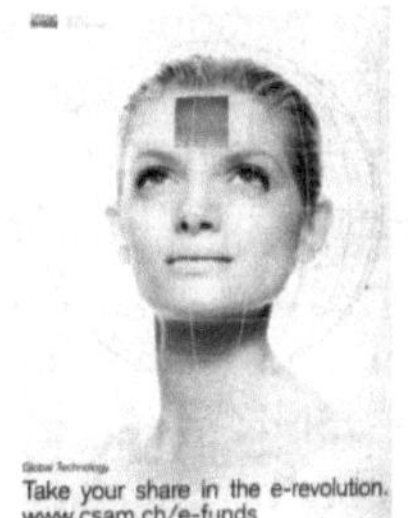

In Switzerland, Germany and Austria the poster could be seen everywhere. In 2001, the Swiss Foundation for the Promotion of Health developed a poster with two blue painted heads without hair, genderless and with a soulless expression. In the

---

[216] Risi, A., *Licht wirft keinen Schatten*, p. 38.
[217] Idem., p. 40.
[218] Idem., p. 42.

middle of the forehead, the on and off button of the computer. This poster hung at all major stations in Switzerland.[219]

Mondex: money on the right hand

Big brother soon found support for his plans from a number of companies, who often are in partnership. One of them is called Mondex, an international company that produces and promotes smart cards.[220] Mondex is a combination of the word *money* and the Latin dexter (right hand). Mondex promotes money *on the right hand* and thus makes cash unnecessary. Frank Sunn, who studied mathematics, physics and astronomy, is well versed in esotericism and has a leading position in the computer industry, has discussed Mondex since the nineties. Hundreds of companies from many countries already do (smart card) business with Mondex. The European Union is also in favour of the smart card (although it does not say so openly). Mastercard has a 51% participation in Mondex. The other 49 % are in the hands of about twenty shareholders. All banks, with the exception of communication company AT&T.[221] The Mondex card is intended to function as a 'leading smart card' for a while, also known as a Universal Biometrics Card. Ace of spades as a trump card!

The cradle of the Mondex system lies in England. With the elite bankers Tim Jones and Graham Higgins of the Natwest Bank, the personal bank of the English royal family! By the way, almost all seventeen original financiers of the Mondex system come from the London banking world and belong to the Club of the Isles, a bank cartel of the House of Windsor, which has an influence on the entire world economy.[222] All smart card financial transactions are secured via the SET protocol, and all systems for the transactions carry the SET character. (SET here stands for Secure Electronic Transaction.)[223] In Egyptology, Set was the brother and opponent of Osiris. According to the myth, he is associated with the

---

[219] Idem., p. 43.

[220] Update: Mondex history on Wikipedia: https://en.wikipedia.org/wiki/Mondex

[221] Sunn, *666*, p. 99-100.

[222] Idem, p. 100 and 102. Also see Icke, D., *The Biggest Secret.*

[223] Sunn, *666*, p. 100.

darkness and killed Osiris, the god of light, who later rises again. In Hebrew he is called *Satan*, adversary, slanderer. The electronic SET system can be seen as the opponent of the awakening light in man.

The Motorola biochip

Another international company that supports big brother is Motorola. Motorola not only produces the Mondex smart card microchip for more than two hundred companies in twenty countries, but is also one of the companies that developed the biochip. This chip can be implanted quickly and without anaesthesia under the skin in the human body. The chip is the size of a grain of rice and contains an answering transmitter and a lithium battery. Information required from the outside is passed on by the answering transmitter. The lithium battery is permanently charged by the temperature fluctuations of the body. Once in the skin, it can't get out.

In order to find out where in the human body the fluctuations are the greatest Motorola spent a sum of $1.5 million. It turned out to be the *head* (just below the hairline) and the back of the hand. Especially the right *hand*, because most people are right-handed. This way, a reading device can easily read the desired information.[224] Since 2004, Mondex has produced more than one million biochips per year and Mondex keeps the momentum going, because the biochip will be *the* solution to all 'card problems'. You can't copy it, nor lose it. The propaganda machines are already running at full speed. There is money to be made. A lot of money.

A mark for slaves?

Li Ka-shing, a multi-billionaire from Hong Kong, befriended the Rockefellers and Rothschilds and entered into a partnership with a number of companies, including Motorola and AT&T.[225] Asia is highly ranked for both the production and consumption of future chips. In 1996 Gemplus and Mondex entered into a contract with Gemplus, currently number one in the world in the field of chip cards, to produce the smart

---

[224] Idem., p. 107-109.
[225] Springmeier, F., *Bloodlines of the Illuminati* , p. 169-171.

card worldwide.[226] Until 2004, Gemplus already made about five billion chip cards, with yet a bigger memory than the traditional smart cards Motorola had participated in. In 2006 Gemplus and Axalto switched to a new company Gemalto. There is no shortage of types of chips. There are more than 200 of them. Plenty of choice.

Marc & Mark

With the U.S. Department of Defense, Gemplus developed an advanced identity card with a chip, the Marc (Multi-technology Automated Reader Card). Not the Marc card, just the Marc. The Marc gets tried out first by the military after which it becomes 'available' to all civilians. The chip in the Marc contains a series of data, including the military and medical file. Furthermore, the soldier can make all his purchases with it. Some of the soldiers were suspicious of the reasons behind it and refused the card. They were sent to prison for a while or sacked. Mark, pronounced the same as Marc, 'sign' or 'mark'. Initially, the code name for the development of Marc was *tessera*, an idea of the National Security Agency (NSA) and the U.S. military defense intelligence agency (DIA). *Tessera* (Latin) means 'identifier'. In Roman times, a *tessera* was the mark that slaves were branded with (on the forehead, in the hand or in another place). It was a piece of mosaic. Meanwhile, the code name *tessera* has been changed to Project Mosaic, and the chip that goes into the identity card is called Capstone (top stone). This 'top stone', or control of man via the computerized identity ship, is seen as an important means of the New World Order to make us gradually dependent on this power pyramid. The last move that the power elite has in mind is the chip in our body, symbolized by the 'sinking' of the top stone on the pyramid, so that the top stone is anchored with the pyramid. If we allow that we are completely subordinate to the power elite and we have become modern slaves,[227] fully governable.

---

[226] Update: https://www.bs2.lt/en/search/?searchtxt=Gemplus
[227] See Sunn, *666*, p. 101-102 and Marrs, *Project L.U.C.I.D.*, 1996, p. 70 –74.

Worshiping the statue

Seated in worship in front *of the image of the beast* (screen of the computer), which was given a 'voice' by speech technology so that it could *speak*, all acts of *buying or selling* will soon be carried out via the internet by the human being who wears a *mark* (chip), *the name of the beast*, on his right *hand* or *forehead*. Those who refuse this *mark* and do not worship the image of the *beast* cannot participate in this system of buying and *selling* and will be ostracized, '*killed*'. Anyone who re-reads the text from the Book of Revelation quoted at the beginning of this paragraph will notice that John's prophetic vision, if viewed outside the time space it was received in, says a lot. One does not need to be a Christian to realize that in our time from the *sea* (Revelation 13:1) of the collective unconscious a powerful electronic 'beast' (the computer) has risen, that has already spread its tentacles all over the world. The beast of the *Earth* (Revelation 13:11) gave the 'breath of life' to a silicon monster that produces chips,[228] anyone who learns to understand the images and symbols in John's vision understands the hidden message. The Western mind is maybe too conditioned in its causal thinking and linear sense of time with the result that John's vision becomes difficult to see for what it is and the meaning of the archetypal language is ignored. Past, present and future are not separated within time space, an ongoing flow of interlocking events, like a snake that bites into its own tail again and again. Anyone who peels off the ingrained past will notice that 'the mind can beat time', the way physicist Fred Alian Wolf expressed it during an interview in the documentary *What the 'bleep' do we (k)now!?).*[229]

Past, present and future can also be manipulated in our consciousness which is evident from Orwell's book *1984:* 'He who controls the past, controls the future; whoever controls the present, controls the past.'[230]

---

[228] The raw material of the chip is silicon, one of the main components of the Earth's crust.

[229] Wolf, F.A., *The yoga of traveling in time*.

[230] Orwell, G., *1984*.

666: the mark of the beast?

'He who uses his brain can calculate the number of the beast, for it is the number of a man and his number is six hundred and sixty-six' (Book of Revelation 13:18).

The basic number of the chip is the number 666. The owner of the Marc (or chip card with a different name) gains access to the internet via an 18-way digitally traceable number, which consists of three groups of 6 numbers. The base number is 666, then follows the country code, then the local number and then the personal number made up of 9 digits (for example, a nine-fold insurance number). Because of the protest of quite a few Christians who recognized the number 666 as the number of the beast (the antichrist), the 18-fold number was quickly changed into a 16-fold digital number. Two non-consequential figures were omitted, but not 666. The personal number is recognized by the reader. With this personal number, everyone will soon be able to enter the internet and *buy* and sell what they want (depending on their income). First via the smart card, then via the *mark* in the body. The number *six hundred and sixty-six from* Book of Revelation does not indicate Emperor Nero, as some people thought. It is the number of man himself, the *new* man in the *new* world order. Man reduced to a number, a digital number that can be traced everywhere: 666. Man fallen into the hands of a dark force that created an artificial intelligence, artificial light, artificial speech. A power with a face like a screen. An electronic monster that performs 'great signs' and is already adored by many. This critically acclaimed 'beast' has created a pseudo-omnipresence through its worldwide web that anyone who connects to their mega-brain is at risk of being absorbed by an artificial consciousness, stripped of warmth, feeling, or compassion.

A consciousness turning knowledge (but which knowledge?) into power. This 'beast' has become a counter force because of its *addictive* and *enslaving* effect. An opposing force to the omnipresence, the all-pervading life-giving power of love, that liberates, is creative, creates space and stimulates life to achieve its highest goal, which the non-seeing scientists so often deny, but something that mystics experience. The 'beast' from Book of Revelation manifests itself in its ultimate form in the internet, which is continuously connected to 'the Beast' of the NSA (the supercomputers), controlling everything and everyone with its 'evil eye'. 'The evil eye' increasingly curbing the spiritual growth of man by dehumanizing him, endeavouring to fence in all of humanity, and to distort love on a daily basis. Enticing us with offers we cannot refuse luring us into that cage until the iron gates are being shut behind our backs.

What do you think: the admonishing finger of the pastor, or his devout word as an epilogue or a theologian who lost his way? They themselves will undoubtedly also work with the internet. Until the claws of the sparrowhawk are deeply embedded the oblivious dove's rich plumage will not turn red. We shall elaborate further on the internet in the next, as well as in the last chapter. But now let's first listen to one of the discoverers of the biochip and then take a look at the company of the 'digital angels'. That way we will learn more about the various plans of our digital guardian angels. They put on sly and cunning ways to convince us step by step that a chip in our body is an absolute necessity. Apparently, they have a couple of trump cards in hand they intend to play against us. If we recognize those for what they are, we might possibly all wake up.

When love fills your life,
all limitations fall away.
The medicine that this sick world so desperately needs
is love.[231]

Peace Pilgrim

---

[231] Peace Pilgrim, *De weg naar Vrede (The road to Peace)*. www.peacepilgrim.org

3.2   Our digital angels

And no wonder, for Satan himself masquerades as an angel of light.
It is not surprising, then, if his servants also masquerade
as servants of righteousness.
 Their end will be what their actions deserve.

2 Corinthians 11:14-15

Executive officer Tim Willard of the *World Future Society,* which boasts 27,000 members worldwide, confirmed more than a decade ago that the technology for the human chip is ready. American author and futurologist Alvin Toffler (dec. 27 June 2016) was one of the members worldwide and was known for his numerous high-profile publications, including the book *Future Shock.*[232] In the seventies and eighties, he already predicted a digital and technological revolution together with a revolution in ways of communication, which would radically change society. In the nineties he also studied the increasing power of the proliferation of military hardware, weapons and technology.[233]
At an early stage though, there were eyes that looked over the shoulders of those who researched the chip and its application with a completely different intention.

Discoverer of the biochip misled

In 1979, Mike Beigel from California introduced a prototype of the biochip (implantable microchip). Since 1991, predominantly animals in zoos and endangered species have been chipped in more than a hundred countries. One of the inventors of the injectable or implantable biochip in the body (both terms appear in the literature) is Carl W. Sanders, electronics engineer from the UK. In his laboratory, he worked on a chip

---

232 Marrs, T., *Project L.U.C.I.D.*, p. 102.
233 https://en.wikipedia.org/wiki/Alvin_Toffler

that can reconnect damaged nerves, for example in patients with spinal injuries. With the discovery of his biochip (also called 'biochip transponder' or 'biochip answer transmitter') Sanders hoped to contribute to reduce pain of disabled people, improving their quality of life. He was unaware however, that the CIA was behind his investigation pursuing a completely different goal. He was oblivious of the fact, that through his discovery, he took part in a lurid project that aimed to introduce the subcutaneous microchip on a global scale with the aim to control and identify humans. Parallel with his research, the American Jewish scientist Daniel Man also produced a biochip. He is in favour of every Israeli citizen having such a chip implanted[234] to put an end to the kidnapping and terrorism. From the start Sanders was against the lithium battery in the biochip. He knew that should the chip break, for example during a surgical procedure to remove it, a tumour full of pus could develop. Some Christian groups relate this to the text from The Book of Revelation 16:2: '... and there arose an evil tumour among the people who wore the mark of the beast and worshipped his image.'

When Sanders was working on his project, it didn't occur to him, that in the near future an attempt to remove the chip would be immediately discovered by the GPS system, automatically alerting authorities. He was shocked to the core when someone drew his attention to chapter 13:15-18 of The Book revelation and he got wise to the hidden intention of the chip project. He stopped his research immediately, became a Christian and nowadays gives a lot of lectures and seminars on the biochip, especially its abuse, often encountering strong resistance.[235]

'... as if people were cattle.'

Sanders tells *Nexus Magazine* (June/July 1994) that his project was stolen by the 'one-world-brigade', another name for representatives of the new world order. He had attended some seventeen meetings with them in

---

[234] https://searchsecurity.techtarget.com
[235] Sunn, F., *666.*, p. 108-110; Icke, D., *... and the truth shall set you free*, p. 438-439; Icke, D., *Children of the matrix*, p. 370-371.

places such as Brussels[236] and Luxembourg. 'The joining of all the money systems in the world' was always the objective. Sanders reported on one of those meetings: 'I was at a meeting where it was discussed how to control a population if you can't identify them. People like Henry Kissinger and members of the CIA [including Bob Gates] attended these meetings. The point of discussion was the question: how to make people aware of the need for something like this chip? Suddenly the idea arose to alert them to the issue of children getting lost and so on. The CIA came up with the idea to put photos of lost children on milk cartons. Since then, the chip has been accepted but you don't see those pictures anymore, or do you? The objective has been achieved.' [237]

Sanders said the manipulators wanted the chip to include name, portrait photo, international social insurance number, fingerprint identification, physical description, family composition, medical history, address, occupation, income, tax information, and a person's police record. Furthermore, to tell people that once they were chipped, they would no longer need a passport or other personal administrative correspondence. He also said that the biochip he manufactured could be used to change behaviour. Already during the Vietnam War, the so-called 'Rambo chip' was used to stimulate the adrenaline levels. Timothy McVeigh, who was responsible for bombing the Alfred P. Murrah Federal Building in Oklahoma City (April 19, 1955), said he was microchipped when he served in the U.S. Army. According to Sanders, the chip can also be used as a birth control tool for the masses or to induce feelings, such as depression, agitation, aggression, sexuality. He expressly calls for the forbidding of the biochip.[238]

---

[236] Brussels is often mentioned in the literature as a meeting place of the power elite because of NATO and the EU residing there. Also underground, allegedly, there is a huge computer system, like at the NSA, called the 'crypt', where everything is stored.

[237] Icke, D., *Children of the Matrix*, p. 370-371; Icke, D., *... And the Truth Shall Set You Free*, p. 438-439.

[238] Icke, D., *Children of the Matrix*, p. 371; Icke, D., *... And the Truth Shall Set You Free*, p. p.439. More on the Oklahoma bombing p. 321-324.

Digital angel: the VeriChip

In the past, a lot of children were raised with the idea that every child has a guardian angel and with bedtime prayers like: "four corners to my bed, four angels at my head, one to watch and one to pray and two to bear my soul away." These have been replaced by the *digital angels* of the electronics companies who want to guard and protect our children, ourselves, our animals and our goods unsolicited. The feather wings of the former guardian angels have been replaced by 'intelligent' chips. The digital angels of L.U.C.I.D. are intruding taking on different identities.

One of the largest digital 'angel companies' is Applied Digital Solutions (ADS) in America. This company operates worldwide as a provider in the field of safety technology and manufactures GPS systems and chips, among other things. ADS supplies governments, companies, individuals, pharmaceuticals, the military, commerce and telecommunications companies. ADS also maintain close contacts with the FBI, the CIA and the Pentagon. Since 9/11, ADS has been experiencing a huge boom in an unfolding world market.

Digital Angel Corporation (DAC), the Cooperative of Digital Angels from Palm Beach, Florida, make chips for devices, animals and people, among other things. Especially well-known was the VeriChip, also called 'digital angel', the first implantable microchip for humans in the world with the size of a grain of rice. (The VeriChip uses RFID technology. RFID is the abbreviation of Radio Frequency Identification, or identification using radio waves.) In addition, Digital Angel Corporation make other chips, such as VeriPay, VeriKid and VeriMed. (The second part of the name gets altered to fit the different applications of the chip.) VeriPay is a type of credit card in the VeriChip with which money operations can be carried out the same way as with a regular credit card. VeriKid focuses on the supervision of children *(kids)* and VeriMed is a chip that is implanted for medical supervision and registration of medical data. The VeriMed program is already operational in the United States and in Mexico. In the emergency departments of hospitals are medical equipment that can read and therefore consult medical records of all implanted patients in the database because they are connected to the internet. Digital Angel Corporation has granted the license of the

VeriChip technology to VeriChip Corporation, a subsidiary of Applied Digital Solutions. ADS has entered into agreements for the sale of chips in Europe, Russia, Asia and Central and South America. [239]
Scott R. Silverman, one of the directors of DAC, had a VeriChip implanted in himself, to entice the customers. 'My chip is located in my upper right arm and has been there for about three years. It's just a simple injection, just like getting a penicillin jab'[240] (just to mention something 'healthy'). Always under the guise that this digital angel makes our lives safe and that the stored medical data on the chip could possibly save us in a critical situation. Peter Zhou (former scientist at the Max Planck Institute in Stuttgart, chief scientist of DAC), who developed the VeriChip, stated: 'The digital angel will be a connection of yourself with the electronic world. He will be your guard, your protector. You will take advantage of it. We will become a combination of electronic intelligence and our soul.' Such a 'mix'[241] is a blatant attack on human dignity and the spiritual evolution of man. This is how the 'digital angel' shows his true identity – that of a demon.

A closed meeting

On the evening of October 30, 2000, the prototype of the VeriChip was demonstrated in New York at a closed meeting. A limited number of people were invited, i.e., Government representatives, soldiers, private investors and analysts from Wall Street. Just a selective number of people from the media were also invited. A number of attendees were not just surprised by the presence of the Secretary of Transportation, Norman Mineta,but moreover, as the main speaker of the evening. Mineta, a strong supporter of the chip, was warmly welcomed by Richard Sullivan, president of Applied Digital Solutions. He emphasized Mineta's role as

---

239 Necerato, P., *The Shocking Truth About The Verichip…*, p. 11-13, 63. 'The microchip implantable in humans. The step that one should not take', 2005. Source: C.R.A.P. (Collectif Résistance A la Puce), www.stop-puce.be
240 Update: http://whale.to/vaccines/tag6.html
241 Icke, D., *Children of the Matrix*, p. 372.

Bill Clinton's personal adviser on trade, economics and digital disclosure.[242]

For the undiscerning reader : former President Bill Clinton is a great promoter of the smart card and of the internet. He maintains good contacts with Bill Gates of Microsoft. In *The Washington Times* of October 11, 1993, journalist Martin Anderson warned that the smart card could herald the subcutaneous chip.[243] At the above-mentioned meeting, Mineta was portrayed by Sullivan as a 'champion in forging a partnership between the public and the private sector,' and he added that this quality was precisely the reason for Mineta's presence. The compliments kept coming. Sullivan: 'I just want to say how pleased we at Applied Digital Solutions are to launch a sensational new partnership with you and the federal government in the important field of digital access.' Mineta, guarded by a number of bodyguards, deftly played the ball back and stressed the importance of working with companies like ADS so that the 'elderly and less wealthy' can benefit from the 'great technological revolution'. He underlined the 'historic opportunity to spread the benefits of information technology to everyone in society', emphasizing 'the importance of digital technology for the U.S. economy and of information technology for the economic success of the United States'. At the end of his speech, Mineta said, 'I congratulate you, Dick Sullivan, on your success and the direction in which you are going with Applied Digital Solutions. (...) As a nation, we cannot afford to miss out on this technology.'[244] Since then, Richard Sullivan was sidelined after he expressed, in an overconfident mood, that he thought that it could be very beneficial in following all foreigners who visit the United States. His successor, Keith Bolton, emphasizes the use of the chip was voluntary.[245] Back to October 30, 2000. The highlight of the evening was the demonstration of the technology, described as a 'show', by Peter Zhou. A

---

[242] Necerato, *The Shocking Truth...*, p. 27-28.

[243] Sunn, *666*, p. 97; Marrs, *L.U.C.I.D.*, p. 117; Risi, *Light wirft boulders Treasures*, p. 39.

[244] Necerato, *The Shocking Truth...*, p. 28-29.

[245] Draulans, D., 'The sign of the beast', in Belgium Magazin *Knack* (April 13, 2005), p. 33 and 36.

large screen showed how an ENGINEER from ADS, equipped with a VeriChip, could be fully tracked via GPS and how the information was wirelessly routed to the internet, where the position and movements of the subject could be tracked from a great distance and stored in a database. The expected market turnover for the 'digital angels' in the coming years is worth the effort.: between seventy and one hundred billion dollars will be pocketed.[246]

CEO Randy Geissler of Digital Angel Corpora tion says it is working with Raytheon-Hughes (ao. arms manufacturing), the U.S. Department of Energy and the pharmaceutical giant Schering-Plough. Geissler was former head of the company Destron Fearing, which makes RFID chips for animals and he is therefore obviously not a novice in this sector.[247] The main customer, however, will be the U.S. military. More and more soldiers are being chipped,[248] making it even easier to follow orders, i.e., promoting the will to fight, because the chip can affect the entire hormonal system.

VeriChip approved by the FDA

Much to the dismay of many, the Food and Drug Administration (FDA), the federal U.S. health authorities, approved the use of the VeriChip for medical purposes on October 13, 2004.[249] There was a strong reaction from the public. Not only would the VeriChip be 'the mark of the beast' (a theological approach), but it would also grossly violate human privacy and could lead to identity theft. In 2004, the Department of Health and Human Services, similar to the Department of Health, announced its intention to allocate a $139 million grant to realize president Bush's encouragement to electronically record most Americans' medical records within a decade.[250] Whereas it elicited little comment when a chip for animals was launched, when the FDA approved the VeriChip, there was

---

[246] Necerato, *The Shocking Truth*, p. 26 and 30-32.
[247] Idem, p. 30.
[248] https://www.digitalangelcorp.com
[249] Necerato, *The Shocking Truth*, p. 16; https://www.digitalangelcorp.com
[250] Idem, p. 16-18.

commotion here and there. Especially so, when it became apparent that the chip for humans did not differ much from that for animals.

A few months later, on 9 December 2004, the RFID Networking Forum was established at the Renaissance hotel in Heathrow, London. Top - people in the RFID world, Microsoft, pharmacy, trade and banking assembled there and most certainly *not* for an early Christmas party. With the FDA's approval of the VeriChip the VIPs anticipated making huge profits in the near future and the market was ready to be conquered with astronomical amounts of money expected to be made.[251] Almost everything and everyone should be chipped. Safety, security and control became the slogans. Swarms of chips of all kinds could now be unleashed onto the world. One plan after another was born. Governments and businesses were soon in agreement. Laws were amended, new laws passed.

The citizen has long since lost the plot. He feels it's all taking place behind his back. A broad public debate is still not taking place. All kinds of products are already being chipped to create familiarity. Convenient, safe and efficient. At the same time a number of international campaigns being launched to make it compulsory to chip all animals within a few years. Pets, livestock, poultry, migratory birds, zoo animals and in the wild; everything that moves, crawls, runs, flies... Chip it. Simultaneously a lot of attention should of course be paid to chips for the elderly, children, prisoners, mentally and/or physically disabled people, called the 'socially vulnerable'. Special campaigns for children are in the making. After all, do parents not like to see their child in safe hands? The digital angel looks like the solution that fits all. The fear of terrorist attacks and the increasing sense of insecurity are exploited in surreptitious ways with noticeable effect. With the captains of business, politics and in the health sector the VeriChip for people is an ever-increasing point of discussion. The publicity mills have been switched on and rice grain microchips and other types of chips are being strewn around Hoping to settle in our minds for us to grind.

---

[251] https://www.well-tech.it

The Chipsons

After approval of the FDA, the VeriChip could not complain about publicity. The media in America and England paid a lot of attention to it. The VeriChip, the 'true' chip *(verus* is Latin for 'true', 'true', 'real'), increased in fame. The 'digital angel' was allowed to get closer to man. Pros and cons were flying around and after several television broadcasts and full-page advertisements, several thousand potential candidates volunteered for the chip. A special 'chip mobile' visited retirement centres in Florida emphasizing the amazing benefits of the digital angel for staff, the elderly and their children. Not much later, the state of Florida even began to advertise the subcutaneous microchip and its link to the internet, to make it easy for everyone to buy and sell what they wanted swiftly. Out of the thousands who had applied, Applied Digital Solutions chose the American Jacobs family to be the first to be chipped. Father and son were broadcasted on TV in a big way in typically American style: A well-timed stunt that sent the digital angel into millions of living rooms. After the 'sacred' moment of chip implantation, they were given the 'baptismal name': the Chipsons. Soap and chips in one. 'Imagine being able to communicate with your computer by just thinking about it,' said Derek Jacobs (the son) enthusiastically, who dreamed of one day being 'the first *cyborg'* (a fictional or hypothetical person whose physical abilities are extended beyond normal human limitations by mechanical elements built into the body).[252] VeriChip Corporation broadly advertises the VeriChip: How to get chipped and where to obtain further information. [253]

VeriChip to the Netherlands

When by January the 1st, it became apparent, that the electronic patient file was going to fall through, cardiologist Menno Baars, director of the company Spare Capacity, advertised the VeriChip. He is going to import the VeriChip into the Netherlands. Baars sees this subcutaneous micro-

---

[252] Draulans, 'Het teken van het beest' ('The mark of the beast'), in Belgium magazine *Knack* (April 13, 2005).
[253] Update: http://www.verichipcorp.com

chip as the perfect substitution for the electronic patient healt file which is likely to take another ten years at least before it is completed. Baars is already in consultation with various hospital managements and government to lobby for support, hopeful to succeed in arguing that the VeriChip can save lives. But the KNMG (Royal Dutch Society for the Promotion of Medicine-Art) is not very enthusiastic about the VeriChip. It sees privacy violations hazards and the misuse of data. According to the British Medical Association, there are 'no ethical reasons why this chip should not be inserted as long as the safety of the patient is guaranteed and it is not done under duress'.[254]

It might be a good suggestion for Dr. Baars to contact Tommy Thompson (1941), former Minister of the Department of Health and Human Services to discuss the preferred method of propaganda. Mr. Thompson namely, after leaving the Bush administration became a board member of both VeriChip Corporation and parent company Applied Digital Solutions. He is very busy advertising the subcutaneous chip as a means of payment as well as an electronic medical record for all Americans. Moreover, in mere seconds the chip can be implanted in your arm.[255] Spokesman for VeriChip Corporation John Procter has it, that Thompson himself, on the other hand has not been implanted with the chip because he is 'too busy', and adds, 'has no concrete plans to do so in the future.' *In seconds, Mister Thompson!'* Thompson was considering running for president in 2008.[256] If he'd been elected, would all Americans then have been called Thomp-sons or Chip-sons? Time will tell. [257] Henri Schein Inc. (HSIC), largest supplier of pharmaceuticals, vaccines, surgical instruments to hospitals, surgical centres, physicians and veterinarians in North America and Europe (in more than 125 countries), has already signed a contract with Digital Angel Corporation for the distribution of the VeriChip. 'We believe that the agreement with

---

[254] *MedNet, Onafhankelijk nieuwsmagazine voor medisch Nederland (Independent medical news magazine in The Netherlands)* (November 4, 2004).
Also see: https://www.mednet.nl
[255] www.spychips.com
[256] https://en.wikipedia.org/wiki/Tommy_Thompson
[257] Necerato, *The Shocking Truth...*, p. 74-75.

Henry Schein will soon allow us to achieve one of our market goals through the medical sector,' said Scott R. Silverman. Not only Schein has big plans with the VeriChip. Recently, the Italian Ministry of Health granted permission for a six-month experiment to try out the VeriChip in hospitals. On a voluntary basis, it is maintained. Could it be a coincidence that Digital Angel Corporation received the prestigious 'Well-Tech' award for its innovative technology and the improvement of 'the quality of life' in Italy?[258] What is meant by this quality is not explained. Some awards sometimes hide a bomb, like with the Nobel Prize, instituted by the dynamite king Alfred Nobel (1833-1896), Swedish chemist and industrialist.

Fast and painlessly injectable

In short; the *digital angel* (digital angel, as the VeriChip is called in the corridors) is on the rise. If it's up to Digital Angel Corporation, it's going to take us to great heights. He pretends to be a fine guardian angel, who may completely replace the real one, if he needs a break. *Digital angel*: safe, convenient, cannot be stolen, is always in the same place, replaces all your paperwork, passwords, PINs and signatures, surpasses the biometric passport and cannot be copied, or so it claims. Furthermore: easy to inject! Done in a minute. A painless 'operation'. No hospital required. A local anesthetic suffices. Best place: between the skin and the three-headed muscle in the upper arm or in the back of the hand. Similar to a mosquito sting, peanuts. It doesn't even itch. While you are still contemplating all the benefits, a syringe with an oblique opening ejects a strong glass tiny cylinder underneath the skin of your hand. In the cylinder is the microchip the size of a grain of rice. As soon as the glass cylinder leaves the syringe, it is covered with a self-adhesive biomaterial, which both isolates the cylinder from the body and clings to the local tissue. Congratulations, you are now chipped and a member of the Digital Angels Cooperative! From now on you will be protected day and night and traceable day and night and henceforth at the mercy of 'the servants of righteousness.' Your privacy has is a hollow phrase from a half-

---

[258] https://www.well-tech.it

forgotten dictionary. You are trapped in the electromagnetic safety net of big brother, the matrix. Surely, we won't let this happen? [259]

Peace I bring onto you, my children,
the sevenfold peace from the earthly Mother
and the heavenly Father.
Peace I bring your body,
led by the angel of heavenly Power.
Peace I bring your heart,
led by the angel of Love,
Peace I bring your spirit,
led by the angel of Wisdom.[260]

(The Essenes Gospel of Peace)

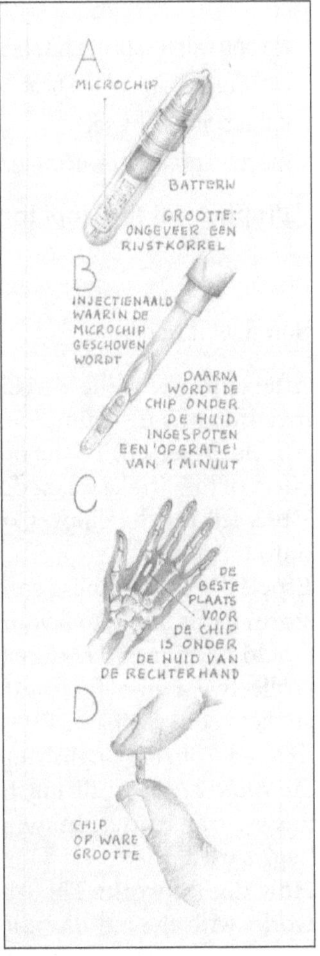

---

[259] 'De microchip implanteerbaar bij de mens. De stap die men beter niet zet'. ('The microchip implantable in humans…'), Source: C.R.A.P. (Collectif Résistance A la Puce), www.stoppuce.be.

[260] *The Essene Gospel of Peace*. vol. 2, p. 61.

3.3   RFID: identification with radio waves

No one will be able to buy or sell
without the sign of the bear.
If this sign can be seen,
the third great war will come.[261]

Prophecy of the Hopi Indians

How does it work?

After approval of the VeriChip by the FDA and after several international
meetings of VIPs, numerous representatives of the Cooperative of Digital
Angels dispersed. To the north, the south, the west and the east. And the
effect of their treks was soon visible. Wherever they went, more and more
VIP's fell for the chips. Contracts were closed, hands were shaken and
onto the next.

Especially the business community, large supermarket and department
store chains began to favour the RFID technology in their products. They
would not mind to replace the barcode with 'intelligent' electronic labels
(collective name for plasticized strips, photo identification , labels,
stickers etc.) with an RFID chip. The term 'intelligent' electronic label is
derived from the English equivalent *smart tags*. Other terms for *smart tag*
are *radio tag* or RFID tag, because of the technology used, or *responder*,
answer transmitter. In the more day to day practice the collective name
'tag' is used.

How does it work? The RFID system (Radio Frequency Identification)
works with the aid of radio waves and consists of an RFID tag and an
RFID reader. The RFID tag (or tag for short) is no larger than a grain of
sand. It consists of a microchip with a mini antenna, always cast into a

---

261 Sunn, F., *666*, p. 90.

certain shape factor or the antenna would break off from the chip. It can have a cylindrical shape (for the biochip) or a plastic shell (label, label, sticker, badge, credit card). Sometimes a tag is no bigger than apinhead. Convenient to apply in clothes. In the literature, the terms RFID tag and RFID chip are used interchangeably. The RFID reader, the device that can read tags, consists of an antenna and demodulator. The microchip is programmed with a unique identification number and possibly other data. If the chip comes within reach of the RFID reader, it is activated via radio waves emanating from the 'reader'. The built-in mini antenna captures the radio waves and transmits the unique identification number via a radio frequency signal to the demodulator in the reader, which converts the original data on the chip into digital data. The digital data can be forwarded to a database and processed and stored. The database can be linked to other databases via the internet.

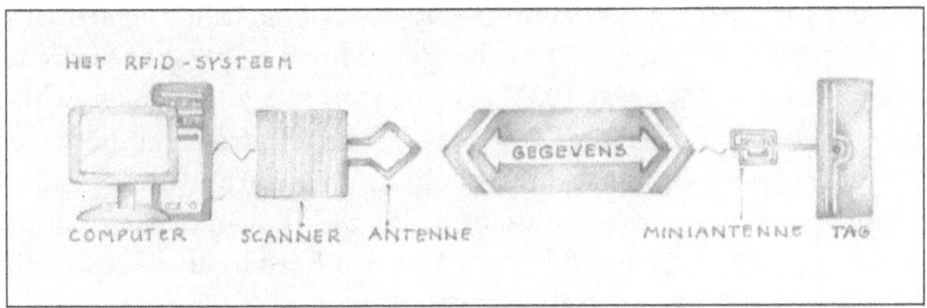

Active and passive chip

RFID chips can be *active* or *passive*. The active chip has its own energy source, a battery, so that the chip can be read from a great distance (from about a hundred yards to a few miles). The information on this chip is rewritable. The passive chip does not need a battery. It uses the energy from the radio waves that the reader emits, generating power in the mini-antenna. The passive chip is much lighter and cheaper than the active one (currently still about 5 euro cents and soon even cheaper) and has a longer lifespan than the active chip, but can only be read from nearby (from about 1 inch to plus minus 2 yards). The information in this chip is not rewritable. The operation of the passive chip is close to that of the barcode.[262] An antenna, available in many shapes and sizes, can be built in anywhere. For example, in a door, where the antenna receives the data of the person who passes the door and is chipped. Or in a toll gate to control passing traffic. The chips can also be read with fast passing cars. The antenna can emit a constant electromagnetic field. When constant monitoring is not required, it is possible to switch the particular area on and off with a sensor.[263]

Hi high tech tag

Right now, all kinds of laws concerning Trade and Traffic are being adjusted or changed with the speed of lightning and new laws are passed to clear the digital highway for the tag. That is how products worldwide will soon be tagged starting in the United States with the government in front. As early as in the second war with Iraq the U.S. Department of Defense used RFID 'to streamline supplies.' The U.S. Department of Homeland Security use RFID for border control of persons and goods. The beginning of this year(2006) saw the start of a pilot project with the tagging of migration papers. This way border controls can be handled faster.[264] Europe does not want get behind. The European Commission wants to speed up the promotion of RFID and is even of the opinion, it can catch up with the United States. (Not that hard to do since Europe is one of the biggest purchasers of American tags.) Where the US and Europe differ from each other though, is that European legislation

---

[262] https://www.rfidjournal.com/frequently-asked-questions and https://www.rfidjournal.com/wp-content/uploads/2019/07/18.pdf; Schaar, P., 'Working document on data protection issues related to RFID technology', January 19, 2005, p. 3, 19- 20, an issue of ARTICLE 29 Data Protection Working Party, an independent advisory body on data protection and privacy. The secretariat is supported by Directorate E (services, copyright, industrial property, and data protection) of the European Commission in Brussels. See also: the website http://www.ec.europa.eu/ with the search term 'privacy'.

[263] Mourits, R., 'RFID: de barcode voorbij. Tussen productieregistratie en privacy' ('RFID: the barcode beyond. Between product registration and privacy'), (October 28, 2004). Source: ZDNet.

[264] Update: articles on www.rfidnederland.nl/

dictates which personal data may and may not be collected.[265] In any case, it is certain that billions of tags are already being produced, while all kinds of discussions about promotion and privacy are still ongoing and the public debate is yet to be started. As if the radio signals have rushed ahead of the representatives of the Cooperation of Digital Angels to make the world 'tag-ripe'. The world?... Well, not *really* the world but rather those who are in control. The general public does not even know the word 'tag' and stumbles over the word RFID, nor knowing what the abbreviation stands for. Lately the media is starting to publicize a bit more about the influence of the chip in general, but in spite of that, it is not sinking in properly with the public in general what revolution we are facing in this area. 'Only 10 percent of the Dutch are familiar with RFID. And yet, in a few years' time, this system will have as much of an impact as the introduction of the internet at the time.'[266] In other countries, the percentage is certainly not much higher either.

From barcode to RFID

RFID technology represents a major breakthrough. Soon the miniscule RFID chip with small radio antenna will replace the barcode. In the Netherlands, the RFID Netherlands Foundation was founded for this purpose in January 2004. Participants include Accenture, HP, KPN, Philips, Rabobank, SAP and Erasmus University. Their main objective is to stimulate the development of RFID applications. Philips has been researching how to read chips from a distance since the sixties. The company gained worldwide fame for RFID chips. The fact that it took a while for the business community and the government to become interested in RFID had mainly to do with the costs and with the size of the chip. However, now that the tags are already as small as a pinhead and have become cheaper and cheaper, they are the ideal replacement for the much larger barcode. Meanwhile, companies such as IBM and Sun have also entered the RFID market.[267] Apparently, Philips benefitted

---

[265] Update: Source: www.rfid4u.nl/nieuws/ no longer available.

[266] Jansen, J., 'Big Brother en de snuffelchip', in: *Het Financieele Dagblad*, in Dutch (March, 19 2005), pp. 34-35.

[267] Mourits, 'RFID' : the barcode over'.

hugely from the Semiconductors in recent years, because this chip division of Philips was recently sold for 6.4 billion euros to three investment companies: KKR, Silver Lake and the Dutch Alpinvest. 'The profit that Philips make from the sale should not go to the shareholders, but should be invested in new technology and growth of jobs in the Netherlands', say the Trade Unions.[268] We can only hope, that this 'new technology' does not mean the further expansion of the military production department, where, among other things, engine parts are built for the Apache and the F-16, recently delivered to the air force of Israel. Food for thought, when we speak about arms supplies from Iran and Syria to Hezbollah, while Philips supply weapon components to Israel, who have been bombing Lebanon and the Palestinians for years. [269] How many electronics companies have a 'military production' department that is kept quiet? Where is our conscience

In the meantime, Philips and Sony have already developed something new: *Near Field Communication* (NFC), a smart form of RFID. Whereas RFID is primarily about storing and sending information in one direction, NFC communicates in two directions and can also process received signals itself. NFC will be used, among other things, in mobile phones as a means of payment and in ticketing systems. For the application possibilities in phones Philips worked together with Nokia. Payment company VISA investigated the payment system. There is good cooperation in an area that the average layman can no longer follow.[270]

If the barcode is still scanned by hand, the decoding of tags is automatic. This saves time and money. With RFID, each tag on a product contains a *unique* identification number (ID number) This ID number can be linked to the person who buys the product with their credit card or loyalty card which is scanned upon payment.[271] The barcode of a bottle of

---

[268] Voorn, E., 'Bonden willen chipwerk in Nederland houden', in Dutch newspaper *Algemeen Dagblad* (August 5, 2006).

[269] www.philips.com: in Dutch newspaper *de Volkskrant* (March 23, 2004).

[270] Update: https://www.sony.com/en/SonyInfo/News/Press_Archive/200312/03-059E/

[271] Update: http://www.worldlii.org/int/journals/EPICPrivHR/2006/PHR2006-Radio_Fr.html

mineral water of the same brand in Amsterdam as in Brussels has the same barcode but with a tag each bottle will soon have its *own* number. Before you pay with a credit card, the bottle and you are still separated from each other but after paying at the cash register with a credit card or scanning your loyalty card (which will soon also receive a tag) they can in principle be connected to each other. The issue is that we don't always know if it's happening. Supermarkets and other chain stores do not like talking about this. However, given the great interest in the customer's buying behaviour, it is very plausible.

The number 6-6-6 in the barcode

Just a little while before we're finished with the barcode. The barcode or UPC (Universal Product Code) was mainly introduced to easily scan item type and item price. Each dash and each double line represent a number. The dashes are scanned at the cash register or they are pushed over a glass plate under which the scanner is located. If you pay in cash and give your loyalty card to the cashier, the items you have purchased can already be linked by the barcode system. On your loyalty card there is also a bar code and so not only all items that you bought are registered, but also your name, address and customer number can be linked to it. In that case, all that data is of course stored in a database. This is to get a better understanding of the buying behaviour in general and in particular into ours. Soon, when the tag is introduced, this will have an even more personal touch. After all, Big brother is really interested in us. Or in our wallets? The customer is king, but Big Brother sits on the throne and likes to wield the sceptre. He is quite willing to give us some discount for our (usually unknowing)co-operation for the registration. Needless to say, that the discount has been calculated in the price.

Take a look at the two barcodes shown. Maybe for all those years you never wondered what is actually in that code. These are the barcodes of the book *The Bush family* (by Kitty Kelley) and that of a ripe mango. Maybe not the ideal combination, but hopefully clear enough as an example.

The barcode consists of 12 (sometimes 13) digits and 24 dashes of equal length, but of different thickness. On the far left, in the middle and on the far right there are three times two identical stripes that are longer than the other 24. They are also called *guard bars* ('protect'-stripes). There is no number in those three pairs of longer, identical stripes. However, they represent the same number three times – the 6. This means that each barcode has 6-6-6 as the base number.[272] Even though the computer does not show the number 666 in the UPC (barcode), for the human eye it is clearly perceptible (see images).

The inventor of the UPC, now retired, is George J. Laurer, former engineer at IBM. In 1971, he was commissioned to design a waterproof code for all the products of the world industry. In 1973, the time had come. Laurer himself admits on his website that the double stripes 'indeed resemble the code for a six,' but adds that it is 'mere coincidence' and that there is no connection to the text from Book of Revelation13:18. 'I'm sorry, but as I said in November 2000, I won't answer questions about the UPC and the New Testament.' [273] Laurer is known for his accuracy with numbers.

Every barcode has therefore been carrying the number 666 for years (curious 'coincidence' right?), which can be found on almost all products.

---

[272] Erdmann, S., *Banks, Brot und Bomben*, dl. 2, p. 265-267.

[273] More information: www.tribulationcentral.com/image/mk-barcode.gif. and on Laurer and *guard bars*: https://en.wikipedia.org/wiki/George_Laurer

On bags, boxes, cans, bottles, cardboard packs, medicine boxes, toothbrushes, soap, toilet rolls, packed mobile phones, books. Every store or supermarket have them on their items. Countless six-six-sixes on countless products. The power of this number for years. For years we have been sticking barcodes on fruit and vegetables in the supermarket. For years, 666 has played a key role in the process of buying and selling. For years, 666 has accompanied us as our 'faithful guardian angel', making itself stronger and stronger, dispersing more and more, without most people knowing. Visible yet invisible...

Radiation harmful to health

If every product is 'tagged', this will of course have great advantages for distributors and suppliers of goods. Scanning is fast and efficient. Fog, snow, ice, rust, paint layers, plastic or anything else do not interfere with scanning. The radio waves go right through it. And through us! Including all the harmful consequences. Scientific research has shown that electromagnetic energy (known as EMF: Electromagnetics Frequency), which is emitted by mobile phones and RFID readers, causes damage to the DNA. The Reflex research project, funded by the European Union, has demonstrated this after four years of study. (Body) cells, exposed to electromagnetic energy, showed 'a remarkable increase in fractures in single and double DNA strands'. Mutated cells are considered a possible cause of cancer. Franz Adlkofa, leader of the project, advises us to use a landline. [274]

The last word on this has certainly not yet been said, even though on 6 June 2006 (6-6-6) a Swiss study by the University of Zurich had published that statistically 'no significant differences' were found 'between non-exposure and short-term exposure' (45 minutes) to the radiation of a UMTS transmitter. Even before the official results of the investigation were announced, State Secretary Van Geel drew the incorrect conclusion that UMTS is completely safe and that municipalities can cease their objections to the installation of UMTS transmitters. The media adopted this erroneous conclusion without criticism. Scientists, GGDs and

---

[274] Update: Newsbrief on http://www.spychips.com no longer active.

municipalities sharply criticized the hasty conclusion of the State Secretary.[275] 'However, no scientist can state with absolute certainty that the radiation has no effect whatsoever. It can never be scientifically proven that something does not exist. Moreover, all the studies, including the Swiss one, only speak out on the health effects of mobile telephony in the short to medium term. The reason for this is simple: mobile phones have not existed long enough to make definitive statements about the health risks over a period of more than ten years.'[276] Incidentally, the mobile telephone industry paid for 40% of this research, as announced on Radio 1, 6-6-6.

The conclusion of Doctor Neil Cherry of Lincoln University in New Zealand on electromagnetic radiation comes close to the RFLEX study. 'Electromagnetic radiation is harmful to the brain, heart, embryos, hormones and cells. It is therefore a threat to (intelligent) life. Electromagnetic radiation acts on bodies and cells via resonance, it disrupts communication between cells and the growth and the control of cells. It damages the genetic basis of life.'[277] Let alone the huge contribution to 'electrosmog'. According to specialists, this is massive.[278]

RFID standards

'All parts of an RFID system are or will be subjected to a standard, such as the design of tag and reader, the storage of data in the tag, the communication between tag and reader, the management of the data collected by the reader, and so on.'[279] EAN International, the organization that deals with the standardization of the barcode in Europe, and the Uniform Code Council (UCC) have entered into a partnership

---

[275] http://www.stopumts.nl/ in Dutch, under 'Artikelen'.

[276] Hoove, S. ten, and M. Persson, 'De zendmast op een appartementsgebouw kan de de boosdoener niet zijn', in Dutch newspaper: *de Volkskrant* (June 7, 2006).

[277] Teule, G., *GSM radiation*, in Dutch, p. 40 and 55.

[278] 'Electropollution. Keeping Safe in a Sea of EMFs'. A Living The Field/Nuts. What Doctors Don't Tell You Publication. See for this: https://www.wddty.com See also Teule, G., *Elektrosmog*.

[279] Schaar, P., 'Working document on data protection issues related to RFID technology', January 19, 2005, p. 12.

(EPCglobal) to standardize the Electronic Product Code (EPC). EPC-global is, among other things, involved in the standardization of communication between tags and readers and wants to develop network standards to determine how EPC data is distributed between companies and other organizations. The standards for the distribution of data are the work of Auto-ID Labs. The International Organization for Standardization (ISO), which has already developed many RFID standards, is working on standards that can track goods in the supply chain that use high and ultra-high frequency tags.[280] U.S. policymakers want to avoid developing too many different RFID standards. They opt for world standards, so that the producers can coordinate things better, reducing costs.[281] Besides EAN International and the UCC, EPCglobal's board consists of representatives of The Gillette Company, Procter & Gamble, Walmart, Hewlett-Packard, Johnson & Johnson, and Auto-ID Labs.[282] Thus, centralization from the top. The bottom layers can't follow it anymore. EPCglobal's top executives in other words, are committed to the application of EPC technology in combination with RFID technology and the infrastructure of existing communication networks. The universal Product Code (UPC) or barcode is still a unique identification number for a product type but the EPC is a unique identification number for each manufactured product *separately.* The EPC consists of a series of numbers and letters, which consists of a main code and three data parts. The first part identifies the manufacturer of the product, the second the product type and the third the unique serial number of the item in question.[283] Making good strides on the way from UPC to EPC, with the internet playing centre role. The end goal they have in mind is buying and selling through the internet. The EU is also doing its best, investing 7.5 million euros in a three-year project to research and develop RFID technology based on EPCglobal standards. In this project 31 universities and companies are involved, such as British Telecom, Carrefour, Kaufhof, Nestlé, the TUG (Technological University Graz), Sony,

---

[280] Idem, p. 12-13 en www.rfidjournal.com, faq 21 en 22.
[281] http://www.rfidnederland.nl
[282] Update: http://zombiewire.com no longer active
[283] www.rfidjournal.com: faq 23.

VeriSign UK. The project started on the 1st of July 2006 with the 'connecting' name BRIDGE (**B**uilding **R**adio frequency **Id**entification solutions for the **G**lobal Environment).[284]

General Food Act

Since January1st 2005, the European *General Food Law* (GFL), the General Food Act, was enforced. The legislation is divided into two parts. The first part deals with food, the second with animal feed. Article 18(1) of the General Rules on Trade in Food provides: 'Food, fodder, food-producing animals and any other substance destined to be or expected to be incorporated into groceries or fodder shall be traceable at all stages of production, processing and distribution.' And Article 18(4): 'Food or fodder which is or is likely to be placed on the market in the Community shall be adequately labelled for the purposes of their traceability...'[285] This has opened the sluices for a myriad of tags for billions of products. The aim of the new food law, which applies to all Member States, is food safety and traceability, so that 'suspect' products can be withdrawn immediately.[286] The 'tagging' of the world has begun.

And with that stream of tags, 666 will soon travel again as the basic number, but this time *completely* invisible. The chances that we will be told are virtually nil. The number 666 can also be read regularly on countless recommended articles, especially electronic articles. Prices such as € 666, € 66.60 or vice versa € 999 or € 99.90 are regularly practiced. This number can often be seen also in telephone numbers used in commercials. Perhaps reason to investigate yourself?

'The third great war'

The prophecy of the Hopis quoted in the beginning of this paragraph is closely related to the already quoted prophecy from The Book of

---

[284] http://www.bridge-project.eu.

[285] Food law on food safety and traceability of food is laid down in Regulation (EC) No 178/2002 of the European Parliament and of the Council of 28 January 2002. Source: www.hellolaw.com

[286] Idem.

Revelation (13:15-18). Authors such as De Soeten and Buschenreiter already pointed out similarities between the prophecies of the Hopis and those of the bible. Naturally, the tribal elders of the Hopi did not know the *barcode* but they *did* know a kind of 'bear code': 'The sign of the bear'. They predicted that if this sign appears, 'the third great war' will come.[287] If you look at the image, you will

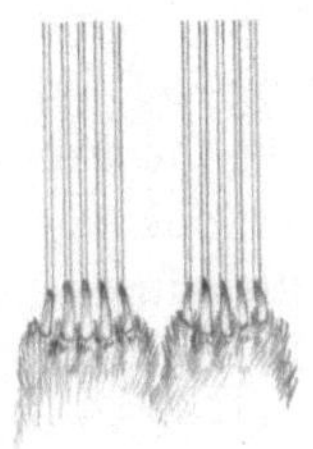

unmistakably see a similarity with the barcode. The Hopi had already predicted the first world war very accurately on the basis of the symbol of the Illyrian and Germanic 'foot cross'[288] (the German iron cross [1]) and on the basis of the swastika [2] (Germany) and the sun symbol [3] (Japan) the Second World War.[289] They also foresaw that man would one day reach for the moon

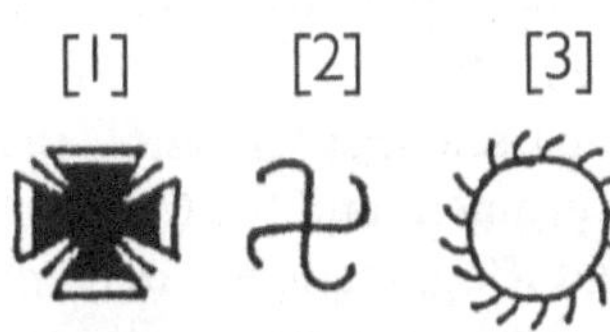

[1]   [2]   [3]

in his 'unimaginable urge for power'.[290] And again, and again they repeat that humanity is in 'the last phase' of a great age, in which everything that is not in harmony with nature will be destroyed.[291] The third great war or destruction, the Hopi links to 'the sign of the bear'. According to them, this sign is only fully understood when 'the day of purification' has arrived. Then the big cleansing will take place and Mother Earth will react in an extremely violent way with an increase in earthquakes, volcanic eruptions, storms, floods, droughts, fires. It's our time. 'But time is of the essence. The day of the cleansing is nigh. We want this to be understood,' the Hopi Thomas Banyacya Sr. told Alexander Buschenreiter on August

---

[287] Sunn, F., *666*, pp. 90-91. The drawing 'the sign of the bear' is inspired by the drawing in this book, p. 91.

[288] Buschenreiter, A., *Unser Ende ist euer Untergang*, p. 203. Buschenreiter spreekt over het *Tatzenkreuz*. In *Duden* staat onder *Tatze*: 'foot, paw of a large predator (especially of a bear)'.

[289] Idem, p. 203-205 and Soeten, D. de, *Hopi*, p. 78-79.

[290] Soeten, D. de, *Hopi*, p. 103-104.

[291] Idem, p. 107-108.

21, 1981.[292] Since that time, the tribal elders have repeatedly sent their warnings out into the world. All the more reason to think about that, because the prophecies of the Hopi are renowned, as well as their harmonious way of living with nature and with the Great Spirit of all life. Countless indigenous peoples who lived with the ways of nature were, as we all know, exterminated, destroyed or decimated by the so-called civilized countries. On several occasions, the tribal elders of the Hopi also warned the heads of government in Washington and addressed the UN and other organizations to make their prophecies known, in particular about the rapidly changing climate. Bar a few, the powerful of Earth replied with an indulgent smile. They are too busy dealing with worldly affairs and don't have time to listen to these people of 'peace,' who have announced the total collapse of the world system.[293]

In January 2004, the internationally renowned scientist, climatologist and chief scientific adviser to the 'British Government and the Office of Science and Technology' in London, Sir David King, made a statement that is very similar to the insights of the Hopi: 'In my opinion, climate change is the toughest problem we face today, even more serious than international terrorism.'[294] But that also fell on deaf ears, just like the warnings in recent climate reports from, for example, the Pentagon and the United Nations. Many still think that 'after rain comes shine', as Prime Minister Balkenende promised. When do we wake up? 'The sign of the bear' has appeared. Whether it is a polar or grizzly bear, the near future will tell. What is for sure, is that the 'sign of the electronic bear' is now becoming visible all over the world. The 'tagging' of the world continues.

RFID conquers supermarkets and department stores

From 1 January 2005, the suppliers of the largest American supermarket chain Walmart will only be allowed to supply their products if they are

---

[292] Buschenreiter, A., *Unser Ende ist euer Untergang*, p. 147.

[293] Idem, p. 150-202: 'The Hopi's message to the world', narrated by Thomas Banyacya Senior (August 21, 1981 in New-Oraibi). This contains the Hopi's prophecies, especially about our time.

[294] *Science* (January 2004), p. 176.

equipped with RFID chips. All their pallets and boxes have 'intelligent' stickers by now. Walmart presents itself as a great advocate for RFID, like it did in the eighties for the barcode.[295] Following Walmart, the department store chains Colruyt, Delhaize and Carrefour in Belgium want to use RFID. Like Walmart, they want to condition their suppliers to equip their pallets with RFID tags. For now, these are pilot projects.[296] The international supermarket chain Metro in Rheinberg has also begun using RFID technology. IBM and Microsoft invested in this 'supermarket of the future'. This supermarket not only tagged the products, but also the loyalty cards and shopping carts, all without the custom being aware of it. By means of these *spy chips* or 'sniffing chips', the customer's buying behaviour could be investigated, even how much time he spent at a certain shelf. When this abuse of the RFID chip leaked the whole of Germany was in total uproar.[297] Partly as a result of this, the German digital civil rights organization FoeBuD (similar to the Dutch Civil Rights Organization Bits of Freedom, non-operational since last September 2006) organized a demonstration against the use of RFID chips.[298]

To think that one of the forerunners of RFID technology was an espionage device using radio waves, invented in 1946 by a certain Leon Theremin for the Soviet government, you realize that so many years later there is nothing new under the sun.[299] But the first to use RFID devices were the English in the Second World War to be able to distinguish returning English aircraft from German aircraft flying back home. Through Identification Friend or Foe (IFF) Transponders they could distinguish friend and foe by the different 'bleeps' on the radar screens.[300] Whether supermarkets and department stores also want to distinguish 'friend from foe' is not entirely clear, but given the 'price wars' and 'trade

---

[295] Mourits, R., 'RFID : de barcode voorbij', In Dutch. Source: ZDNet.

[296] *Industrie Magazine* (Belgium magazine). Source: www.rfidnederland.nl.

[297] Jansen, J., 'Big Brother en de snuffelchip', in Dutch, *Het Financieele Dagblad* (March 19, 2005), p. 34-35.

[298] http://www.foebud.org/rfid: Update: foebud.org is https://digitalcourage.de

[299] https://en.wikipedia.org/wiki/Radio-frequency_identification

[300] Update: Source http://zombiewire.com no longer active.

wars' that regularly take place, one can also learn to understand the 'bleeps' at the cash register differently.

In any case, more and more supermarkets are switching to the RFID system. Even paying through fingerprinting is already possible, as in the *Piggly Wiggly* supermarket in the United States. With the push of a button on the Pay by Touch System (pay by touch) it takes about ten seconds for the transaction to complete. Also in Portugal, and soon in Spain, it is possible to pay via fingerprint at GALP petrol stations. Apart from the fact that the 'system' turns out to be efficient, it is 'much easier, more practical, safer and much more fun', says the director of *Galp Energy*.[301] In the Netherlands, the plan is to have as many supermarkets as possible fully automated by 2010. Digital gates, scans, tags and paying with a credit card (in preparation for a cashless society) are the keywords for the new type of shopping. You drive your plastic cart across the floor at the cash register and in one go everything is scanned and possibly automatically debited from your account, provided that the balance is sufficient. Cashiers are no longer needed. A lot of small cameras, hardly noticeably. Ordering via the internet is by then probably quite normal. For marketing purposes IBM has since developed the programs Foot-Prints and Blue Eyes. Foot-Prints mean small sensors installed in the floor of the supermarkets registering every step the customer takes. Blue Eyes recognizes the direction in which the customer is looking and his overall attitude. On the basis of this info, one can determine what products in the supermarket interest the customer and which don't.[302] Theft becomes almost impossible. Combating shoplifting is an important motive for the Dutch Retail Council to use RFID.[303] 'Catch the thief!', might soon become 'Chip the thief!'

Look at us doing it!

Tesco is not only the largest British retailer, but number three in the world of retailers, with thousands of department stores in Europe and

---

[301] Update: Source www.niburu.nl becomes www.ninefornews.nl.
[302] Reischl, G., *Unter Kontrolle*, p. 76.
[303] Mourits, R., 'RFID : de barcode voorbij', In Dutch. Source: ZDNet.

Asia. Almost 30% of the groceries purchased in the UK come from Tesco. Tesco has been in disrepute lately for being one of the biggest promoters of RFID spy chips. In 1300 ware houses the company has installed more than 20,000 RFID readers and antennas. Millions of tags will soon be purchased, which of course will be included in the sales price. On top of that Tesco wants to expand the pilot project of the use of UHF tags (ultra-high frequency tags) from two to ten department stores, extending the traceable products. (Mostly 'high frequency tags' are used.) Numerous organizations that stand up for privacy and civil rights have already protested, including Electronic Frontiers Australia.[304] As early as 2003, Tesco was in the habit of spying on its customers with spy chips, hidden on shelves and in products.[305] There was the Gillette scandal. Customers who bought Gillette razor blades were spied on via hidden RFID surveillance vessels in the packaging of the Gillette products. It would give them better understanding of the buying behaviour of the customer.[306] RFID was also used to combat shoplifting. 'When a customer picked up a packet of razor blades from the shelf, an RFID reader sent a signal to a video camera that took a short picture of the customer. At the cash register, this process was repeated. Staff could always see afterwards who had not paid and these customers would be banned henceforth.'[307] This pilot project has now been discontinued, it is said. Either way, it shows what consequences RFID technology can have for privacy. Already via the loyalty card, Tesco had been known for a while to store all the customer's data when scanning. In fact, Tesco even invited other companies to come and check out their way of spying.[308] Both Walmart, Metro and Tesco choose to buy RFID chips at the lowest

---

[304] Update: http://strike-the-root.com/52/lfb/lfb1.html

[305] Update www.boycotttesco.com. The Tesco Boycottwebsite is a project of CASPIAN (Consumers Against Supermarket Privacy Invasion and Numbering). Two other types of tags are low frequency tags and microwave tags.

[306] Update: Idem and at the time a similar boycott of Gillette: www.BoycottGillette.com.

[307] Mourits, R., 'RFID : de barcode voorbij', In Dutch. Source: ZDNet.

[308] Update www.boycotttesco.com.

price i.e., 5 cents each.[309] Before long the RFID chip will only cost 1 euro cent. For that price, espionage will soon be within everyone's reach.

RFID is advancing at the speed of lightning

As of January 1, 2005, the U.S. Department of Defense also demanded that its suppliers 'tag' all goods and products. Mountains of tags are waiting for distribution. Everything must have a tag in or on! Clothes and shoes, medicines and expensive objects, on suitcases at airports, in the bottle top of mineral water. In household appliances, so that e.g., a washing machine can choose a washing program completely independently and a refrigerator can give a signal once an expiry date of a product has passed.

In the Netherlands, a pilot project was launched at the Academic Medical Centre in Amsterdam, where doctors, nurses and medicines are tagged. In this way, people and products are 'monitored'.[310]

Children, patients, soldiers and prisoners

In the Danish amusement park Legoland, the children are given an RFID bracelet. This way they can be traced quickly if they get lost, plus, one can check and see how much time a child spends at one particular attraction. Safety and commerce go hand in hand. In Osaka (Japan), a number of schools decided to apply chips to satchels, nameplates and in clothing, and install scanners at crucial places in the school. [311] Manufacturer Kyowa Corporation in Tokyo made a start with making satchels equipped with an active chip. Thanks to a security system from the company Secom, the parents can track down their children on a website that uses waves of mobile phones and satellites to indicate where the satchel (and thus also the child hopefully!) is located. As a result of the horrific attack on the school in Beslan in North Ossetia by Chechen rebels, the children in Moscow will soon be wearing metal tags also used

---

[309] https://en.wikipedia.org/wiki/Radio-frequency_identification
[310] Persson, M., 'Vervanger streepjescode vatbaar voor virussen ', in Dutch newspaper: *de Volkskrant* (March 15, 2006).
[311] Mourits, R., 'RFID : de barcode voorbij', In Dutch. Source: ZDNet.

for dogs. In America, single children and Alzheimer's patients are given armbands or ankle bands with a chip. (In many nursing- or care homes it has already come to that.) Soldiers in Australia and New Zealand are chipped, in Australia also the banking personnel and in America, thousands of prisoners have already been 'tagged'. (Some even involuntarily) 'Prisoners who already wear an electronic ankle band for the monitoring of their day-to-day movements by GPS, say that they do not wear that band around their ankle but in their head.'[312] In a new prison in Lelystad, six inmates will soon be placed in one cell. They all get a wristband with an RFID chip in it. This determines, among other things, the exact place of the detainee and allows him to gain access to entertainment (radio, TV, video). Username and passwords become obsolete. The guards are also going to wear an RFID chip on their keyring. This way, the guards can be 'guarded' from the control room. [313]

VIP chip clubs and tags in teeth

Some visitors to the Baja Beach Club in Barcelona and Rotterdam had a subcutaneous microchip (VeriPay) (Also called VIP chip) implanted to facilitate quick automatic payment via RFID.[314] Other clubs, such as the Sobabar in Glasgow, is just as good with the biochip as an 'electronic wallet'.[315] For those who have forgotten, VIP means *very important person*, but, depending on the situation, the second meaning is *very idiotic person.*

Researchers from the Catholic University of Leuven (Belgium) are testing RFID tags in the teeth of humans. 'You put your ID card in your pocket, we put it in a tooth,' said forensic dental Patrick Thevissen.[316] All personal information is stored on the chip, so that, for example, in the

---

[312] 'The microchip implantable in humans' (see chapter 3.2). Bron: C.R.A.P., www.stoppuce.be

[313] www.rfidnederland.nl/

[314] Persson, M., 'Vervanger streepjescode vatbaar voor virussen', in Dutch newspaper de *Volkskrant* (March 15, 2006).

[315] www.barsoba.co.uk

[316] Randerson, J., 'Chip in Tooth. Scientists Point Way to New Identity Tag', in: *The Guardian* (February 28, 2006).

event of natural disasters and terrorist attacks, forensic teams can swiftly identify the victims Useful for tsunamis or hurricanes. If the body is no longer identifiable, then at least the teeth are. Your 'tag-doctor' of the future is skillful; With a chipped tooth you can go places! 'It's your ID-card you'll never lose or forget to carry with you – unless your tooth falls out of course,' writes science journalist James Randerson in *The Guardian*.[317] One is at a loss for words. The tag in the tooth is resistant to repetitive chewing movements, heat and cold, but there are still problems with the expansion and shrinking of the teeth due to heat and cold. According to Thevissen, the tooth is the best place to store data, because it is the strongest part of the body and lasts the longest. He refers to excavated tooth fossils of extinct primates. The tags for people's teeth, by the way, look like the tags for animals.[318] Hopefully it doesn't come with animal feelings too. The iris scan and a tooth tag give the biblical phrase 'An eye for an eye, a tooth for a tooth' from Leviticus 24:20 a possibly prophetic meaning.

Book and ball

Since the 1st of April 2004, RFID tags are applied widely in public libraries. All new books that the libraries purchase through the Dutch Library Service (NBD) already contain tags. Sometimes the corresponding CDs, DVDs and CD-ROMs are also 'tagged'.[319] 'Every year NBD/Biblion sells about 2.7 million books to Dutch libraries. That's 80% of the Dutch book market', writes Jonathan Collins. He continues to say that the chips were supplied by Philips Semiconductor (the branch of the company which was sold, as we saw earlier) and the labels are supplied by two other companies, UPM Rafsec and Smartag.[320]
The tickets for the World Cup in Germany (spring 2006) also contained RFID chips. The world football federation FIFA, wanted to prevent falsifying and black trading of tickets and to ban rioters and hooligans

---

[317] Idem.

[318] Idem.

[319] www.nbdbiblion.nl/

[320] Collins, J., 'Publisher Tags All Library Books', an article on
www.rfidjournal.com.

from the stadium. It was the first time that RFID technology was used at a world football championship to identify cardholders. It was the largest international project with RFID access cards to date as well. The football fan was eligible for getting an entrance ticket after filling out his/her personal information on the FIFA internet site: name, address, telephone number, e-mail address, date of birth, nationality, identity card or passport number, bank account number, credit card details, 'and even his favourite football club'.[321] When asked what information would be on the chip, FIFA remained ambiguous. Rumours that there were wearable RFID readers in the stadium were denied by the organization. The chips would only be read at the entrance.[322] Be that as it may, even with minimal data stored, a lot of information of the owner can be traced by linking his data with the central databases. The fact is that counterfeiters, black traders and hooligans serve big brother well and play straight into the (chip) hand of the fast-growing control society.

The RFID tickets project was a co-production of FIFA, the German Ministry of the Interior and Philips, sponsor and supplier of the chips.[323]

Banknotes in the microwave

In order to prevent counterfeiting and theft of banknotes, the European Central Bank (ECB) were in consultation with its partners already back in 2001 about putting RFID tags in the banknotes. Some people will have it that since the beginning of March 2004, the euro and dollar banknotes already contained tags. It is suggested we can find out by placing a note in the microwave oven. The RFID tag will apparently explode?[324] Katherine Albrecht and Liz McIntyre, who invented the word 'spy chips', have tried this method using dollar bills, but do not recommend it. It is risky with fire and smoke.[325]

---

[321] http://www.rfidnederland.nl, and Jansen, J., 'Big Brother en de snuffelchip'. In the Dutch magazine *Het Financieele Dagblad*, March 19, 2005.

[322] http://www.rfidnederland.nl,

[323] News in 2006 on www.emerce.nl.

[324] Update: https://www.emerce.nl/achtergrond/rfid-optimaliseert-voorraadbeheer

[325] Albrecht, K., and L. McIntyre, Spychips, pp. 145-148.

Airports also participate, naturally

KLM, in collaboration with Schiphol Airport will be equipping all luggage with RFID chips to simplify the tracing of luggage that is underway. Hand luggage and shoes go through a safety gate to check for metal and/or explosives. Scanners check passport and ticket. Just before boarding the plane, a second passport and ticket check follows. If all goes according to plan, around 2011, the departure halls of Schiphol will boast dozens of columns and gates checking passports, checking in passengers and taking in luggage all to reduce waiting times for passengers. This new equipment must bring down the exponential increase in the airport's security costs (EUR 295 million for 2006). Schiphol's competitive position is jeopardized for the first time. Before anything else though, new electronic systems are going to make our faces more recognizable and read our fingerprints better. After all, it is the 'wish' of the United States that all airports in the world have such a system by the end of 2007. [326] So, we comply, 'Big brother' has spoken. In the future, Schiphol wants to install cameras using radiometry (electromagnetic radiation) that can detect concealed weapons and explosives (e.g., under clothing). TNO Defense and Security developed this 'through-the-wall radar'. It can look through walls, cars and clothes.[327] Before we know it, we will be naked. 'Clairvoyance' through technology. No need for detection gates any longer. Schiphol has already tested this body scan on staff, causing confusion amongst the staff. They did not like the way they were portrayed and are scared the radiation might be harmful. Airport management claims that the images will not be kept, that faces are not recognizable, that the radio waves are not harmful and fewer people have to undergo an embarrassing physical examination.[328] Under the guise of 'safety', the methods of control are becoming increasingly shameless. Ethics no longer seem to play any role and there is not even a law against technology abuse. The American company Militech has been supplying

---

[326] Veldhuijzen, A., 'Super fast to the trunk at Schiphol' and 'Doe-het-zelf op Schiphol', in Dutch newspaper *Algemeen Dagblad* (August 5, 2006).

[327] http://www.europarl.europa.eu.

[328] https://www.nu.nl/economie/715631/luchthaven-test-bodyscan-on-staff.html

these kinds of 'see-through cameras' to the US military at ten thousand dollars apiece for years. Military electronics supplier Raytheon did not stay behind and developed methods to detect metallic items like knives and hand weapons with the aid of radio waves.[329] Civilian airports are gradually turned into military airports. The marshals are already there and is the waiting for the generals to take over the 'steering wheel' in the cockpit.

Participating countries in the European Civil Aviation Conference (ECAC), the European Civil Aviation Conference, have been negotiating since April 1995 the introduction of biometrics as an identification system. At the twelfth meeting in Cairo (from 22 March to 2 April 2004), Germany, Iceland, the Netherlands, Spain and the United Kingdom (all, bar Iceland, EU countries) reported on initiatives and experiences with the application of biometrics.[330] Were you also aware of this? Partly through pressure from the United States, biometrics as an identification method was accelerated Despite the advanced techniques of big brother, terrorists manage to strike again and again to achieve their frightening objectives. 10 August 2006, the world was rocked by the news of a series of foiled attacks by the British secret service MI5. The plan was to blow up ten aircraft destined for America (New York, Washington, Boston) in the air with partly liquid, partly solid explosives, smuggled through in hand luggage and mixed in the air.[331] Keeping in mind, this was in spite of the fact that Heathrow Airport (London) had just been equipped with a high-tech eye identification system.[332]

Dialogue instead of even more security

Perhaps the Western heads of government should gather the courage to enter into a dialogue with groups that concoct those attacks. The question is whether or not a lot of goodwill has not been lost already? Emphasizing the image of the enemy or speaking of 'fascist fundamentalist Muslims', as did the US President following the foiled attacks by MI5, do not

---

[329] *New Scientist* (November 4, 1995).

[330] www.icao.int (International Civil Action Organisation).

[331] Dutch newspaper *Algemeen Dagblad* (August 11, 2006).

[332] Update: http://home.wanadoo.nl/henryv/

contribute to understanding the cause of the problems. As long as the West is not willing to get to the bottom of the pressing problem of terrorism and does not dare to involve itself in what the causes may be, even more advanced techniques, even more security systems will be found, without ever providing the citizen with any real security. On the contrary, indirectly, this approach could well fuel terrorism and it would demonstrate moral courage to enter into dialogue. It would be of crucial importance to examine one's own contribution to the highly inflammable situation in the Middle East, in a historical and critical way.... only then can the constant tension with regard to Iraq, Iran, Syria, Lebanon, Israel and the Palestinian community be understood and resolved in completely different ways, other than using brute force. Wisdom, patience, forgiveness and the realization that to combat hate with hate never solved anything, will ultimately be the only effective 'weapons' leaving no painful wounds. Because everything is connected to everything. Several countries played a dubious role in the colonial past in different parts of the world where major tensions are now revealing themselves. We might have thought too lightly of the major hurt inflicted on those who were exploited in the past and who are getting their own back.

All the advanced techniques that are now being applied (biometrics, chips, scanners, RFID readers, cameras, mobile phones, GPS, sensors) to secure society do definitively not contribute to a solution for the conflicts and wars but rather pave the way for even more RFID technology and ultimately for the subcutaneous microchip. Those who do benefit from this are the 'digital angel cooperatives' and the security industries. They are an affirmation of the lost trust in each other, of a world gone adrift. Researchers from VU University Amsterdam have shown that RFID technology also has a weak spot. 'The new chip on food, consumption resources, passports, people and animals are susceptible to viruses and can therefore be abused.' Andy Tanenbaum, professor of computer science, 'sees doom scenarios of suitcase bombs being transported unnoticed over baggage carousels'.[333] Thus, everything has it's 'Achilles' heel and there will always be people with evil intentions that will target it.

RFID for delinquent detection policy?

Mr. H.N. Brouwer, president of the College of Attorneys-General, gave a lecture on 10 November 2005 in Zeist on the occasion of the eighth Netherlands Congress. He made a strong plea for the RFID system that coudl facilitate the investigation policy, although Mr. Brouwer also saw possible hazards associated with the violations of privacy. 'There is no denying that we are moving towards a situation, in which it is the exception rather than the rule that a company or an organization does *not* use RFIDs at all. This obviously means the Public Prosecutor's office and the police have to reflect on what consequences this carries for the detection and prosecution of criminal offences.' He proposes well-known motives such as the prevention of crime and efficient stock - management.

The step from the electronic monitoring of offenders via wristbands and ankle straps to the subcutaneous microchip no longer seems so big.

In Belgium, Senator Jacques Brotchi recently introduced a bill to make it possible to implant a chip in sex offenders so that their movements can be monitored. 'My main aim is that this proposal might start a public debate', says Brotchi. Paul De Hert, professor of law and criminology at the Free University of Brussel, thinks this legislative proposal is premature and reprehensible. This is probably a sliding scale because once you start with implanting a chip in sexual offenders, where do you end up?[334] The answer is not that difficult...

Our car fully guarded

RFID technology is also booming on motorways and in cars. As long as the right RFID chips are in the car, the TrafficWatch system can follow

---

[333] Persson, M.,'RFID -chip blijkt niet onfeilbaar', in Dutch newspaper *de Volkskrant* (March 15, 2006).

[334] 'Pro & Contra. A chip for sex offenders?' in Beglium magazine Knack (July 26, 2006).

us exactly via telecommunications and satellite. The car we drive where and when, how fast, and so on. A safe feeling, right? Radar control is old-fashioned. An electronic toll system, connected to a biometric Traffic Watch system, can match the license plate number of all vehicles with that in the database. If the camera signals a stolen vehicle, an alarm automatically goes off on the control panel. Traffic-Watch can also be utilized as an access system in parking spaces of companies, to control bus or taxi lanes, short-term parking or for the monitoring of containers.[335]

Even more ingenious is that via the internet, it will soon be possible to check where a car is located at any moment. The company Geospatial in Santa Ana, California, launched the product GST Tracker ('tracker') in 2000. A built-in level transmitter in a car, will locate and trace the car via the internet. 'Anyone who is logged into this system can be followed by the government, by the company or from their home, alternatively they themselves can also follow everything.'[336] Just log in on the website, enter code and password. Tracking the car can also be done from a mobile phone that is connected to the internet. Wherever the car is, it will be found, because localization is done by satellite.

In England, the Electronic Vehicle Identification (EVI) project is in the pipeline. EVI foresees that in a few years' time every car will be equipped with a chip with all the details of the car, and its owner! Traffic congestion can be combated, unsafe driving behaviour can be prevented and in the event of theft, the car is quickly recovered. Safe and convenient. We are being reassured that EVI will not affect privacy, because only the vehicle is traced.[337] Yeah…right! Within the EU, a similar system as in England is being contemplated. A driver's license with an RFID chip for the whole of Europe, a registration certificate with an RFID chip[338] and improvement of the electronic control and ticket system is on the books.

---

[335] Reischl, G., *Unter Kontrolle*, p. 158-159.

[336] Idem, p. 158.

[337] Update: at the time to be found on http://ec.europa.eu/transport/ on the page on road safety.

[338] https://nl.wikipedia.org/wiki/Radio-frequency_identification

At the same time, discussions are on the go in Europe (by specialists of course) whether we could check the cars, just like the planes, via a 'black box' or 'data recorder' (English DAT stands for Digital Audio Tape). Electronic chips in the box register non-stop, the speed, acceleration, deceleration, braking, use of car lamps or turn signal. Only 30 seconds before and 15 seconds after a collision all data is stored. In the United Arab Emirates, people are ahead of the West: thousands of cars carry a black box. If the speed limit is exceeded, the driver will first hear a warning. If he does not reduce his speed, the black box passes on his identity to the police together with the speed and the place where he was speeding. This plan should be completed by 2011 and reduce the number of fatal accidents by half.[339] The police are the invisible co-driver. Perhaps rather buy either a Public Transport chip card or a ticket for train, tram or bus via the internet or ticketing machine after all? The European Commission is pushing for the installation of an e-call in every car. In the event of a collision this electronic device emits an emergency signal to the emergency service via the built-in mobile phone equipment in the car giving its exact location. As from 2007, all emergency services of the European Union can receive *e-calls*. There is already an agreement with the European Car Construction (ACEA) to equip all new vehicles with this system as from 2009.[340] Insurance companies are also exerting pressure. The car, motorway, parking spaces, everything will soon be electronically monitored and organized. The internet will play a pivotal role in this. There was a time that your car was your mate. Soon he will be your auto-mate-ic (an 'automatic'). For our safety?

Attacks on our privacy

Because of the almost daily attacks in the world, many are inclined to ignore the fact that since 9/11 our privacy is attacked on a daily basis too, all for our own 'security'. Anyone who follows the developments of the countless decrees and laws will see that the noose of the electromagnetic

---

[339] Hayez, V., 'The black box. Chips record what you do', in: Touring Explorer (April 2006).
[340] Idem.

net is gradually tightening around the human neck and therefore also around all other life forms. Caught in that net, the matrix, man's free choice to act will be restricted. More and more citizens are forced by banks, companies and politicians to take the digital route quicker. With a 'soft hand' he is forced to participate as much as possible in the world-wide electronic process via the internet.

After the European Union first met with the industry for a couple of months about RFID technology (i.e., with specialists), public debates have been organized since 3 July 2006 regarding the applications and limitations of RFID, under the grotesque name 'Your Voice in Europe'.

All Europeans have a say in this matter![341] And then to think that less than 10% actually heard of the word RFID. An even lesser amount of people is aware of this technology, and of that, a tiny percentage is actually familiar with the subject. Since some time now, Democracy has lost all its meaning. The decision-making processes have progressively come into the hands of specialists, technicians, VIPs, businesspeople, politicians and lobbying circles internationally, not to mention the secret societies 'in the background'.

There is a constantly growing concentration of power in all manner of groups in which the elite cohort jeopardizes the democracy. The valid question can even be asked whether one can still speak of democracy in today's complicated electronic society in which the average citizen has long since lost track of many of the developments. It looks more like a power elite, a plutocracy or a new kind of 'aristocracy' that determine everything whereby the 'subjects' are occasionally permitted to make their voices heard on issues that have anyway long since been decided upon behind the scenes by large European or global paper-producing organizations with their thousands of civil servants. Citizens trying to orientate themselves are being sidelined in their first attempts because of the complicated laws and fast-spinning paper mills.

Article 29 Working Party

---

[341] Update: https://ec.europa.eu/commission/presscorner/detail/en/MEMO_06_378

As has been repeatedly pointed out in this book, our privacy is at stake. For the first time in human history, it is getting engulfed in a tsunami like wave of information and technology making the average human being manipulable.

The Article 29 Data Protection Working Party, the Working Group established under Article 29 of Directive 95/46/EC of the European Commission, is an independent European advisory body on data protection and privacy.[342] The committee aims to initiate a broad discussion about RFID by providing information. Its agenda on data protection and privacy in relation to RFID technology is an important document, which, however, doesn't reach the public opinion. Hopefully the Thematic Committee on Technology Policy, of the House of Representatives will include this discussion paper for public debate. On April 5, 2006, such a debate took place, organized in collaboration with EPC.NL and the RFID Platform Nederland (note: interest groups!). It was the first time that Dutch politicians had been informed on this subject at this scale.[343] If even politicians need to be informed, how can we expect the average citizen to be updated, let alone make his 'Voice in Europe' heard? If citizens were to be widely informed about RFID technology and grasp that in addition to a number of advantages, there are also major disadvantages and dangers connected to it, this could stagnate political decisions and probably even halt them. There is much at stake and Banks and Companies (BB) will of course do everything to circumvent obstructions. Not pleasant for policymakers. That's why it is of vital importance that we wake up!

There is another issue that should start all the alarm bells ringing; the 21st of February 2006, the European Ministers of Justice and Home Affairs agreed on the European Directive to the compulsory storing of telecommunications data. Telephone and internet companies must keep all data of landline and mobile phone calls and emails of the 450 million

---

[342] Schaar, P., 'Working document ...' [see note 262]. The tasks of that committee are defined in Article 30 of Directive 95/46/EC and Article 15 of Directive 2002/58/EC. Website: Update: https://ec.europa.eu/info/law/law-topic/data-protection_en

[343] www.rfidnederland.nl

inhabitants of the European Union for a minimum of half and a maximum of two years 'for the purpose of investigating, detecting and prosecuting serious crimes'.[344] This makes every citizen a potential suspect. According to Franco Frattini, vice-president of the European Commission, it is only for 'traffic and location data' (who calls or emails with whom and when and for how long, and with a mobile phone also from where). Without the court's permission, police, judiciary and intelligence services from all over the European Union can get to this valuable data.[345] Nobody will make confidential phone calls or write intimate emails any longer. Why is no one standing up? Are we all willing to sacrifice our precious privacy for the 'so-called' security? The Article 29 Working Group calls the obligation to hold on to data 'in violation of the personal lifestyle' (Article 8 of the European Convention on Human Rights), but the European Commission dismisses all objections. After all, during the ongoing investigation into the London attacks, the telecommunications data has turned out to be 'invaluable', right?

Is there a privacy issue?

Wim van Rooijen, director of Media Plaza, is of the opinion that there are many misunderstandings about RFID and that it is impossible for instance, to follow someone in the city wearing tagged clothing. 'Is there a privacy problem with RFID in the first place?', he wonders.[346] Professor Cor Molenaar, chairman of the RFID Platform Netherlands representing the interests of technology in the Netherlands, also sees no privacy problem. 'Informing the public about the presence of RFID and about data stored in the chips is fine. However, deactivating the chips [at the

---

[344] Vander Velpen, J., P. De Hert and J. Maebe, 'Terreurbestrijding brengt privacy in gevaar', in Belgium newspaper *De Morgen* (March 7, 2006). Vander Velpen is a lawyer and president of the League for Human Rights, De Hert professor at the Vrije Universiteit Brussel and Maebe member of the Working Group Privacy and of the League for Human Rights.

[345] Idem.

[346] Rooijen, W. van, 'Column: Privacy bij RFID géén issue meer' (October 16, 2004)Update: https://webwereld.nl/nieuws/security/logo-moet-privacyzorgen-rond-rfid-tags-wegnemen-3769071/

till] goes too far.'[347] He says this in response to the above-mentioned basic rules of the recently non operational digital civil rights foundation Bits of Freedom (BoF), who advocated the introduction of a law to stop the tracking of people via RFID. Both Molenaar and van Rooijen conveniently forget the fact that the unique ID number in the tag can easily be linked to the identity of the buyer when he pays with credit or debit card or gets his customer card scanned. This besides the fact that the tag can be read from a distance without the person's knowledge,[348] e.g. upon entering a store with 'tagged' items from another store, which are not removed or disabled. By the way, if the frequency range of the tag is enlarged, it will be even possible to follow the wearer of a tag (in clothes, shoes, bag) at a great distance which of yet cannot be done with the regular tags. Tesco has shown, that 'ultra-high frequency tags' are already in use, making the range only bigger. Not so long ago, the European Telecommunications Standards Institute (ETSI) adopted a new European standard for the use of RFID systems. The permissible power of the RFID reader and the available frequency figures in the UHF (ultra -high frequency) band was stretched.[349] A plus for the retail, but is it for the consumers? It won't be long before the 'intelligent RFID reader' will hit the market, which can read the tags independent of the instructions of an underlying network. If the network fails, the RFID reader can still store the data of about ten thousand tags.[350]

According to electronics specialists, nowadays everything can be linked to everything and databases can be cracked. Specialists and certainly super specialists at the NSA can do that in a split second via the Echelon eavesdropping system but the average layman can't do that.

Everything that gives off a signal can be traced by Echelon, as we saw.

For some time now, the trust of countless people has been seriously violated by a power elite, who, by abusing the electronics and under the pretext of the war on terror, is turning against the civilians in an attempt to submit them to a new world order. Big brother is much more advanced

---

[347] Mourits, R., 'RFID : de barcode voorbij', In Dutch. Source: ZDNet.

[348] https://nl.wikipedia.org/wiki/Radio-frequency_identification

[349] Schaar, P., 'Working document ...' [see note 262].

[350] https://www.emerce.nl/achtergrond/rfid-optimaliseert-voorraadbeheer

than many suspect and the reality is to not be naïve in these matters, but to wake up quickly!

Disadvantages outweigh the advantages

Anyone who reads the very well-documented book *Spychips* by Katherine Albrecht and Liz McIntyre will no longer speak lightly about the misuse of RFID technology. It describes in detail how this technology is already being (ab)used to control *everything* from stamps and shoes to the people themselves and what the 'master plan-makers' still have in store. All without our knowledge. Katherine Albrecht, a graduate of Harvard University, and Liz McIntyre, well in the know of the ins and outs of the banks, conducted an investigation into the use of RFID in global corporations, retail, marketing organizations, banks and the U.S. government. Katherine Albrecht is founder and director, and Liz McIntyre director of communication of CASPIAN (**C**onsumers **A**gainst **S**upermarket **P**rivacy **I**nvasion and **N**umbering), an organization that opposed, among other things, practices of Tesco, Piggly Wiggly and other supermarkets.[351] Albrecht is one of the first to ring the alarm bell about the great dangers of RFID technology. On Caspian's website, Albrecht and McIntyre make a strong appeal to inform people and to take action as soon as possible, because the benefits of RFID do not outweigh the enormous risks. They immediately disclose RFID scandals on their website. According to Albrecht, the 'security industry' costs ten billion dollars per year.[352]

Influence on our psychic and spiritual well-being

Thanks to the worldwide use of RFID technology, trillions of extra radiations will soon enter the ether every day in addition to the existing radiations from mobile phone and UMTS masts, television, computer and all kinds of other equipment. All these radiations will have an increasingly intense influence on our psychological and spiritual well-

---

[351] See CASPIAN, update: www.boycotttesco.com
[352] Update: www.spychips.com and
   https://www.motherjones.com/politics/2005/12/total-surveillance/

being. Undoubtedly, they will bring about a radical change in the earth's electromagnetic field and possibly even lead to blockages in our spiritual evolution. We know that both the alpha rhythm of the human corresponds with the electric waves emanated by our planet at ca. 10.6 hertz and thus we come to the inevitable conclusion that this has a great influence on our consciousness. [353]

HAARP

And then, insult to injury, the disastrous influence of HAARP, in Gakona, Alaska, an electromagnetic transmission system virtually unknown to most. HAARP is the abbreviation of High Frequency Active Auroral Research Program. It is the greatest ionosphere heater ever built on Earth, made possible by the genius physicist Nikola Tesla, contemporary and friend of Albert Einstein.

The ionosphere is essential to our atmosphere. HAARP, a Pentagon project, consists of a complex of 360 antenna towers regularly emitting high frequencies into the ionosphere. This recharges the ionosphere and creates the so-called ELF waves (extremely low waves) that are radiated back to earth. This way the ionosphere becomes a kind of cell tower, sometimes hundreds of miles long, which, with a force of 10 Gigawatts (10 billion watts!) can emit its diabolical radiations. HAARP can substantially influence or control the weather, the electromagnetic field of the earth, the communication system, air traffic, the ecosystem and the consciousness of humans. It is an ultimate weapon that most people hardly know about and that far exceeds the power of nuclear weapons. The immense influence of

HAARP, Gakona, Alaska, USA.
Source: Wikipedia

---

[353] Bruce, L.C., *Die Harmonie des Weltraums*, p. 156-157.

HAARP is underestimated by many. Under the guise of scientific research, things are taking place in faraway Alaska that are intolerable. Specialists who have made a study of it see HAARP as one of the biggest threats to all life on our planet.[354] In the foreseeable future, it is of the utmost importance that man regains his inner peace, and does not become a plaything of forces which cayse divisiveness everywhere and try to realize their new world order through creating chaos. Such a world order runs counter to nature's harmony and rhythm and will eventually lead to a world catastrophe unless we wake up and take countermeasures in the very near future. We can do this! Joining forces.
Gather courage and perseverance and wear it like your coat of arms. Stoke the fire of peace in the heart, soothe the mind, to calm and cleanse it until it is like the still surface of water. These forces are supported by the all-penetrating spirit of the universe, by the inexhaustible reservoir of energy that can be applied for peace by those who seek peace, by those who are weary of all world violence.

---

[354] Begich, N., and J. Manning, *Angels Don't Play This HAARP* , p. 8-9; Heerd, U. (red.), *Das HAARP Projekt*.

'The first peace, which is most important, is the peace that descends into the hearts of men as they realize their union, their oneness with the universe and all cosmic forces, and once they realize that in the center of that universe Wakan-Tanka (the Great Mystery) dwells and that this center is truly everywhere; it can be found in all of us. That is the true peace and the others are only a reflection of it.
The second is the peace between two people and the third is the peace that is made between peoples.
But above all, you have to understand that there can never be peace between peoples, before that true peace is known which, as I have said many times, can be found in the hearts of the people.' [355]

Black Elk, Oglala Sioux, Dakota, 1948.

---

[355] Bruchac, J. (eds.), Indian wisdom, p. 78-79.

3.4   Animals and children as an intermediate step

'Their goal is to microchip every human being on the planet and every child from
birth. This is not science fiction.
It's already happening. Of course, they don't come out with that and they're not
honest about that, because they know that a lot of people will resist it
(well, some anyway).
They do it step by step to keep the actual game hidden.
They start by microchipping animals, first voluntarily and now often by law, and
the same method is used in humans.' [356]

David Icke

Trying it out on animals first

As more and more people become accustomed to tagging all sorts of
products and objects, to the chipping animals and the socially weak, the
soldiers and famous people (that always does well!), the time is ripe to
chip people on a collective scale. An attack that pales in comparison with
9/11 pales, or another catastrophic event in the world, would make a
drastic decision of this kind more acceptable. Let us please not be naïve
about what the power elite stand for. Katherine Albrecht writes; 'An
outbreak of smallpox, the news of a 'dirty bomb,' or the obvious need to
control a special part of humanity, can be seen as the justification for
gathering the targeted human groups, to chip them and track them with
this technology'.[357] Of course, we will hear more often that a
subcutaneous chip is the best protection in the event of accidents,
diseases or attacks and should it not have dawned on us yet, the chip is of
course also a solution to safely conduct financial transactions in these

---

[356] Icke, D., *Children of the Matrix*, 2002, p. 368.
[357] Albrecht, K., *Spychips*, p. 169.

violent times. Useful to be trailed in the financial field as well. Cash money must go.

First let's get used to chipping animals and then finally it's man's turn. Like a herd of cattle, ready to be enslaved to those who have more interest in a fascist-administered society than in a society in which trust, respect, frankness and love are central. You don't believe it? Exaggerated? Delusional?

Chip for all livestock and all pets

The digital angels are busily chipping animals. They were way ahead of the laws. Or.... did they come about through close collaboration and inspiration? The special Department of Animal Identification Systems (AID) of Applied Digital Solutions (ADS) has been producing tags for animals for a number of years. Millions of them are sold and millions are earned. Mountains of tags are awaiting distribution. Why? In the foreseeable future, the chip will be mandatory for all livestock and all pets throughout Europe and America. You read that right, yes. For *all* livestock and *all* pets, while many animals in reserves and zoos, as well as migratory birds, have been chipped for some time.

Years ago, the digital angels went out with scanners for animals in veterinary practices and veterinary clinics. A market was opening up. Thousands of devices have been sold since 2005. Turnover per year on the world market: one hundred fifty to two hundred million dollars. From 2005 onwards, growth to five hundred million dollars a year was predicted.[358] By making all herds electronically traceable creates fortunes. The dance around the golden calf has begun. America by now has a three-phase plan in the drawer. Canada will soon make a start with tagging all cattle. But Europe is the true 'cash cow'. With about a hundred million head of cattle, about two hundred million sheep and goats, there is work to be done in the chip shop. Add to that, a hundred and fifty million pigs that are slaughtered every year. The newborn piglets immediately get

---

[358] Figures and names from Digital Angel Powerpointpresentatie 2005, from bij
    Allen & Caron, representatives of ao.VeriChip. Source: www.allencaron.com:
    Update: website no longer active; also www.digitalangel.com no longer active.

chipped of course. The more is slaughtered, the bigger the chip market. Bread from the dead. The digital angels find vegetarianism not really fashionable. Europe is expected to have fully switched to 'electronic monitoring' of all livestock by 2007/2008. European Commissioners, ministers and other representatives managed to push things through in such a way that there was no whining. Who, by the way, reads all these decisions? Mountains of paper are often the best blanket to muffle democracy. The National AID system in America is supported by well-known names: National Cattlemen's Beef Association, Pork Producers, Walmart and McDonald's. Our non-partial non-elected representatives of the people. Their logos are everywhere. Logos often mean more to a lot of people nowadays than the Logos...

The digital angels, in consultation with the governments, will soon want to chip everything that crawls, walks, flies and swims. Another step. Cattle alone require tens of millions of tags in America every year. By 2009, the hundred million head of livestock in America must be tagged.[359] Now that they are well advanced in the process of introducing this system, it appears that the animals that are equipped with a passive RFID chip, can hardly be 'read'. They like to walk in groups and the passive chips can only be read at a very short distance because they have too little transmitting power.[360] So, the active RFID chip is looming. Didn't they know this in the first place.? Oh well, double production means double merit, right? And then ultimately there's the multimillion-dollar market for tagging pets. We all let it happen. As if paralyzed. It gets crazier, by the way. Recently, millions of salmon have been chipped so that they can be followed in their migration through the dams of the Snake and Columbia Rivers.[361] RFID chips are even placed in the stomach of some cows. The Animal Industry Lab in the Japanese city of Takayama devised a 'health care' system for cows last year. Temperature and weight of the cow are monitored via the chip. Useful with childbirths too. Twenty-four hours before calving, the body temperature of the pregnant cow drops

---

[359] Update: www.digitalangel.com no longer active.
[360] http://rfid.emerce.nl
[361] Update: www.digitalangel.com no longer active.

and the 'intelligent' RFID chip with transmitter gives the farmer timely warning. [362] Unbelievable that cows used to do this unaided for thousands of years. By constantly talking about the 'market' of animals or the 'meat industry', consisting exclusively of producing millions of kilos of meat, one forgets that in those perfectly wrapped 'pieces of meat' there was ever a warm beating heart, and eyes that could see, had vocal cords that could make a sound, and have a soul and feeling. But hey… it's just cattle. 'I'll have that smoked sausage thank you, that piece of steak.' If you love to own a herd, that apparently does not automatically mean that you love cattle.

Hormones are still a 'finishing touch' for the hormone mafia to make animals fatter, thus the wallet. Meanwhile, the number of diseases is expanding (or are they being released?): mad cow disease, swine fever, foot-and-mouth disease, rabies, blue tongue, bird flu... For the digital angels all the more reason to propagate that all cattle, all pets, all migratory birds, all wild animals in reserves and zoos must be chipped. For our health! The health of the animals does not count, unless it benefits ours. In often unworthy conditions, animals are slaughtered, life after life from generation to generation. For the palate's pleasure. For our pleasure. Millions of hectares of forest or tropical rainforest have been sacrificed. For even more burgers... And now? Tag collectively! Should the animal still be bound by an instinct, in the meat industry all those have been destroyed.

Tagging or coercing

On April 25, 2005, the U.S. Department of Agriculture launched its Draft Program Standards ('St'; Draft Programme Guidelines) and Draft Strategic Plan ('Plan'; Draft Action Plan) on the National Animal Identifcation System (NAIS).
'From 1 January 2008, the NAIS will be mandatory (Plan, p.2, 10, 17).
Anyone owning only one horse, one cow, pig, chicken, sheep, pigeon, or owns an entire herd is required to register their habitat, including name, address, and phone number of the owner, and GPS satellite monitoring

---

362 www.rfidnederland.nl/

in a federal mega database under a 7-digit ID number (St., p. 3-4, 10-12; Plan, p. 5). Each animal will be assigned a 15-digit ID number, which will also be kept in a federal mega database. 666 as the base number? Preferred ID form is an RFID tag or microchip that can be read at a (large) distance (Plan, p. 10; St., p. 6, 12, 20, 27-28). The Plan also includes the collection of the DNA and/or retinal scan of each animal (Plan, p. 13). The owner is obliged to report the following: date of birth of the animal, the insertion of each ID tag of the animal, time at which an animal leaves or enters the area, loses a tag, or when a tag is replaced, the slaughter or death of an animal, or if an animal goes missing. Such cases must be reported within 24 hours. (St., p. 12-13, 17-21). Veterinarians are obliged to report 'sightings' of animals (St., p. 25). In other words, if you call a veterinarian to treat your horse, cow, or any animal and he sees an animal without the mandatory 15-digit computer-readable ID number, he is required to report this to you. If you do not comply with this (St. and Plan), the ministry will impose 'coercive measures' such as fines and/or confiscating your animals. No exceptions. Everyone is forced to register and report on their animals, even if breeding is for their own consumption.'[363]

From 2007 onwards, this can still be done voluntarily. Nice, isn't it? Mike Johanns, secretary of state for agriculture, says that this measure aims to prevent an outbreak of dangerous viruses. (Clever thinking!) However, Jay Truit of the National Cattlemen's Beef Association thinks that encouraging RFID technology is the true motive. According to John Clifford, chief veterinarian of the Ministry of Agriculture it is not necessary to register animals that are moved, only animals that have come into contact with other animals. According to him, it is about being able to register viruses quickly.[364]

Some sort of rabies.

Gandhi once said that the level of a civilization is known by the way man treats his animals. Many no longer know that animals are creatures with

---

[363] https://educate-yourself.org/cn/animaltaggingandbigbrother03mar06.shtml
[364] www.rfidnederland.nl/

a soul. This must first be scientifically proven. Animals have all too often become an object. If necessary, we use them as laboratory animals. How would we feel about becoming laboratory animals of the power elite? The English *animal* comes from the Latin *anima*, soul. A 'civilization' that still has the 'factory farming' ('industry of life'!) as the basis of animal policy and chips its animals on a collective scale, is fast on its way to losing its dignity or suffering from rabies? Such a 'civilization' reduces life to efficiency, production, profit. Any kind of relationship with the animal disappears as a result. One should read *Animal Liberation*[365] (with some shocking photos) by Peter Singer, philosopher and ethicist. In this 'bible of the animal liberation movement', as this book is often called, Singer exposes the unbridled suffering of the animals and makes a warm plea for the rights of the animal. Singer is a vegetarian and rejects any form of violent action.

'We are a part of Earth and Earth is a part of us. The fragrant flowers are our sisters; the deer, the horse and the mighty eagle are our brothers. The rocky heights, the grassy meadows, the body warmth of pony and man – everything is interrelated,'[366] is what Seattle said, the chief of the Duwamish Indians, in 1854 in a speech to Governor Isaac Stevens who wanted to buy the land of the Indians on behalf of the white farmers. Fortunately, more and more people are becoming aware of such situations. Fortunately, there are also more and more animal protection organizations that stand up for the rights of the animal. Gradually, more people are beginning to work in a critical but peaceful way for their brothers and sisters; the animals.

Freemasons and chips

A group that has recently become vigorously committed to the protection of children are the Freemasons from the state of Indiana. They developed the Child Identification Program, abbreviated as CHIP. CHIP is claimed by the Freemasons lodge in Indiana to be the 'largest and most common program of child identification currently available'. Propaganda material

---

[365] Singer, P., *Animal Liberation*.
[366] 'My words are like the stars, they don't change', *Seattle's speech*.

and their website say FREE CHIP. An allusion to FREE (by) CHIP, or FREE (MASONS) (for) CHIP? At the bottom right of the image, a child holds the math's compass that cuts through the triangle pointing upwards containing the letter G, which can indicate both God and grandmaster. The same in the top left plus the name of the lodge and the website. In the 'C' of the word chip a fingerprint is visible. Such a picture is of course also a good advertisement for Freemasonry, for many still a 'great unknown'.

Through identification, CHIP wants to protect the children from a lot of misery. A noble initiative in itself. You could carefully ask yourself if digital angels might be behind it, because the Order of Freemasons consists of initiated and uninitiated

members and lots goes on behind the veil of the portals. CHIP being the portal of the real chip? Surely not?

CHIP-Indiana is based on the successful program started by the Massachusetts Grand Lodge. Every year, about one million children disappear in America, according to the lodges. With a statement like that you lay a solid foundation, attract attention. The protective measures include e.g., a digital video, called 'the cornerstone' of CHIP. In a short interview with the child, it shows the personal characteristics (face, speech, body-postures). In the event of abduction, the parents or guardian immediately make the video available to the media for distribution. They also have computer prints of the child's fingerprints with the date of disappearance and the child's name, age, height and weight. In addition, they get a DNA set: three sets of small bags (DNA bags), three hundred in total, and one set of larger pouches (to store the DNA material), one hundred in total. The three small ones are for hair samples, nail clippings and a sample of a saliva smear (biometrics!) Finally, a CHIP flag from the Indiana lodge. Ten safety tips complete the program, such as teaching children what their name, address, phone number and zip code is, who their friends are, what kind of activities they undertake, not forgetting to mention the emergency number 911.[367] That was the way it started, wasn't it? In any case, the lodges are successful with the duty-free CHIP program and the word becomes familiar. The data remains with the parents or guardian, they say, but still; a lot of data together in a short time.

Schools put children on a leash

Several schools in America are already successfully introducing the RFID tag from the company Texas Instruments for children. For their safety. Katherine Albrecht and Liz McIntyre investigated the situation. The first school to introduce RFID was the Enterprise Charter School in Buffalo, New York, in 2003. Enterprise is part of a network of sixty state schools in New York, where about seventy-five percent of the children come from the poor layers of the population and their lunch is subsidized by the state). The four hundred and sixty children of this school are forced to wear an RFID tag from Texas Instruments around their necks. Upon entering the school or moving up to the second floor, they are scanned and at that moment the tag reveals the children's photos, dates of birth and further registered data. 'I labeled the devil,' said the headmaster of the school, who looked at this project quite critically— but at the same time was proud that no parent had protested. Understandable perhaps, because the school has a waiting list and students have to re-register every year.

In the Spring Independent School District, north of Houston, Texas, it is being considered whether to tag twenty-eight thousand students for the route to and from the school bus. A representative of Hewlett-Packard's, in favour of the spy chip, is chairman of the financial committee of the board of this school and a member of the technology committee of this school district. The children say they do not feel any safer with tags but rather feel humiliated and insulted. A fifteen-year-old child said, 'It makes me feel like some sort of animal.'[368] *The New York Times* reported

---

[367] www.tryfreemasonry.com and www.4chip.com. Update: the last website is no longer available.

[368] Albrecht/McIntyre, *Spychips*, p. 173-174.

that it has been suggested that the subcutaneous RFID chip is a safer alternative to the tag, because the children cannot lose or exchange it. It is not surprising that this district has persevered in introducing the spy chips, because Texas is the home of the company that makes the chips. [369]

Every new baby a digital file

The digital angels have more big plans, having started with the chipping of children. Children, like the animals, are for the power elite an important intermediate step on the way to massively chipping the world's population. In America, they are seriously working on a bill to chip children at birth. But not only in the US. As early as 1997, the CDU/CSU in Germany proposed the subcutaneous chip for children. To protect them from kidnapping. It caused violent reactions and a sharp debate in parliament followed. The seed of 'getting used to it' had been sown. However, the Dutch government also has fancy plans. Not for a chip (yet) but it smacks of it. 'Every new baby an electronic file' was the news item of 12 September 2005 on the website of the Ministry of Health, Welfare and Sport. (Smart to announce this the day after the opening of parliament) 'From 1 January 2007, every new baby will receive an electronic file containing information about the child, the family situation and the environment. The files will be kept and updated by doctors and nurses from the youth health care. Secretary of State Ross spent 25 million euros on it. The electronic child file is linked to a social security number.[370] Should the child move home it won't be 'lost' and possible 'derailment' can also be prevented. In case of surreptitiously considering chips, it is perhaps best to consult cardiologist Menno Baars who can tell you that there is a shorter route than the 'electronic file'. What would the digital angels whisper behind the scenes: 'Let the children come to us?'

---

[369] Idem, p. 174.

[370] Update: www.minvws.nl/nieuwsberichten/djb/2005/elke-nieuwe-baby-een-eigen-elektronisch-dossier.asp is no longer available.

In the eyes of the child, I saw the one Self,
in his voice I heard the keynote of the universe,
in his youth I felt eternal life.
When it was violated, a star lost its luster.

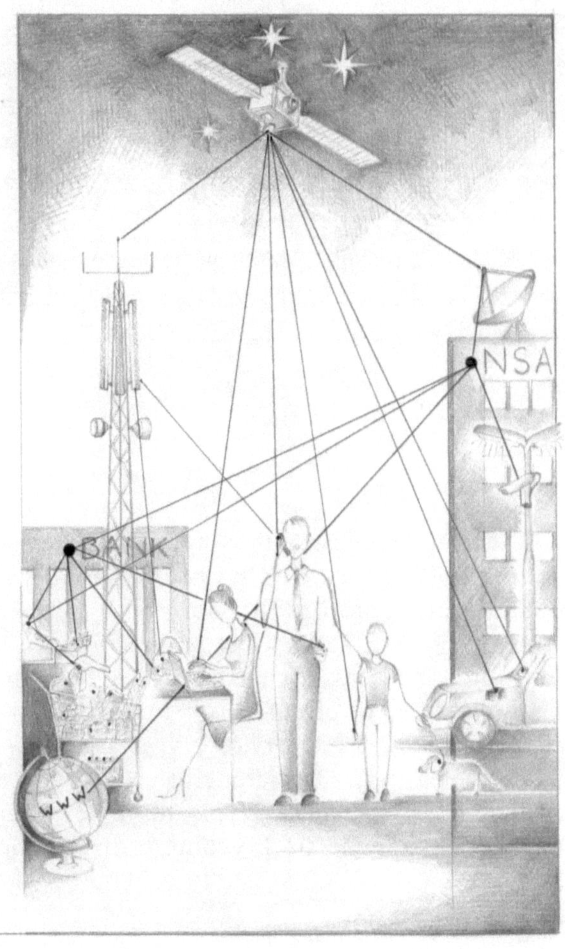

3.5   The completely controlled man

'In the pursuit of a totalitarian state, the power elite can now access and control our consciousness in an unprecedented way. As a result, it also has control over our humanity and can do whatever it wants with us. The means of creating global slavery are in sight and the implementation of this technology is advancing day by day. The signs are visible all around us. Many suspect that there is an overall philosophy that staged the crises and the chaos of the latter part of the 20th century, and I believe they are right. Behind the scenes, forces are at work to propagate a new world order not fundamentally different from the negative utopian world state described in George Orwell's 1984.
If this elite is cold-blooded enough to knowingly create war, famine and disease - and many suspect it has already done so - what conscientious objection could stop it from bringing about global mind control?' [371]

Jim Keith.

The battle for the human spirit

Jim Keith was a leading American author in the field of research into the forces behind the world stage. He died in 1999, as a result of a mysterious accident. Keith's books gained great notoriety.[372] In *Mind Control, World Control,* he discusses some secret projects that aim at the total control of human consciousness, such as MKULTRA and MONARCH. Keith also describes the involvement of secret services and large companies in these projects. Secret services also appear to have infiltrated the world of psychology, art, literature, religion and new age. Drugs, perverse sexuality, abuse of psychiatry, psychosurgery and electronics (chips), criminal brain experiments, injections of viruses and bacteria –

---

[371] Keith, J., *Mind Control, World Control*, p. 9-10.
[372] https://en.wikipedia.org/wiki/Jim_Keith

all this appears to be seriously used by the power elite to destroy man's mind. Billions of dollars of taxpayers' money are spent on it. Yet another shocking book. Stay silent? And soon face the accomplished facts? The Buddha is said to have fought the demons with the flaming sword of insight and truth. This theme is depicted on various tankas of the Buddhist life wheel. Let us wield this sword too. We are potential Buddhas, although the power elite prefers to see us as slaves.

The domain of demonism

In his article 'Josef Mengele and the Monarch Programme', Robin de Ruiter describes the Monarch Total Mind Control Program, which wants to enslave man through long-term systematic traumatization of the mind. At the basis of this project is the Nazi doctor Josef Mengele, who during the Second World War in Hitler Germany did his cruel research on children and adults, often from concentration camps. After the collapse of the Nazi regime, he fled, according to many, to the US, where he continued his experiments with predominantly children with subsidies from the power elite.[373]

When brain surgery and technology of the chip fall into the hands of those who want to manipulate the consciousness of man, the terrain of demonism is entered. 'The last stronghold of freedom is of a biological nature: the brain protected by bones. This stronghold of nature has so far been undefeatable for those who wanted to impose their will on others. As long as the thoughts remain free, control ends there, with the brain. What, however, if one can manipulate the brain directly? (...) What happens if people's thinking can be directly interfered with?'[374]

Dr. Luukanen-Kilde on Mind Control

Rauni-Leena Luukanen-Kilde points out that the NSA's Signals Intelligence Department can remotely control human brain information by decoding the transmitted frequencies of the brain (3.5Hz, 5 milliwatts). 'Experiments on prisoners in Gothenburg and Vienna clearly

---

[373] In *Frontier* 12.3 (juni/juli 2006), p. 33-38.
[374] Scheflin, A.W. en E.M. Opton, *The Mind Manipulators*, p. 9.

showed brain injuries. Where brain implants are usually in operation, decreased blood circulation and lack of oxygen follow in the frontal and temporal lobe. Tests on a Finn showed atrophy of the brain and interim attacks of unconsciousness due to lack of oxygen.' The author describes that (military) intelligence services, in collaboration with psychiatrists, have been secretly applying mind-control techniques since the 1980 -ties, without the knowledge of the civilians and soldiers, and without the knowledge of the subjects! Patients were used as guinea pigs from electronic, chemical and bacteriological forms of Mind Control. Viruses were also tested in this way in different countries. All international conventions relating to human rights prohibit the manipulation of people without their consent, even in prisons, and so most definitively of the civilian's population.[375] The victims of MC were diagnosed as 'mentally ill'. Psychiatry and secret service that go together... A well-known Gulach-archipelago theme.

Will our thoughts soon be controled?

Article 18 of the United Nations Universal Declaration of Human Rights states that everyone has the right to 'freedom of thought, conscience and religion...'[376] DARPA, an institute of the Pentagon, has been subsidizing a lurid program called Brain Machine Interfaces through a number of universities for years. With this BMI software, thoughts can be read from the brain, but also entered into the brain. Purpose: to govern the human mind. That's called psych-cybernetics. [Greek *kubernao* = govern; *psyché* = mind]. We are also working on a technology to be able to control machines via the brain. The prestigious Massachusetts Institute of Technology already made great strides. Monkeys and rats are used as laboratory animals and can be 'controlled' like a remote-controlled car. This technology can also be put to use for the Mind Control of entire populations. An example is the Wireless Cloud Experiment. The University of Georgia, together with the local government, founded

---

[375] Luukanen-Kilde, R-L., 'Microchip Implants, Mind Control and Cybernetics' in *Spekula* (1999).
[376] https://www.ohchr.org/EN/UDHR/Pages/Introduction.aspx

WAG (Wireless Athens Group). Through the creation of a Wireless Cloud (a kind of 'cloud' with radio waves) over an area where anyone can get free internet, one can communicate with MMEA chips (Multiple Micro Electrode Array) that are implanted in humans.[377] But with that, one can also implant thoughts and feelings so that the person is totally under the control of the people who operate the MBI software. Yet another example of perverted science; there are plenty more to give unfortunately. John Kenneth Galbraith, a well-known historian and professor at Harvard, had been asked to be part of the team that was to write 'The Report from Iron Mountain', a think tank study commissioned by the Department of Defense. The aim of the study? to explore new ways to make the masses submissive. When a copy of this report leaked to the press, the government said it was a joke. Galbraith, however, confirmed that it was completely authentic.[378] What is the UN actually doing about these extraordinarily gross violations of the Universal Declaration of Human Rights, besides staying silent in all cases?

'Thought police'

In Orwell's *1984* there is talk of the 'Thought Police', who have to control 'crimethink' and 'doublethink' (deviating from the Party's philosophy), even the murmurs whilst sleeping. In *1984* there is also talk of the 'newtalk' dictionary. In each new print, words are destroyed. Every party member learns the same language. In this way, critical thinking is eradicated. Those who still think on their own or have sharp views are 'vaporized', cleaned up, destroyed. 'People always disappear during the night. Your name is taken out of the registry office, your entire existence is denied and then forgotten. (...) If the past and the outside world both exist only in the mind, and if the mind can be controlled – then what?', Orwell writes. History is always be rewritten at will. One has to learn that two plus two is five if the Party says so. 'Things will happen to you from which you will never recover.(...) Never again will you be capable of any

---

[377] Update: https://today.duke.edu/2002/08/darpacontract0802.html
[378] Griffin, G.E., *The Creature from Jekyll Island*, p. 404.

human feeling. Everything inside of you will be dead. (...) You'll be hollow. We will squeeze you empty and then we will fill you with ourselves.' [379]

Alan Yu, former lieutenant colonel of Taiwan's defense ministry and later emigrated to America, announced that a 'thought detection machine' already exists in America. When he was still working at The Ministry of Defense in Taiwan, such a machine was purchased from the United States. The device sends electromagnetic waves to a person who one wants to examine (without his knowledge). The brainwaves are collected and translated into words or images. Even dreams can be drained. The device can also make consciousness foggy, cause cardiac arrest or brain damage and even kill a person using too high frequencies. [380]

On the way to the robot man?

Dr. José Manuel Rodrigues Delgado, born in Spain and is still rumoured to have been a Franco supporter, is now 90 years old. In the seventies he was professor of physiology and director of the institute of neuropsychiatry at the well-known University of Yale, the university that often pops up in relation to Skull & Bones. Delgado is a controversial scientist and already applied Mind Control in the fifties. He developed the first radio-wave-controlled brain implants, which he called 'stimoceivers'. His program was funded by the Intelligence Service of the Navy and Air Force. Delgado was best known for his (unethical) experiment, in which he managed to remotely stop a bull with a chip in the brain ('brainchip') with a transmitter.[381] All over the world, photos of this experiment appeared in newspaper articles, including in the *New York Times*.[382] His research paved the way for the modern brain implantation technique. The 'brainchip' is also called 'nerve prosthesis' because one has been able to associate every facet of the mind, 'from the mental images to the moral sense, from the collective memories up to acts

---

[379] Orwell, G., *1984*, p. 25, 61, 92, 236-243, 288-289.

[380] www.thewatcherfiles.com.

[381] Keith, J., *Saucers of the Illuminati*, p. 26 en Keith, J., *Mind Control*, p. 52-53.

[382] Osmundsen, J.A., 'Matador with a Radio Stops Wired Bull Modified Behaviour in Animals the Subject of Brain Study', in *The New York Times* (17 mei 1965).

of genius, with a particle of the nerve connections'.[383] The 'brainchip' is henceforth used in patients with epilepsy, Parkinson's, paralysis, blindness and deafness.[384] The military purposes are, of course, are not revealed. In films such as The Manchurian Candidate, The Terminal Man and The Matrix, these 'brain chips' make their return. To get used to the idea...

In August 2005, Delgado had himself photographed with a brain implant in each hand, referring to the old adage: 'Know thyself', which according to him can now be altered into 'Construct yourself'.[385] A number of proposals of his chilling ideas can be found in the minutes of Yale University. For example, the minutes of 24 February 1974 (number 26, part 118) state: 'The individual may think that the most important reality is his own existence, but that is only his personal point of view. It shows lack of historical perspective. Man does not have the right to develop his own mind. These kinds of liberal views are very appealing. We need to control the brain electronically. One day, armies and generals will be controlled by electronic stimulation of the brain.'[386] According to generalissimo Rodrigues Delgado. These kinds of ideas would have gone down quite well in the years 1940-45. If the 'brainchip' or another biochip will be connected to the GPS system, we are in the middle of the most chilling control scenario ever conceivable.

THEREFORE, SAY 'NO' TO THE BIOCHIP!

Another controversial scientist is Kevin Warwick. (*What's in a name?*) Warwick is professor of cybernetics at the University of Reading in England. On August 24, 1998, he had a silicon chip surgically implanted

---

[383] 'The microchip implantable in humans. The step that should not be taken', January 2005. Source: C.R.A.P. (Collectif Résistance a la Puce) and Update: www.stop-puce.be not longer active.

[384] Horgan, J., 'The Forgotten Era of Brain Chips', in *Scientific American* (oktober 2005), p. 55.

[385] Ibid, p. 55

[386] https://www.wireheading.com/jose-delgado.html. Also see Delgado, J., *Psychical Control of the Mind*. p. 89-96.

in the middle nerve fibres of his left arm under local anesthesia. Via a computer he can open doors, create light, control heating and other computers in his institute. And that without lifting a finger. Warwick sees this experiment as a preparation for the next step: using a brain implant to merge human and computer into a *cyborg*, a type of concocted being, consisting of part being and part computer. He likes to think of himself as the first cyborg: a cybernetic organism or a cross between man and machine.[387] On March 14, 2002, Kevin Warwick and his wife Irena had a chip implanted that allows their central nervous system to be connected to, among other things, data processing systems. 'This is the next step of merging man and machine. We will be able to get two central nervous systems to communicate over the net.' [388] Warwick wants to work in two directions: to pick up signals from the brain and send signals to the brain, directly, without an intermediate step. 'We are really thinking about thought communication. The way we communicate now, with language, images, e-mails, is really very cumbersome: slow and prone to errors. Language is really a limiting way of communicating. If we could send our thoughts directly, we would understand each other much better.'[389] According to London's *Daily Mail*, Warwick is sponsored for half a million pounds by major internet companies from the United States. He is also in favour of chipping children so that children can no longer be abused and can be located immediately in the event of disappearance and abduction.[390] Warwick feels a close relationship between the chip and himself. 'It's like an arm or a leg'.[391] In the near future he expects machines that are more intelligent than humans. His vision for the future? 'It will be a robot-dominated world with chilling consequences for humans. Is a prospective alternative?'[392] We see Warwick's name

---

[387] Draulans, D., 'De machine wordt mens' ('The machine becomes man'), in Belgium magazine *Knack* (15 februari 2006), p. 54-57; www.kevinwarwick.com.

[388] Icke, D., *Children of the Matrix*, p. 369; en www.kevinwarwick.com

[389] Draulans, 'De machine wordt mens', p. 55.

[390] Idem, en Icke, D., *Children of the Matrix*, p. 370.

[391] www.kevinwarwick.com

[392] Idem.

repeatedly when it is about the central role the internet will play in this world.

Apocalyptic horsemen

Milton William Cooper was a former Marine and top official in the U.S. Army. He had ever sworn the prestigious oath to protect his country. When he worked in the secret service, he found out about the plans of the approaching new world order through secret archives his conscience began to speak. In his book *Behold a pale horse,* he exposes the whole structure of the new world order, whereby the world government uses electronics to enslave man and applies consciousness control.[393] Although he realizes that some of the conclusions in his book may not be entirely correct, he still hopes to be able to convince the reader 'that things are going terribly wrong'.[394] Like other insiders, he also repeatedly warns that it is not about ghost stories, bizarre fantasy or science fiction, but about *facts.*

'The government has been completely misled. We are manipulated by a foreign power, which will end in total slavery and/or destruction of the human race. We must use all means to prevent this from happening.'[395]

Several authors also see the government as complicit (Icke, Rétyi, Erdmann, Jimm Marss, Sutton). On May 11, 2001, Cooper was mysteriously killed after surviving two attacks. He was extremely concerned about the developments on our planet. 'Twenty-five years ago, I believed something else, but twenty-five years ago I had not woken up yet.'[396] Barbara Ann says in the preface to his book; 'It does not bring one fame when telling people, the truth. History shows us what happened to the true prophets of the past,'.[397]

'Encrypted microchips, implanted in everyone, will connect us all to a main computer that can track us down in an instant. Whether you like it

---

[393] Cooper, M.W., *Apocalyptische Reiter* (German translation of *Behold a Pale Horse*), p. 435- 442).

[394] Idem, p. 6.

[395] Idem, p. 302-303.

[396] Idem, p. 13.

[397] Idem, p. 11.

or not',[398] says Cooper, 'plans for such a system are already in the making, as is the inoculation program whereby the chip unnoticeably can be included in the inoculum.'[399] Incidentally, he was of the opinion that AIDS was deliberately expelled (via smallpox vaccination) in order to decimate the Africanpopulation.[400] If we do not wake up quickly and do nothing, *everyone* will soon be a slave of what is called the secret government; the power elite that is actually pulling the strings.'

The nanochip

The vaccination program, the one Cooper speaks about, has progressed further than you might suspect. Nanotechnology makes this possible. Martin Rees, well-known professor of astrophysics at Cambridge University and 'Astronomer Royal' of England, warns the world of the immense dangers that threaten our earth. In his book *Our Last Century* he talks about the dark side and great dangers of bio-, cyber- and nanotechnology, dangers that are more imminent than the known nuclear threat.[401]

Nanotechnology escapes not only the naked eye, but also the opinion of the masses. He has been researching the tiniest for about twenty years. Nanontechnology operates at one thousandth of a thousandth of a millimetre (one billionths of a metre). On this scale, the classical laws of magnetism and electricity no longer predominate, but the interactions of individual atoms and molecules take over. The Greek word *nano* means 'dwarf'. A nanometre is one billionth of a metre. From the point of view of nanotechnology, Earth is the size of a marble. A pinhead is one million nanometres (nm) thick, a banknote a hundred thousand nanometres and a human hair about eighty thousand nanometres.[402]

Experts agree that nanotechnology will fundamentally change our entire society and lifestyle in *all* areas in the coming years: in the food chain, power supply, medical sector, cybernetics. There is even talk of a

---

[398] Idem, p. 440.

[399] Idem, p. 440-441.

[400] Idem, p. 444.

[401] Rees, M., *Onze laatste eeuw.*, p. 7.

[402] Kahn, J., 'Nanotechnologie', in *National Geographic* (June 2006), p. 106-127.

revolution in science and technology paling the discovery of radio, television, plane, train, telephone, computer and internet. Richard Philips Feynman (1918-1988), 'the father of nanotechnology' and winner of the Nobel Prize in physics in 1965, already wondered in 1959 why we were unable to etch all twenty-four parts of the Encyclopaedia Brittanica on a pinhead; that is possible since 2006. The technology of the chip in particular is currently undergoing a revolution. As early as 1965, Gordon Moore stated in a speech about the advancement of computer technology that every new chip that came out had twice the capacity of its predecessor and predicted that the computing power of computers would increase exponentially,[403] with nanotechnology having made a major leap forward in chip development. In ten years', time, there will be computers the size of a watch that can connect you to internet and GPS.

'Every small switching element of a computer chip consists of billions of atoms making it very big and awkward compared to the tiniest imaginable switch elements. The latter would only be a nanometre in size – a billionth of a metre, instead of a micrometre (millionth of a metre), like the current chips.' [404] Nanotechnology can also be applied to living systems, such as proteins and enzymes. Then we speak of bio-nanotechnology. Entire laboratories can be etched on one chip.[405] Unprecedented and chilling possibilities present themselves, paving the way for he robotization of humans. In the hands of the power elite a life threatening instrument.

---

[403] https://nl.wikipedia.org/wiki/Wet_van_Moore

[404] Rees, J., *Onze laatste eeuw*, p. 22.

[405] De Jaeger, P., 'Grote toekomst voor kleine technologie', in Dutch *Eos Magazine* (April 4, 2005), p. 34-38 and Kahn, J., [noot 402]; 'Nanotechnology'. See also 'Nanotechnology. Innovation for the world of tomorrow, brochure published by the European Commission and www.cordis.lu/nanotechnology (no longer active) Update: https://www.equipes.lps.u-psud.fr/Launois/IMG/pdf/pdf_coursUVSQ2008.pdf.

Liquid nanochips

Nanotechnology is already working on liquid injectable chips that can be connected to the neurons. The classic biochip and the hand scanner will soon be hopelessly outdated. The nanochip is on the way. The digital angels will soon have to sell old shares to buy new ones, unless… they have been working with nano cooperatives under a different name for a long time. That way you double your earnings. First cast off the 'old-fashioned' chips, then introduce the new ones. The VeriChip the size of the 'rice grain' is a mountain compared to the nanochip. Through vaccination, the nanochip can be injected on a massive scale.Living little nano-robots, electronic creatures, are already in stock. Professor Jean-Piere Petit, internationally known astrophysicist and technical engineer, former director of the CNRS (Centre National de la Recherche Scientifique), the largest scientific research institute in France, warns explicitly against 'the new generations of vaccines' using nanotechnology. He noticed that the chip was first often promoted under the guise of: 'Why refuse this technique if you have nothing to hide?' Petit points out that since then, there is a system available that will chip people through vaccinating without their knowledge. The best place to control us are the brain. To achieve this, you need a microchip finer than the density of the blood. By injecting not one, but several fine balls into the blood to transport them. These spheres fix themselves in a capillary of the ear or in the brain to serve as an antenna to pick up signals from emitted microwaves. This way, hallucinations can be triggered audibly and subliminal messages can do their job. The brain can even be filled with false ideas. Petit emphatically warns that this is not about science fiction, but about techniques that were already tested in the early seventies. Via satellite, telephone exchanges or mobile phones,

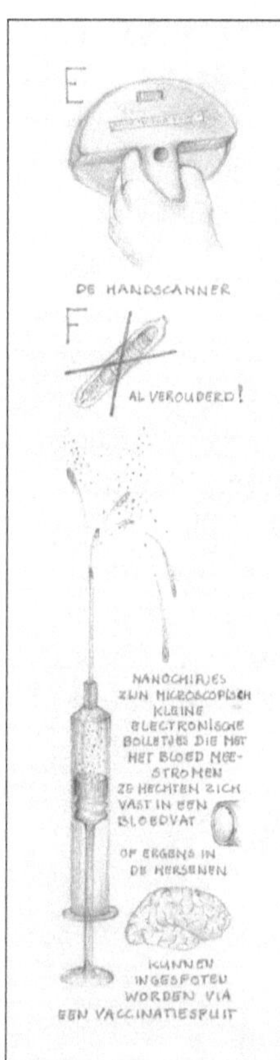

microwaves can be emitted to determine the behaviour. Moreover, Haarp can control the consciousness of an entire crowd ('crowd control'). *to* The Russians also have such a system. 'The United States and Russia already master this technology perfectly,' says Petit. [406]

CIA agent in distress

In 1997, Icke spoke to a scientist who worked a while for the CIA thinking that he could serve his homeland in this way with his knowledge. Until he realized that the real purpose of the CIA was to keep people under control. On his chest was a translucent pouch with an addictive liquid, which had to be replaced every seventy-two hours, otherwise he would die a slow and painful death. A large number of brilliant scientists who could free the world from poverty and hunger are in the same position. This scientist told Icke that, among other things, a lot of beneficial scientific discoveries were stopped by the power elite, because this did not yield any money (such as curing cancer, making deserts fertile, free energy). According to him, it is the intention of the Illuminati (the power elite) to chip all people. On the one hand to be able to follow people *everywhere,* on the other to influence and determine our mental and emotional processes. It is rather the information that goes from the computer to the chip than from the chip to the computer that is the most important. He said people had no inkling of the technology of the Illuminati's secret projects. Once chipped, the computer (via the internet) could make the people slavish, aggressive, sexually aroused or lukewarm and shut down their minds making them like zombies. This man emphatically asked Icke 'to urge people to refuse the microchip at any price, because the moment we allow it, we will be no more than controlled machines...' We need a world campaign 'SAY NO TO THE CHIP' and we need it 'NOW'.[407] He also told Icke ' Microchips in the

---

[406] Petit, J-P. Published several books in which he discusses super technology. Also see for more recent information Foster, L. E., *Nanotechnology* and Fritz, S., *Understanding Nanotechnology.*

[407] Icke, *Children of the Matrix*, p. 369.

secret projects have become so small that they can be injected with a hypodermic needle during mass vaccination programs.' [408]

Chipping through vaccination?

In his work *Biohazard,* the Russian top specialist Ken Alibek a few years ago gave us all the dirt about the chilling world of biological warfare, bioweapons and viruses with the aim of destroying masses of people.[409] Dr. Leonard Horowitz, internationally known for his publications on health, has been writing about bioterrorism, the elimination of viruses and the abuses regarding vaccination for years.[410] We hardly realize what some governments do on the sly. Meanwhile, more and more American doctors are inclined to vaccinate babies as early as possible in order to reduce the infant mortality rate. Ofer Levy, an immunologist at Harvard Medical School, wants to vaccinate babies even immediately after birth.[411] The proponents of vaccination completely ignore the scientific evidence that it provokes a very strong immune response in babies and that vaccination increasingly looks like the cause of SIDS and the 'shaken baby syndrome'. In this syndrome, the baby shows disturbed breathing for months after vaccination of DKT (diphtheria-whooping cough-tetanus) and polio-vaccines. This writes former chief scientific researcher in science Viera Schreibner. From 1980 she did research on vaccines and devoted dozens of publications to the subject.[412] The immune system rather appears to get whacked by the vaccination, and new diseases come about i.e., greater frequency of allergies and meninges. Desirée L. Röver publishes articles for several years on the harmful influence of vaccination and also makes the connection with the power elite associated with pharmacy. [413]

---

[408] Idem, p. 370.

[409] Alibek, K., *Biohazard.*

[410] Horowitz, L., *Emerging Viruses.*

[411] 'Vaccines at birth possibility'. Source: http://news.bbc.co.uk/2/hi/health/4939996.stm

[412] Schreibner, V., 'Vaccinations and the Dynamics of Critical Days', in *Nexus* (October/November 2005), p. 29-34 and 76.

[413] Röver , D., in *Arts & Apotheker* in Dutch: 6 (2003); 2 (2004); 4 (2005); 4 (2006).

Dr. Mark Randall, pseudonym of a former vaccine researcher, who worked for years in the laboratories of major pharmaceutical companies and national health facilities of the U.S. government, states in an interview that he had the feeling he was working in an industry 'based on a range of lies.'[414] His conclusion is as plain as day: 'As far as I am concerned, all vaccines are dangerous.'[415] He is vehemently opposed to mandatory vaccination. With his current knowledge, he would never have his own child vaccinated. He believes that the PR of the medical world, along with the press, often puts people under pressure picturing scenarios of the consequences when you refuse vaccination and almost suggesting you commit a crime when you refuse to have your child vaccinated, for example.[416]

If, in the event of a pandemic, fabricated or not, the power elite were to decide to make the vaccine compulsory, assisted by the approved constitution of the European Union, one does not need to be paranoid when the idea arises that nanochips can be easily administered via vaccines. Moreover, most vaccines come from the America's pharmaceutical industry, where the fear of disease is fertile ground for huge moneymaking. Questions about possible causes of diseases (unhealthy lifestyle, improper nutrition, stress, negative thoughts and feelings) are not discussed in the world of pharmacy. There are pills and vaccines for everything. The *Global Alliance for Vaccines and Immunization* (GAVI) is a global organization (launched in 1999) that is affiliated with a number of well known organizations that paradoxically are advocates for birth control: the Rockefeller Foundation, the Bill and Melinda Gates Foundation, the United Nations, the World Bank, the World Health Organization (WHO) and the Western governments.[417]

---

[414] Rappoport, J., 'Vaccine Dangers and Vested Interests', in *Nexus* (Feb/Mar 2006), p. 11-14 en 74-75. Also see www.nexusmagazine.com.

[415] Idem, p. 12.

[416] Idem, p. 5.

[417] Nield, M., 'The Police State Roadmap', 2005, p. 158-165. Source: http://www.hiddenmysteries.org/freebooks/studies/policestateplanning.pdf

Is it past five to midnight?

Slavery is as old as humanity itself. Almost all colonial countries employed slaves. It made America big. Nowadays, slavery works more cunningly, concealed by sophisticated class systems and imported guest labourers. Whereas in the past the slaves were identifiable by a mark (*tessera* or *mosaic*) or by heavy iron rings or a ball and chain around their ankles, we are presently in danger of becoming *collective* slaves through super technology, vaccination, big brother techniques and the internet. Certain branches of science and technology have for some time been grossly violating the freedom and thought process of man, the emotional life of man and animal. In the meantime, the enormously advanced electronic technology is breaking into the consciousness of man and animal with the preconceived idea to block their spiritual evolution. This evolution concerns the unfolding of the cosmic mind as did all sages and enlightened people through the ages. It is seated in the essence of man to make this conceivable, like a precious gem. It is a seed connected with the awakening of certain spiritual faculties and can germinate in the process of cosmic awakening. Now that man has arrived at the extremely important point of evolution, in which a quantum leap seems possible to a higher consciousness, another dimension, it is for the first time in history that the power elite deliberately attempts in extremely cunning ways to block this leap. Besides a number of positive possibilities, internationally renowned specialists also point out the great dangers of certain technologies. However, refusing to face the dangers, and without doing any genuine research, outright dismissing them as fantasy, science fiction, irrationality or doomsday thinking is contributing directly to the continuation of evil. It might be time to amend the constitution in western democracies when it comes to the 'violability of the body' (in the Netherlands, for example, in Article 11 of the constitution). In the draft European Constitution, October 2004 (full of hitches and snags by the way), part 2 paragraph 63, dealing with 'The right to the integrity of the person', states: 'Everyone has the right to physical and mental integrity'.[418] Our eyebrows are raised and the corners of our mouths are

---

418 https://www.europarl.europa.eu/charter/pdf/text_en.pdf

curled up to such an extent, that a digital photo for a biometric passport becomes totally unsuitable. Are they mocking us, behind our backs or in our face? It is high time that an additional article for the European Constitution were prepared that no *one*, even in the event of a pandemic, can be obliged to get vaccinated and that everyone has the right to decide in his own way with whatever means how to keep his body healthy.

The battle for pharmaceuticals has already erupted on the internet and those who wish to use natural medicines are increasingly being clamped down or attacked by those groups involved in pharmacy. One does not have to belong to a particular religious group to realize the urgency of a constitutional protection against compulsory vaccination. An additional article should also be included, guaranteeing the freedom to be able and to be allowed to choose one's own medicine. But perhaps the whole constitution needs to be scrutinized... It is indeed later than five to twelve but not too late! As long as we wake up quickly, very quickly!

Truly, I say unto you:
The venerable saints who were, are and will be,
all say, speak, proclaim, declare the following:
no animal, no plant, no highly developed being,
no other living entity, may be smitten, dominated,
 overpowered, exhausted or destroyed.
That is the pure, lasting, eternal doctrine,
proclaimed by those who know, because they understand the world.[419]

Mahavira, contemporary of the Buddha and founder of Jainism

---

[419] Mahavira, *Keine Gewalt gegen Mensch, Tier und Pflanze.*

WHAT CAN WE DO?

- Study all aspects of the smart cards and the chip in a group as soon as possible. Inform as many people as possible. Contact the media. If necessary, use email to inform each other quickly. Sometimes greet big brother first. Let him know that you know what he is up to.
-With all your actions you intend to undertake, try to do so with as many people as possible. United you are stronger!
- Avoid telebanking or keep it down to a minimum. Talk to your bank, ask, inquire and decide. Do not straight away run to the bank when asked to come in with your passport. procrastinate...
- Consider handing in your loyalty cards. Make the staff in supermarket or other large stores aware of the why. You may lose a few euros, but you gain a bit of freedom.
- Consider whether you still want to continue buying in supermarkets that will soon completely switch to RFID. First, talk to the management and staff. Realize that they are often ill-informed and of good will. Please show them how you value certain things, but that you cannot go along with decisions without the customer's involvement. Promote ethical thinking about these matters. With kindness and decisiveness together, you achieve the most.
- Enter into a conversation with the government about all kinds of issues that are bothering you. Talk to the people's representatives about it. Attend parliamentary sessions in the House of Representatives. Organize a hearing. Information is the key to understanding. Be persistent with the government until there are results. Keep your humor with overly serious officials.
- Do not part willy nilly ,with your personal details (more) (surveys, subscriptions and the like). Be critical! Discuss the ethical aspects of chip implantation in your working group. Make others aware. Publish the results. Get your local newspapers and door-to-door magazines involved.
- If you are against chipping animals, enter into discussions with the relevant authorities, with animal protection organizations, veterinarians, municipalities. Follow or track down decisions and bills on this topic. Make your voice heard! Get out of your comfort zone!

Once again: together you are strong! Organize a special meeting against the 'tagging' of animals. Let the people bring their dog, cat, rabbit, guinea pig or other favourite animal. Let the animals have their say! Invite children too. Let a clown or cartoonist portray something. Start a conversation about the rights of the animal. And tidy up afterwards. If you have livestock and are against tagging: organize, talk to the government, publish newsletters.

- Provide information about the plans that are there to chip children. Organize meetings. Visit schools, parent councils, boards. Invite the press at the right time. Let your concerns and objections be heard clearly.

- Scrutinize all possible articles in your country's constitution and the draft of the European Constitution. Enter your comments. Publish, make contacts, always be there when it comes to important decisions.

- Think about how you would act if forced implantation were to be carried out in a state of emergency. Investigate the real possibilities and dangers of chipping via vaccination. Publish your vision.

- If you also find that the implantation of the chip in the human body is a serious violation of being human, prepare actions. Quiet, dignified, but determined.

- Let the policymakers know that you are there! And... that from now on you are no longer a docile sheep. These are extremely serious matters. When one sheep leaves the flock, many follow. Chipped, that will be very difficult, if not almost impossible...

Will We Wake UP?

4

Internet:
the Beast 666
or Big Boss?

Take the number 666, which good or badly proportioned either
represents a perfect man or a perfect devil.
Then divide the love of man in exactly 666 parts.
Of those, give 600 to God , give the neighbor 60 and yourself 6,
and you have the equation of the perfect man.
If you want to be a perfect devil however, you give God 6,
your neighbor 60, and yourself 600![420]

Jacob Lorber (1800-1864)

420 Lorber, J., *De Wederkomst van Christus*, in Dutch, p. 95.

4.1   Military background

The next computer you buy may be the last one you need.
In the future, the scientists want to plant chips in our foreheads
to connect us directly to the superhighway for information.
British researchers in cooperation with international teams are working on an
implant to translate human thought into computer language. A group of
scientists will have it, that within a generation people with a chip in the back of
their necks the size of a peppercorn will be able to converse with machines.

Sunday Times, 16 April 1995

What is the origin of the internet?

Under former President Bill Clinton, the momentum picked up. You will
remember the advertisement he made for the smart card. In 1994 he
announced that he wanted to make the internet grow into an Information
SuperHighway. Worldwide. Accessible to everyone, from companies,
e.g., insurance companies, banks, brokers, libraries, producers and
consumers, government money transactions information, travel
agencies, and much more... Wherever you live in the world, in the
mountains, in the valleys, in a village, in the middle of the desert or in the
jungle. The first commandment of the internet is: Thou shalt have access
to the internet. The world wide web is meant for everyone (for those who
can afford it, that is, because with 2 dollars a day to live on you will not
get far). February 15, 2000, two weeks after the World Economic Forum
in Davos, the president of the US at the time, Bill Clinton and the big boss
of Microsoft, Bill Gates, praised the internet. A subsidiary of the World
Bank and the Japanese computer company Softbank, Corp., entered into
a partnership to promote new internet companies in some hundred
developing countries with the aim to reduce 'the global digital divide'
between rich and poor countries. This was the 'start of the globalization

of the internet'. [421] Internet: An artificial brain apparatus with a formidable memory? A nerve centre with countless nerve wires that connects everything and all? An electronic octopus that covers the entire globe with its tentacles? 'A kind of world library that connects everything and everyone?' the way H.G. Wells saw the new information repository of the future almost a century ago. A beast, connected to the Beast? Internet: adored, reviled, praised, despised, praised, ignored.

A military project

Few people know that the internet sprung forth from a military project in the United States. In 1958, in response to the advance of Russian technology – Russia had just launched its sputnik satellite – ARPA was established, the technological research agency of the Department of Defense (DOD), the Ministry of Defense. ARPA is the abbreviation of **Advanced Research Projects Agency**. In 1968, ARPA started the ARPANET project, preceding the internet. Four university computers were connected to each other. Should one of the computers be destroyed during a military attack by the enemy, the data could still be found on the three other computers. We are in the year 1969, at the cradle of one of the greatest inventions of mankind. At least, if you want to see it that way. Not much later, from ARPA flowed forth the more famous DARPA, the abbreviation for **'Defense Advanced Research Projects Agency'**. Darpa, simply put, must ensure that America remains number one in the technological field.[422] Two Big brothers adjacent to each other simply does not work. Electronics and microelectronics will play a central role within DARPA. GPS, internet, manned and unmanned systems (including for monitoring and control), chip technology, translation machines and biotechnology, all that and much more can be found in the DARPA program.[423] Three years later, the FTP service (File Transfer Protocol) and e-mail (electronic mail) were introduced. In 1983 it was complete; *internet*. At that time, there were 390 computers worldwide

---

[421] Risi, A., *Licht wirft keinen Schatten*, p. 38-39.
[422] https://nl.wikipedia.org/wiki/Defense_Advanced_Research_Projects_Agency
[423] https://www.darpa.mil

connected to each other that could exchange data, albeit not having quite reached adulthood. CERN (The Geneva based research centre for particle physics) developed www further. Three years later there was the firstweb browser, a user program to be able to navigate in www (to cruise, look around). The internet began to detach itself from the military and the universities and evolved further. How? Via so-called *websites* that are connected to each other by super connections (*the hyperlinks).* And what do you know?, via the *homepage* the user can now visit all kinds of websites with the click of a mouse. In this way he *surfs* (slides) through a world of information. Data transmission and e-mail are integrated on the internet.[424] This description above could of course be better and more technical, but not by this author.

Now, after so many years, the internet, besides the very many positive possibilities, may also hold a lot of dangers it seems. It sometimes looks like a runaway electronic horse. A world library with an immense and overwhelming amount of accumulated information. You lose your way in a forest of trivialities surrendering you to the spy chips – built-in electronic thieves' guilds – hackers, control signals and much more. A jungle, in which you apparently have to learn to cut your own path and above all make sure you have your solid bodyguards and virus scanners. When Dan Brown wrote his book Digital Fortress he was well informed about the internet by the NSA. Not such a bad place to gather information and perfect advertising... For the NSA that is... The next passage from his book on the internet is still very relevant.

The floodgates opened and the crowd poured in. In the early nineties, the once safe internet of the government had become an overfull wasteland of e-mail and sites. As a result of a number of silenced but very damaging computer cracks in the Navy's intelligence service, it became increasingly clear that the secrets of the government were no longer safe on computers that were connected to the rapidly expanding internet. The president, in consultation with the Department of Defense, issued a secret decree that formed the basis for a new, highly secure government network that was

---

[424] Sunn, F., *666.*

to replace the corrupted internet and function as a link between the various U.S. intelligence services. To prevent more government secrets from falling into the hands of computer hackers, all confidential data was stored in one very secure place: the NSA's new database, the Fort Knox of the American intelligence services. Literally millions of highly confidential photos, tape recordings, documents and videotapes were digitized and stored in an immense storage facility, after which the originals were destroyed. The database was protected by a triple power supply and a layered system of digital backups. It was also more than 200 feet underground to shield it from magnetic fields and possible explosions. All activities within the control room fell under the heading of ultra-secrecy, the highest classification of confidentiality that the country had.[425]

Electronic warfare

So many years later, we hear again from the American Ministry of Defense. Apparently, the internet did not quite manage to shake it. In early February 2006, a report leaked out which they claimed later, was said to be released. Report name: Information Operations Roadmap. It was obtained by a number of individuals from the National Security Archive at George Washington University. They invoked their right to the Freedom of Information Act. Pentagon officials wrote this report back in 2003, and the Secretary of Defense, Donald Rumsfeld, signed it. It had already been published on October 30, 2003, but 'not yet released'. The roadmap shows a fascinating glimpse of America's military plans in connection with the to be waged 'information wars'.

Stop! Born in a military cradle, reaching adulthood in the civil society, all of a sudden electronic machine guns are apparently aimed at this maturing child. Whilst the world becomes one big network, the Pentagon is walking around with wicked plans. It looks as if an 'electronic war' needs to be fought. The roadmap calls, among other things, for 'electronic warfare' whereby enemy networks must be destroyed and psychological operations *(Psyops)* be directed against the computer and

---

[425] Brown, D., *The Juvenalis Dilemma*, pp. 161-162.

television of their own population, whereas such operations were previously limited to foreign countries. The internet suddenly seems to have become a threat to the inventor himself. Maybe not that strange, because in addition to beautiful texts from the sacred traditions, formulas of Einstein, information about Nobel Prize winners, the latest reports about climate change, the latest tip in cooking or the birth of a new star, the internet also contains the not so trivial. Questions about 9/11, information about the Anunnaki ('gods' or 'watchers' of other planets), Illuminati, Skull & Bones, the New World Order, statements of prominent figures about the New World Order, the background of the establishment of the Federal Reserve Bank, the immense influence of certain internationals and their activities in the Second World War, the power of the pharmaceutical industry, the support that capitalism gave to Marxism, the hidden activities of Cecil Rhodes, the influence of the Bilderberg Group on world politics, the worldwide influence of the Rockefellers and the Rothschilds, the involvement of grandfather Prescott Bush in the financing of the Nazi regime and how he excavated the skull of the Apache chief Geronimo in Fort Sill (Oklahoma) for the relics tomb of Skull& Bones... All of those themes that, of course, one would rather not see on the net. It could make people think, maybe wake them up. There are already rumours that the Pentagon would prefer to wipe out or 'blow up' the internet and replace it with a new, totally controllable, net. Of course, fortified with a rock-solid control mechanism. It will probably suffice to execute a number of strong electronic attacks on certain websites and take various websites out on a regular basis, because the World Wide Web, we can simply not do without. The Pentagon in any case has started an electronic war against the user of the internet. After all, so the report states, 'The internet has now become the enemy. *Fight the net'.* So here you are: 'As you make your bed, so must you lie in it.' In the bed of the internet was something explosive. Sooner or later, that becomes visible... That is the Universal

Law that does not need a charter, no judges nor law books. That law is hidden in life itself. [426]

... And that no man might buy or sell,
save he that had the mark, or the name of the beast,
or the number of his name.

Book of Revelation 13:17

---

[426] 'Information Operations Roadmap', October 30, 2003, published by the Department of Defense of the United States of America, special 3.C.8 (u) Develop and Electronic Warfare Investment Strategy, p. 14 and 3.C.9 (u) Increase Psychological Operations Capabilities, pp. 15-16.

4.2   The big Googler

'I believe that the time will soon come that humanity will split, because a computer actually isolates man even further from his surroundings. It gives him a sense of control over his surroundings even more than he already had. We, on the other hand, use the computer to tell the world that it is insane, wrong to isolate oneself from one's environment, possibly a deadly mistake. It is true, the computer is the toy that will dominate everyone's thoughts, while the world collapses.' [427]

John Mohawk, (Seneca-Indian)

The Giant Google

Google is still young, however in a short time it has already grown into a big Googler. Less than nine years ago, Google was founded by two students: Larry Page and Sergey Brin. Brin is a Jewish refugee who traded Russia for America. Google has created a world-famous motto: 'Don't be evil'.

Google became a giant in nine years' time, outgrowing his boots with limbs that are far too large and firm hands that can reach everywhere. Google went public. Google's stock market profits are growing by 100% per year. According to many, Google is the fastest growing company in the world. Apparently, that is how success is measured. Exactly like the electronics company Philips, Google is also trying to conquer China. They're like crusades. But China also built a long wall around various search engines. It is no problem for you to google Tibet or the Dalai Lama or the Heavenly Square of peace (where many peace demonstrators were

---

[427] Buschenreiter, A., *Unser Ende ist euer Untergang*, p. 255-256. Consulted for this paragraph: Belgium newspaper *De Gentenaar* (January 28 and 29, 2006); and Dutch newspapers *Trouw* (February 2 and 8 2006); *Algemeen Dagblad* (March 17, 2006).

killed), but do not expect access to a website. It just doesn't exist or is 'vaporized', as Orwell put it. You *can* look up the word 'freedom'. China has a potential market of 110 million internet surfers. So, we shall simply adapt a bit to the Chinese censorship laws.

Google has become strong. He could easily deliver a huge blow to the book and newspaper industry and to the traditional retail stores. The search engine *Google News* provides the most recent news information. Together with Yahoo, Google seizes the majority of the advertising revenues on the internet. Google currently employs about 5000 people. [In 2021 that number has grown to 140.000] Bill Gates, of course, Microsoft's multibillionaire, wants to surpass Google's success. Giants like devouring giants. He plans to design an even better search engine. With even more possibilities than Google. Gates probably knows even more digital gates. Search engines are the thing. They inspire more confidence in millions of seekers than a quest for the soul. Whereas Parcival still had to trek through a valley of spiritual experience, the digital Parcival is met by digital gates, locks and fortresses. The grail glimmers with electronics and inside is the much sought-after chip…

Is Google indispensable?

For many, Google is almost indispensable. By the way, Google maintains a relationship with the searcher, knows who you are, which websites you visit, with whom you email and the content thereof. Google looks like big brother for he cares about you too. Google wants to make all the information in the world accessible to everyone. It seems like a noble end, a means to real democracy. But what kind of information ? Biased? Filtered? Selected? Even Google has to admit that it needs to adapt to government policies here and there. From *Googleplex*, Google's headquarters in Mountain View in California and from many offices in the world, the great Google invents quite a lot for the probing person. Millions of books are already being scanned. The digital book is progressing everywhere. Also, countless videos and DVDs are going to be indicated. Email and chat services are being proffered and more and more companies around the world turn to Sir Google. With *Google Earth* the big Googler tells you how, starting with a satellite photo, you can zoom in on your own house, until you... presto! have discovered your own home all on your own (even though you were already inside)! Isn't that great? You don't even have to walk around your own home anymore. From your seat, behind the screen, you have found your own home via GPS. You are now cosmically situated. Down on Earth. You are eligible for the Google award! You may go through to next year's annual programming competition at Google's headquarters. All sitting behind the screen. Googling with the great Googler. Would you rather like to see something other than your own home? Perhaps how far they are with the construction of the new Tower of Freedom?? or The Eiffel Tower?  or The Taj Mahal? Or take a peep at the Pentagon? Just zoom in. The star space takes you into the world of Google. Google is like your magician. The Pentagon has already disclosed that with Google it is not difficult for terrorists to carry out a nuclear attack on the territory of America, for example. At least American territory can be examined in detail. 'Fight the net?' [428]

Two Googlers

Is Google going to devour other search giants? Gobble up the privacy of all searchers? Surreptitiously passing on all data working in disguise? In the each computer program Cookies are installed. Cookie is giving you a treat behind your back. Everything you look up is traced and saved. And the big Googler looks after it in his secret googlers box. He who wants to inform everyone, has himself become the best informed on every visitor to his search engine. Of course, Google is not going to just pass on any of it, but still, there will always be secrets hidden in the large google box unbeknown to the ordinary layman.

---

[428] https://www.globalissues.org/article/589/us-plans-to-fight-the-net-revealed en
http://news.bbc.co.uk/2/hi/americas/4655196.stm

There is one more Googler living in America. A googler who has started a 'global war on terror' and of course, is extremely interested in the possibilities of Google. 'Googler' Bush dusted off some of the old laws, spoke of the threat of, i.e., sexprograms for children on the internet, and called in the judge to demand information from Google. For example, he wanted to know which sites the millions of surfers visit (preferably with all the personal details of every seeker). The unfortunate truth is, is that Google provides access to hidden child pornography and other criminal material via a separate search method. Google has a dark backdoor. Once that is opened it gives you access to child pornography and baby sex as if seated in a dark room. Bestial subjects, rape, drug information, and so on. What else is hidden under that big Google hat? Don't be evil... Two faced after all? Moral Knight and Al Capone in one? For the time being, Google said 'no' to Googler Bush. But Bush's magic wand is very powerful. Three competitors, Yahoo, MSN and America online, have already responded 'to the president's call.' The searcher will soon be a potential suspect and can be traced anywhere when he visits certain sites (terrorism for example). Privacy and security clash once again. Could there perhaps be a different game being played behind this whole 'war on terror'? For example, to use this war to possibly take control of the whole of the internet? 'Fight the net'. This can also be done by demanding information from search engines... But....if it's *really* necessary, it won't be a big job for the NSA to just empty the Google magic box. That is always a possibility, possibly even unnoticed? We have to ask Dan Brown that. Google has become the 'know-all'. His giant pants are full of electronic papers. The great Google feeds his manna of the world to the millions of hungry minds. 'In the not-so-distant future', the big Googler announced, 'a kind of shopping service will be started, with which the customer can buy and sell everything via the internet'! That sounds familiar...

4.3   It's all about the internet

'The net is always there, and when we sleep, it keeps on working.
People panic when their computer crashes
and is out of use for a few days.' [429]

Kevin Warwick

Access to WWW

The time is not far off when masses of people will 'communicate' electronically via the internet. Virtually no house lacks a computer, a television, a video, a modern radio and other electronic equipment. A second computer and television are common in many households with children or working parents.
If the *modem*, the additional device that makes it possible to conduct data communication via your phone and the *software* is installed and you are registered with a *provider*, you have access to the internet, to WWW.
Countless people spend hours every day behind their screens, behind the internet or television.
Sometimes entire work weeks in one week. On the internet, anything has become possible. Whoever enters this virtual world, not only enters a paradisiacal landscape of a distant past, but is also at risk of dangers. From *cybersex* (experimenting with sex via the internet) to gambling, from trading goods to buying medicines, from *chatting* with each other about the most inane or serious things to seeing the latest encyclopaedia, from consulting the latest space program to solving loneliness, from requesting advice on suicide to making a dirty bomb, from the latest

---

[429] Belgium magazine *Knack* (February 15, 2006), p. 57. Consulted for this section: *De Financiële Morgen* (November 23, 2004); *Knack* (October 26, 2005 and January 18, 2006); de *Volkskrant* (May 30, June 2 and 10, 2006).

information about the war on *terror* to ordering a new mobile phone (with or without a spy chip) or ordering a shipment of flower bulbs... It's all possible via the internet. Even getting married via the internet is already possible here and there. And of course, there are the hundreds of computer games, a billion-dollar industry. Especially war games, battle games and black magic games are the thing to do. It's all in the game. All these games, according to research, turn out to be extremely addictive. Digital bullying has also become a life-size problem. Many a child succumbs to it.

Internet is growing and growing

Everything seems to revolve more and more around the internet. Meanwhile, the overall addiction to the medium is also increasing. There are those who can no longer sleep peacefully if they have not surfed, played a game, watched the latest news, requested the results of the scratch lottery, heard the result of a football match. Bread and circuses. That statement is as true of our times as it was in the times of the Roman empire where the emperor dictated about life and death with the movement of one finger.

With the click of the mouse, new worlds open and the human mind is all too often enticed, trapped, and dragged along.

Meanwhile, there is a battle raging over who is really the Big Boss of the internet. Is there one big boss? Countless companies turn out to be the Big Boss together, simultaneously competing fiercely. Providers, telephone companies, fibreglass and copper cable companies, hardware suppliers, domain administrators and ICANN (Internet Corporation for Assigned Names and Numbers) all have something to say in the matter. One thing is for sure, America has a very large influence on the world web. As a pioneer of the internet, America has the use of important *root servers*, huge machines whose main task is referring every request from a website to the right domain *server*. A kind of telephone exchange that refers to the right correspondent. Without root servers, the internet just won't work.

The Internet grows and grows and grows. The number of websites around the world runs into the 80 millions. Every day, 50,000 to 100,000 new *weblogs* are added. A weblog, called blog for short, is a kind of personal digital diary, possibly supplemented with news facts and other things. People will probably have to pay extra to get information faster. Perhaps an internet with 2 gears.

Large companies conduct their business more and more via the internet. Paying taxes is already being done via the internet, buying and selling is increasingly done via the web, booking trips, ordering books, requesting information... Endless. The future will be 'wireless' (like the wireless mouse, which has already lost its long tail). But in the wireless future, a gigantic radiation field will also be released. A true bombardment. An electronic war in itself...

Search engine and 666

To consider: if you ask search engines such as Google, Yahoo or Alta Vista to search for the number 666, you will be inundated with a hundred thousand possibilities. Except... the internet itself. Very interesting. And then to know that if you enter WWW on your keyboard to visit a website, you type in 6 three times. In the Hebrew alphabet, the *Vau* stands for both the letter V and W and corresponds in Hebrew number theory, Gematria with the number 6. In the Greek alphabet, the number 600 corresponds to *chi*, the number 60 with *xi* and the number 6 corresponds to *stigma*. *Chi* also stands for God as Father or owner. *Xi* stands for 'condone' and *stigma* comes from the Greek *stizo*, which means 'to sting', 'prick' or 'tattoo', referring to a mark 'implanted' into the body.

Welcome to the internet! Welcome to WWW! It all gets clarified once the new world order will have everyone who sits behind their internet screen chipped. Then via HAARP or another advanced technique, with the help of GPS, the human being can be connected to the mighty Beast of the NSA via his personal computer, his pet. He then has become the slave of the Beast. So, who is the Big Boss? And then who is the slave? Just as a reminder:

... And he causeth all,
both small and great,
rich and poor,
free and bond,
to receive a mark in their right hand,
or in their foreheads:
And that no man might buy or sell,
save he that had the mark, or the name of the beast,
or the number of his name.
Here is wisdom.
Let him that hath understanding count the number of the beast:
for it is the number of a man;
and his number is six six six…

Book of Revelation 13:16-18

4.4   World-Wide Webb consciousness

Within ten years, everything we make
will have a chip that speaks the language of the web.

Kevin Kelly.

World Wide Web

Kevin Kelly is a well-known internet philosopher and author of several books, with the internet as the focal point and co-founder of the magazine *Wired.* July 7, 2006 in a final lecture of the conference *the next Web* (Amsterdam), the web guru emphasized that the internet is only four thousand days old. 'Everything that has happened in the internet area has happened in that time frame. That's in the blink of an eye, compared to the whole civilization and in the next four thousand days I think the changes will be ten times greater.'[430] Nothing is growing as fast as information right now. Kelly believes that we have entered a unique planetary situation, releasing unprecedented opportunities for the internet. And of course, the internet is the place where all this information comes in.

Everything will soon be connected to the internet. A World Wide Web of Information Exchange. Everything, including ourselves, will soon be part and parcel of the internet. And Kelly is not worried about privacy at all. It can be protected, Kelly says, and sensitive information can be made anonymous and encrypted. 'Just as we search the internet, it searches us. With every mouse click we program the web, exactly the same as we tell Google everything we are looking for. Everything is one big machine.'[431] It won't come as a surprise to you, that all actors of the film *The Matrix*

---

[430] Bruin, E. de, 'Het intelligente web', in Dutch newspaper *NRC Handelsblad* (July 10, 2006).
[431] Idem.

were told to read the book '*Out of Control*'[432] and some other books by Kelly before filming could begin. Kelly was at the root of the *Matrix*.[433] He praises the internet. According to him, the internet is the best, the most reliable system that ever came out of human hands. You can't fault it, or so he thinks.

To the question asked during the conference whether the internet can develop consciousness, he gave a fascinating answer: 'There are people who say that it already has, that Moore's Law, which doubles the storage capacity of chips every eighteen months, is an 'idea' of the system. The internet consciousness would have a different type of consciousness than ours anyway. Can we ever communicate with that consciousness? Not during my lifetime, nor during yours. The internet may not even find it necessary to talk to us at all.'[434] Kelly is a member of the 'Long Bets Foundation', an organization that promotes long-term thinking and attempts to make predictions of the future realistic, by betting on it – for money. [435]

Consternation

When reading such a newspaper report, there is bewilderment. I most probably do not belong to this planet, haven't done so for a while. I am hopelessly outdated in my visions of technology and alienated from the latest electronics inventions? It is as if something snapped in me a while ago, a wire that connected my inner space station and the world full of internet wires propelled by chips, that are believed will soon not only store all possible information, but on top of it will also feed the world brain in increasing consciousness. Computer scientist Professor Tanenbaum who has a critical view of chips says; 'With the chip, the real world will be connected to the internet.' [436]

The first cyborg Buddha is already underway. I can already hear his metal footsteps and from his feet grow electronic lotus flowers. I have this

---

[432] Kelly, K., *Out of Control.*
[433] https://en.wikipedia.org/wiki/Kevin_Kelly_(editor)
[434] Idem.
[435] https://longbets.org
[436] Dutch newspaper *De Volkskrant* (October 19, 2006).

vision of the future: for my beloved internet I greet the morning sun, accompanied by the song of birds and flowing mountain streams. And in the evening before going to bed, I can choose the music I want to hear from a website. Or rather a beautiful text or an exciting film. The *Matrix* for example? And when I get up, my intelligent computer greets me, has thought of everything for me, sorted out my day including my shopping list and translated my foreign letters already. Sitting in front of my WWW-er, with a 'pepper ball' in my neck or a 'pinhead' in my forehead, I humbly bow my head to thank the internet for its beautiful appearance and its magnificent creations. I thank him for all his blessings, benefits, cleverness, intelligence, and brilliance. Okay, let me not be cynical: the internet has brilliant possibilities and can of course be used in a positive way for many purposes. And we should certainly not hold back in taking advantage of it and make good use of its possibilities. And not worry too much how much Big Brother can see of us via the internet. That gives him way too much credit. Just let him know that you have it. The internet can be subservient and supportive for a while. Provided...*we* are in charge. The internet is also capable though, of completely destroying our humanity, pulling our consciousness into the gigantic electromagnetic cage, the matrix. You may apparently criticize such an invention, but countless people cannot do anything else but 'worship' the internet. Something deep inside me agrees with the Indian John Mohawk. The Indians know a different 'web'. That is not connected by an artificial network of wires (Wired), but consists of *pure* consciousness, of Wakan—Tanka, 'the Great Mystery,' Great Spirit himself that connects everything in us all.

World Wide Wildness?

Welcome to the World Wide Web. Welcome to the Worldwide Web-consciousness. Have faith. Never believe that your privacy is being violated, even if the *Handbook for Internet and Online Services* says the opposite. Even though Rob Gonggrijp, once a pioneer to get as many people as possible on the internet, says: 'privacy is yesterday'. [437] And that

---

[437] www.destentor.nl.

the computer is filled with 'spyware' we know nothing about, Mr. Kelly, like we don't know anything about 'Trojan horses', which effortlessly track down bank details, insurance details, credit card numbers, emails and phone numbers. They do not whinny and are noiseless. And then there are also the *packet sniffers'*, programs that search the net for passwords and credit card numbers. We have no inkling about that either. So, fill the computer with plenty of *antispyware*.

And finally, dear internet user, do not believe that if you click on the internet icon, your computer *immediately* sends its specific identity number into the room, allowing the NSA, if it wants, to read everything along. Do not believe that the internet will deceive you ever. Don't believe that this Global Webwork has even one weak side. Please realize, that never before was a stronger device made even though one huge solar storm can completely annihilate the internet. Could WWW also be the abbreviation for: World Wide Wildness?

'One thing we know for sure:
Earth does not belong to man. Man belongs to the earth.
We also know: everything is connected; as blood unites the members of a family.
There is a connection between everything.
What happens to Earth happens to her children.
The web of life is not woven by man, he is just a thread in it.
What he does to the web, he also does to himself.' [438]

Seattle, chief of the Duwamish Indians in his 1854 speech.

---

[438] Seattle's speech, p. 28.

4.5   The end of freedom or quickly wake up!

Freedom knows no borders, no space and no time.
Freedom is the eagle that flies to unknown horizons.
Freedom is the child of perfect love,
that is his own birthright.

The apocalyptic scales that the horsemen of the new world order want to pour over Earth contain an ominous content unless we quickly change course and wake up. At all levels of our society. There is no getting around it anymore: the climate is on the way to collapse. And it's hushed up. We have a huge environmental problem. And it's hushed up. The number of earthquakes, volcanic eruptions, flood-like rains, floods, droughts and other catastrophes, is increasing. The signs of the times are more than clear. But maybe we don't want to listen? Would you rather have the latest big brother show on television? Another football match? Our Saturday morning newspaper with a cup of coffee? Our second holiday of this year? Above all, be happy.

Few politicians and spiritual leaders are frank enough to tell you what's really going on. Or they just don't know. But, if a politician is well informed, he won't easily talk about it. After all, it doesn't attract a lot of votes. And we're still entitled to the shine, after the rain, right? In the New Age circuit, many also seem to be asleep, lulled into a false sense of security, followed by ironic utterances, calling it irrational thoughts. With a few exceptions. The Danish philosopher Sören Kierkegaard once let it slip that man will probably 'applaud his own demise'. Like you applaud at the end of a play. We can only hope that he will be proved wrong, although none other than Jesus remarked that if the 'birth pains' of the new Earth were to begin, many people would not even recognize the 'signs of time'. They would just continue to eat, drink and be merry. (Matthew 24:32-35). Better phrased: many just don't *want to* hear it (yet) or admit it. Just as Plato wrote about the time of Atlantis in his *Critias,* has the water reached our lips now too? And what do we do?

Fortunately, something else is going on. People feel a buzz. A number of people are beginning to speak openly about the big transformations going on. Even though not everyone wants to admit that something substantial is going on, the feeling is there. The Mayans, who have the oldest calendars, have warned us repeatedly. They even talk about drastic changes around 2012. Naturally one should not let this preoccupy us or dominate our spiritual freedom. But all old sages knew that everything has a size and number and that the process of creation proceeds in cycles and is part of the understanding of all peoples. And certainly, all the ancient peoples still possess this knowledge.

Now that the earth's electromagnetic field is changing rapidly, solar eruptions are going to increase in all its intensity in the coming years. Climate is really going to bother us, the hertz number of Earth is going up, the photon belt, an immense field of light coming from the Pleiades, is increasing in strength daily, so all in all, maybe there is enough ground for contemplation about what is really going on.

John Perkins, already discussed at length in chapter 1.4 'war on terror', wrote in his book *Confessions of an Economic Hit Man* something significant for our time:

'In almost every culture I know of, the prediction circulates that we entered a remarkable transition period by the end of the 1990s. In monasteries in the Himalayas, ritual places in Indonesia and the Indian reservations in North America, from the heart of the Amazon region and the peaks of the Andes mountains to the ancient cities of the Mayans in Central America, I have heard that we live at a special moment in the history of mankind, and that each of us was born at this time because we have a mission to fulfill.' [439]

Do you feel you have a mission yourself? What could be your mission? Will we be overcome by fear in the coming period? Will we be sucked

---

[439] Perkins, J., *Confessions of an Economic Hit Man.*

into the new world order, robbing us of our free choice and forced to live under the yoke of a fascist state? Or are we going to turn to the greatest power of all time, to the light in our hearts, to the Great Mystery, hidden within ourselves?

Over the next few years, each of us will have to make a choice. That choice will have everything to do with the end of freedom and privacy or the awareness of our freedom, in full consciousness, in full force. Freedom is our natural heritage. Freedom is the manifestation of love. Not cheap freedom of arrogance and egotism, but freedom that is secure within the great laws of life, in harmony and peace. But when matter has sucked us in and we have fallen into a deep sleep, like Sleeping Beauty, pricked by the toxic needle of ignorance and numbness, brainwashed for a long time and sleeping in the tower of misty consciousness, it is now high time to wake up!

Wake up! That's the issue. Not soon. RIGHT AWAY!

Wake up and fast! See what's going on. Without panicking. Be confident that the Great Spirit will shelter and protect us every step of our lives. Be aware that our true essence is boundless, is light and love. Also realize that our true identity cannot be determined by electronics or dark forces behind the world stage. But to truly appreciate that, we must first awaken within the *Matrix*, in which we have been for so long through ignorance, captured by bizarre forces that have overwhelmed and raped our earth.

Come on, let's get up from the dead sleep. Come on, like Star Children choose the way to freedom, go the journey of the stars, unfold our robe of light, escape the electronic tentacles of the Beast. Come on, let's apprehend that everything and all is connected and that the greatest power of life is light and love, two in one. Come on, let us spread our compassion in love and light, even endeavour to love those who want to be our enemies. No matter how difficult this task is. Love is the only force that can calm evil. Love is the only force that can calm the fire of unbridled desire. Love is the source of all that is.

May all living entities
in this wondrous universe
be happy
and live in peace!

Light-Love Meditation

There is light within a man of light
and he lights the whole world.
If he does not shine,
there is darkness.

Gospel of Thomas, logion 24

The essence of all life is light and love.
Both forces are essentially one unmentionable force,
manifesting itself in time and space.
That untold force permeates everything in the cosmos.

Light is the organizing principle of matter.
Our body is completely made of it.
About ten million cells renew themselves in our body, every second.
This is done by the power of light.

The new physics dematerializes matter.
A world made of waves of pure light, opens up before our eyes.

Life constantly inhales order.
This organising principle comes from the sunlight.
Light turns out to be the best(and cheapest) pharmacy for our health.

Without light, no creative processes.
Without light, no star dance.
Right down to the black holes.

Light is joy, love, timelessness.
It is an inexhaustible ocean; which can be experienced if we are selfless,
have respect for life, living the principle of freedom according to the laws
of harmony.

As soon as we forget that light is the basis of everything,
we have forgotten the one and only thing.

All mystics, all enlightened people point out that light and love are the
basis of everything.
Darkness is a temporary state, a misguided attempt to live without light.
To overcome the deepest darkness, one must descend to the source of all
life: light and love.

THEREFORE

That is why every Sunday and Wednesday thousands of people in
different countries unite in spirit.
From 7:00 pm they tune in for ten minutes to a light-love meditation.
Would you like to join? Feel free and don't turn it into a dogma.

Find a spot in your home or garden, in the forest or any other place that
feels right for you.

Sit as upright as possible on a chair or on the floor.
Light a candle as a symbol of the imperishable light.
Now breathe in gently through your nose with your mouth closed.
Let the breath slowly flow into your lungs.
Until it is palpable in your belly.

As you breathe in, pronounce the inner word 'light'.
Then breathe out quietly with your mouth closed, from your belly.
And as the breath from your lungs flows back through your nose, you
inwardly pronounce the word 'love'.

Let this light-love energy flow impersonally for about ten minutes.
The collective light-love field of thousands of people will permeate those
dark places where light is most needed.

If we base ourselves on light and love,
no demon can undermine this power.

Trust that this power will envelop and protect you
as long as it is necessary during our journey through this Earth field.

Give us the wisdom that will lead us along the path of truth.
Keep all that is evil far from us
so that the Sun will never hide its face from us in shame,
and leaves us in darkness.

From a traditional thanksgiving prayer of the Sose-Ha-Wa,
(Seneca Indians)

There is light in people of light

Light.

Breath of Great Spirit
becoming visible
in dancing bodies of light.
Origin of everything that lives
of all energy, all power, all consciousness.
Light in light,
such shining light.

O Light of all light,
which as invisible light
is hidden in visible light,
that burns in the fire of love,
that like innumerable solar eyes
and myriads of stars
radiantly sees itself everywhere
and in the eye of men
reflects itself as shining vision.

I call on thee, O Light,
from the unfathomable being that always is
as force of all force
as life of all life
as breath of all breath
as truth of all truth
as love of all love

In immaculate dawn without time
thou art ever visible
in eyes that sometimes close
against the bright noon sun
in the shadowless life.
Thou art the eternal radiance
who in the material garb of Mother Earth

hides thy spiritual Light
that always is as its being of being
as the I am that Is.

O Light of all light,
which is luminous love
highest vibration of creative power.
Inexhaustible is your might
Unlimited the range of your rays.
Present in all that is visible
thou art beauty and harmony.

O Light of all light,
thou art the inmost of the outmost
the outer of the inner
spaceless in space
timeless in time
and always in many one.

I call upon thee, O Light,
in the north and in the south
in the east and in the west
in the nadir and in the zenith
in fire, earth, water, air and ether.
Thou who art as dazzling Light
being pure Love
in which all suffering will one day turn into joy.

Breath of my breath
light of my light
essence of my essence
love of my love
That which I truly am.
That which art thou in me and I in thee,
not two but one.

O immortal light,
that selfless I am

here and now
always
in rest and motion
in motion and rest.
Voice in voice
silence in silence
breath in breath
amen in amen
immortal…

AUM in AUM...

Literature

Albrecht, K. en L. McIntyre, *Spychips. How Major Corporations and Government Plan to Track Your Every Move with RFID*, Neslon Current, Nashville, Tennessee 2005.

Alibek, K., *Biohazard. The Chilling True Story of the Largest Covert Biological Weapons Program in the World – Told from the Inside by the Man Who Ran it*, Delta Publishing, New York 2002.

Bancroft, A., *Zen. Direct Pointing to Reality*, Thames & Hudson Ltd., 1980.

Begich, N. en J. Manning, *Angels Don't Play This HAARP. Advances in Tesla Technology*, Earthpulse Press, Anchora, Alaska 2002.

Black, E., *IBM and the Holocaust; The Strategic Alliance Between Nazi Germany and America's Most Powerful Corporation*, Crown, New York 2001.

Blix, H., *Disarming Iraq: The Search for Weapons of Mass Destruction.*, Pantheon, 2004.

Bredenhoff, A. en J.T. Offringa, *Greet Hofmans. Occult licht op een koninklijke affaire*, Kok Lyra, Kampen 1996. [in Dutch]

Breitman, R., *Heinrich Himmler. De architect van de Holocaust*, Verbum/Vitataal, Oostum 2005.

Brown, D., *Digital Fortress*, St. Martin's Press, 1998.

Bruce L.C., *Die Harmonie des Weltraums. Die geometrische Analyse ungeklärter Phänomene*, Neue Energien, Peiting z.j.

Bruchac, J. (red.), *Indiaanse wijsheid. Het huis van dauw*, Mirananda, Den Haag 1996. [in Dutch]

Brzezinski, Z., *Between two Ages: America's Role in the Technotronic Era*, Viking Press, New York 1970.

Bülow, A. von, *Im Namen des Staates. CIA, BND und die kriminellen Machenschaften der Geheimdienste*, Piper, München/Zürich 2005.

Bülow, A. von, *Die CIA und der 11. September. Terror und die Rolle der Geheimdienste*, Piper, München/Zürich 2006.

Burke's Peerage, Baronetage and Knightage, ed. Ch. Mosley, Burke's Peerage & Gentry, Buckingham 2003, 2 volumes.

Burns, C., *Billy Graham and His Friends. A Hidden Agenda?,* Sharing, Mt. Carmel 2002.

Buschenreiter, A., *Unser Ende ist euer Untergang. Die Botschaft der Hopi an die Welt,* Lamuv, Göttingen 2004, 2 volumes.

Bush, G.W., *We Will Prevail. President George W. Bush on War, Terrorism and Freedom,* Bloomsbury Academic, 2003.

Chomsky, N., *Power and Terror: Post-9/11 Talks and Interviews,* Seven Stories Press, 2003.

Cooper, M.W., *Apocalyptische Reiter,* Pandora, Peiting 2002.

Danielou, A., *La fantaisie des dieux et l'aventure humaine. Nature et destin du monde dans la tradition shivaïte,* Le Rocher, Monaco 1988.

Delgado, J., *Psychical Control of the Mind. Towards a Psychocivilized Society,* Harper & Row, New York 1969.

Denslow, W.R., *10.000 Famous Freemasons,* Missouri Lodge of Research, Missouri z.jr., 4 dln. in 2 bdn. (repr. ed. 1957-61).

Dhammapada. Des Buddhas Weg zur Weisheit, ed. Nyanatiloka Mahathera, Jhana Verlag, Uttenbühl 1992.

Eckhart, *Van God houden als van niemand. Preken,* ed. F. Maas, Gottmer, Haarlem 1975. [in Dutch]

Ellwood, W., *The No-Nonsense Guide to Globalization,* New Internationalist, 2006.

Erdmann, S., *Banken, Brot und Bomben,* Ama Deus Verlag, Fichtenau 2004, 2 dln.

Essene Gospel of Peace, The. The Unknown Books of the Essenes, ed. Szekely, E.B., International Biogenic Society, Cartago, Costa Rica 1981.

Foster, L. E., *Nanotechnology. Science, Innovation and Opportunity,* Prentice Hall (Pearson Education, Inc.), Upper Saddle River, NJ (etc.) 2006.

Fritz, S. (red.), *Understanding Nanotechnology,* Warner, New York/Boston 2002.

Gandhi, *All Men are Brothers, Autobiographical Reflections,* ed. K. Kripalani, Continuum, New York 1990.

George, S., *Het Lugano Rapport. Of: hoe ons kapitalistische systeem kan standhouden in de eenentwintigste eeuw,* Lemniscaat, Rotterdam 2005.

Greenberg, K.J. en J.L. Dratel, *The Torture Papers. The Road to Abu Ghraib.* Cambridge University Press, 2005.

Griffin, D.R., *The 9/11 Commission Report. Omissions and Distortions,* Olive Branch Press, Northampton, Massachusetts 2005.

Griffin, D.R., *The New Pearl Harbor. Disturbing Questions about the Bush Administration and 9/11,* Olive Branch Press, Northampton, Massachusetts 2004.

Griffin, G.E., *The Fearful Master. A Second Look at the United Nations,* Western Islands, Boston/Los Angeles 1965.

Griffin, G.E., *The Creature from Jekyll Island. A Second Look at the Federal Reserve,* American Media, Westlake Village 2005.

Hanus, B., *Drahtlos überwachen mit Mini-Videokameras. Eigenschaften, Anwendung und Installation von Mini-Videokameras zur Objektüberwachung,* Franzis Verlag, Poing 2003.

Heerd, U. (red.), *Das HAARP Projekt. Über Mobilfunk zur Strahlenwaffe, über Wetterveränderung zur Bewußtseinskontrolle,* Michaels Verlag, Peiting 2003.

Hermes Trismegistus, *Hermetica. The Ancient Greek and Latin Writings which Contain Religious or Philosophical Teachings,* ed. W. Scott, Shambala, Boston, 1985. 4 dln.

Hogue, J., *Nostradamus and His Prophecies,* Gramercy, 1988.

Horowitz, L., *Emerging Viruses: Aids & Ebola-Nature, Accident or Intentional?* Tetrahedron Press, z.pl. 1998.

Icke, D., *The Biggest Secret,* Bridge of Love Publications USA, Wildwood 2000.

Icke, D., *... and the Truth Shall Set You Free,* Bridge of Love Publications, Cambridge 1998.

Icke, D., *Tales from the Time Loop,* Bridge of Love Publications USA, Wildwood 2003.

Icke, D., *Alice in Wonderland and the World Trade Center Disaster. Why the Official Story of 9/11 is a Monumental Lie,* Bridge of Love Publications USA, Wildwood 2002.

Icke, D., *Children of the Matrix. How an Interdimensional Race has Controlled the World for Thousands of Years – and Still Does,* Bridge of Love Publications USA, Wildwood 2002.

Keefe, P.R., *Chatter, Hoe iedereen wereldwijd wordt afgeluisterd,* Balans, Amsterdam 2005.

Keith, J., *Saucers of the Illuminati,* Adventures Unlimited Press, Kempton, Illinois 2004.

Keith, J., *Mind Control, World Control,* Adventures Unlimited Press, Kempton, Illinois 1998.

Kelley, K., *The Family. The Real Story of the Bush Dynasty,* Doubleday, 2004.

Kelly, K., *Out of Control. The New Biology of Machines, Social Systems and the Economic World,* Perseus Books, Reading, Massachusetts 1995.

Korten, D.C., *Het bedrijfsleven aan de macht,* Lemniscaat, Rotterdam 2003. [in Dutch]

Laszlo, E., *You Can Change the World: The Global Citizen's Handbook for Living on Planet Earth,* SelectBooks, Deventer 2010.

Laurent, E., *Bush's Secret World: Religion, Big Business and Hidden Networks,* Polity, 2004.

Lorber, J., *De wederkomst van Christus. Een ontwikkelingsbeeld der mensheid* (bloemlezing), De Ster, Breda 1985. [in Dutch]

Mahavira, *Keine Gewalt gegen Mensch, Tier und Pflanze. Ein Beitrag zur Ethikdiskussion,* ed. K. Titze, Zerling, Berlin 1993.

Marrs, J., *Inside Job. Unmasking the 9/11 Conspiracies,* Origin Press, San Rafael, Californië 2004.

Marrs, J., *Rule by Secrecy: The Hidden History That Connects the Trilateral Commission, the Freemasons, and the Great Pyramids,* William Morrow Paperbacks, 2001.

Marrs, T., *Project L.U.C.I.D. The Beast 666 Universal Human Control System,* Living Truth Publishers, Austin, Texas 1996.

Middelkoop, W. en Dollee, T., *Patronen van Bedrog,* Amsterdam University Press, 2018. [in Dutch]

Moore, M., *Dude, Where's My Country,* Penguin Books Ltd. 2003.

Necerato, P., *The Shocking Truth About The Verichip ... And How It May Quickly Change Life As You Know It,* Liberty Rising Production, Austin 2004.

O'Harrow, R. jr., *No Place to Hide,* Free Press, New York (etc.) 2005.

Orwell, G., *1984.*

Paradin, C., *Alliances genealogiques des rois et princes de Gaule,* Jacob Stoër, z.pl. 1636.

Pastouna, J., *Guantanamo Bay. Gefangen im rechtsfreien Raum,* Europaïsche Verlagsanstalt, Hamburg 2005.

Peace Pilgrim, *De Road to Peace.* www.peacepilgrim.org

Perkins, J., *Confessions of an Economic Hit Man,* Plume, 2005.

Pike, A., *Morals and Dogma of the Ancient and Accepted Scottish Rite of Freemasonry,* Charlestone 1871.

Quigley, C., *Tragedy and Hope. A History of the World in our Time,* Macmillan, New York 1974.

Quigley, J., '*What Does Joan Say?' My Seven Years as White House Astrologer to Nancy and Ronald Reagan,* Carol Publishing Group, New York 1990.

Rees, M., *Our Final Century? : Will the Human Race Survive the Twenty-First Century?* Gerdners Books, 2003.

Reischl, G., *Unter Kontrolle. Die fatalen Folgen der staatlichen Überwachung für Wirtschaft und Gesellschaft,* Redline Wirtschaft bei Ueberreuter, Frankfurt/Wien 2002.

Reisegger, G., *Die Bildbeweise, 11 September,* Hohenrain, Tübingen 2004.

Rétyi, A. von, *Macht und Geheimnis der Illuminaten. Verschwiegene Weltgeschichte,* Kopp Verlag, Rottenburg 2004.

Rétyi, A. von, *Skull & Bones. Amerikas geheime Macht-Elite,* Kopp Verlag, Rottenburg 2003.

Risen, J., *State of War: The Secret History of the CIA and the Bush Administration,* Free Press, 2006.

Risi, A., *Licht wirft keinen Schatten. Ein spirituell-philosophisches Handbuch,* Govinda-Verlag, Neuhausen/Jestetten 2004.

Ruiter, R. de, *George W. Bush en de mythe van al-Qaeda. De verborgen macht achter de terroristische aanslagen van 11 september 2001,* Mayra Publications, Enschede 2005. [in Dutch]

Scheflin, A.W. en E.M. Opton, *The Mind Manipulators,* Paddington Press, New York 1978.

Seattle's Speech: (1854)

Seligmann, S., *Die Zauberkraft des Auges und das Berufen,* J. Couvreur, Den Haag 1921.

Singer, P., *Animal Liberation,* Random House, Londen (etc.) 1995.

Singer, P., *The President of Good & Evil: Questioning the Ethics of George W. Bush,* Plume, 2004.

Soeten, D. de, *Hopi. Deur van verleden en toekomst. Problemen, profetieën, ceremoniën, overleveringen van een oeroude Indiaanse cultuur in Arizona*, Ankh-Hermes, Deventer 1984. [in Dutch]

Springmeier, F., *Bloodlines of the Illuminati*, Ambassador House, Austin 2002.

Stiglitz, J., *Globalisation and Its Discontents*, WW Norton & Company, 2003.

Ström, P., *Die Überwachungsmafia. Das gute Geschäft mit unseren Daten*, Hanser Verlag, München/Wenen 2005.

Sun Bear and Wabun Wind, *Indian Prophecies for the Millennium that Reveal the Fate of the Earth*, Dutch Edition, 1993.

Sunn, F., *666. Die Zahl des Tiers im Internet*, Wilhelm Goldman, München 1999.

Sutton, A., *Wall Street and the Bolshevik Revolution*, Buccaneer Books, Cutchogue, NY 1993.

Teule, G., *GSM-straling. Nieuwe feiten en inzichten*, Sigma, Tilburg 2000. [in Dutch]

Teule, G., *Elektrosmog. De verborgen vervuiler. Over de negatieve effecten van GSM en UMTS en andere draadloze communicatie*, Schors, Amsterdam 2006. [in Dutch]

Tocqueville, A. de, *Oeuvres complets*, J.P. Mayer, z.pl., 1951, 12 volumes.

Toffler, A., Future Shock, Bantam Books, New York 1971.

Van Lennep, J., *Alchemie. Bijdrage tot de geschiedenis van de alchemistische kunst*, Gemeentekrediet, Brussel 1984. [in Dutch]

Vermeeren, C., *9/11 Complex. De dag dat men de wereld veranderde*, Obeliskboeken.nl, 2020. [in Dutch]

Vidal, G., *Perpetual War for Perpetual Peace: How We Got to Be So Hated*, Nation Books, 2002.

Wahl, G., *22 neue Minispione. Neue erprobte Schaltungen für Spionage-Profis*, Franzis Verlag, Poing 2004.

Wolf, F.A., *The Yoga of Time Travel*, Quest Books US, 2004.

Wolferen, K. Van en J. Sampiemon, *Een keerpunt in de vaderlandse geschiedenis*, Meulenhoff, Amsterdam 2005. [in Dutch]

Woodward, B., *Bush at War*, Simon & Schuster, 2003.

Ziegler, J., *Die neuen Herrscher der Welt und ihre globalen Widersacher*, Goldmann Verlag, München 2005.

About the author

Marcel Messing studied anthropology, philosophy and comparative god-service sciences, was a staff lecturer in higher education, independent collaborator of the international *Bibliotheca Philosophica Hermetica* based in Amsterdam, is the author of numerous books, articles and poetry collections and gave hundreds of lectures and seminars in different countries. A number of times he stayed in India, was taught by various teachers there and exchanged knowledge between East and West. For several years he has been living with his life companion in the French Pyrenees again, where he still writes some about the hidden history of mankind in relation to the fast and risky global development and the Universal Law.

In 2021, Marcel Messing also wrote *Code Red Alarm*. This important manifesto attempts to briefly reveal some of the things that the existing power elite would rather keep hidden, leaving ordinary people ignorant of what is really going on in the world. It is impossible, Messing says, to understand world history without knowledge of the occult.

The manifesto can be found at:

www.worldofconsciousness.com

For Marcel's website, visit:
www.marcelmessing.com